D1498447

About This Book

Why Is *Building Expertise* Important?

This is a book about the psychology of expertise and how instructional professionals can leverage mental processes to grow expertise in the workforce.

Whether you are a class facilitator, course developer, or both, your job is to build expertise. There are many books available on the *how's* of training, full of useful tips and techniques. But for the most part, these books don't explain the *why's* behind the how's. Unlike what's in these books, I present guidelines based on how people learn and on evidence of what works during learning. What distinguishes a professional from a paraprofessional approach to education and training is a depth of understanding of how learning occurs and how to adapt evidence-based guidelines to unique situations.

What's New in the Third Edition?

In the 21st Century, the global economy has become a reality. To stay competitive, organizations must increasingly rely on innovation—innovation emerging from expertise that can be adapted to diverse and unpredictable contexts. Throughout this new edition, I draw on evidence about how to build innovative forms of expertise and translate that evidence into useful guidelines for instructional professionals.

I have rewritten all of the chapters that appeared in the second edition. In some cases, I divided chapters to reduce the mental load. In my rewrite, I updated the research on the various techniques discussed throughout the book. Since the second edition, we have seen growth in e-learning with expansions into synchronous as well as asynchronous delivery methods. I have incorporated new examples to reflect these changes.

Finally, this is the first time *Building Expertise* has benefited from a professional production effort. Newly published by Pfeiffer, this edition reflects professional editing and layout.

What Can You Achieve with This Book?

If you are a designer, developer, facilitator, or evaluator of instructional environments for classroom or digital delivery, you can use the guidelines in this book to ensure that your courseware meets human psychological learning requirements. In particular you can learn the best ways to build expertise by:

- Reducing unproductive mental load during learning

- Directing attention

- Leveraging prior knowledge of your learners

- Helping learners build new mental models through implicit and explicit training methods

- Supporting transfer from the instructional environment to the workplace

- Using guided discovery design architectures that build problem-solving skills

- Building mental monitoring and learning management skills

- Motivating learners to invest the effort needed to build expertise

How Is This Book Organized?

From music to chess to programming, psychologists have learned a great deal by studying experts in various domains. Part I includes Chapters 1 through 4, which lay the foundation for the book by summarizing what recent research tells us about expertise—what it is and how it grows. These chapters introduce key concepts relevant to the rest of the book, including the features of expertise, four learning architectures, and an overview of how learning happens.

Part II is the heart of the book, containing eight chapters that focus on the core psychological learning events proven to build expertise. These chapters explain the psychology of each learning event and describe techniques to:

- Minimize unproductive mental load in working memory

- Support early events of instruction, including focus of attention and activation of prior knowledge

- Help learners build mental models through implicit and overt activities

- Create an environment that promotes transfer of learning to the workplace

Figure I.1. The Structure of Building Expertise

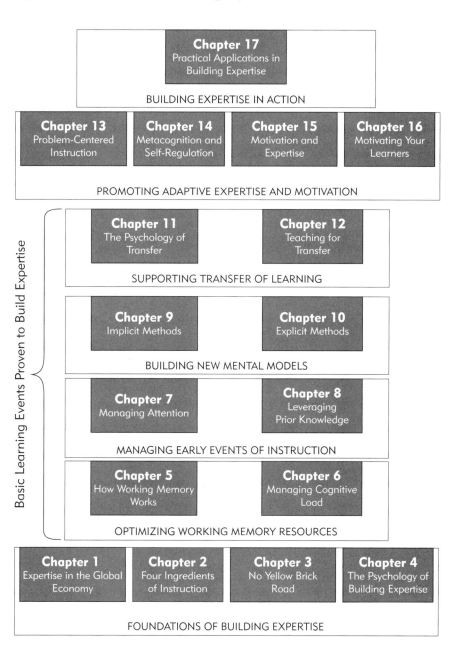

Chapter 17
Practical Applications in
Building Expertise

BUILDING EXPERTISE IN ACTION

Chapter 13
Problem-Centered
Instruction

Chapter 14
Metacognition and
Self-Regulation

Chapter 15
Motivation and
Expertise

Chapter 16
Motivating Your
Learners

PROMOTING ADAPTIVE EXPERTISE AND MOTIVATION

Chapter 11
The Psychology of
Transfer

Chapter 12
Teaching for
Transfer

SUPPORTING TRANSFER OF LEARNING

Chapter 9
Implicit Methods

Chapter 10
Explicit Methods

BUILDING NEW MENTAL MODELS

Chapter 7
Managing Attention

Chapter 8
Leveraging
Prior Knowledge

MANAGING EARLY EVENTS OF INSTRUCTION

Chapter 5
How Working Memory
Works

Chapter 6
Managing Cognitive
Load

OPTIMIZING WORKING MEMORY RESOURCES

Basic Learning Events Proven to Build Expertise

Chapter 1
Expertise in the Global
Economy

Chapter 2
Four Ingredients
of Instruction

Chapter 3
No Yellow Brick
Road

Chapter 4
The Psychology of
Building Expertise

FOUNDATIONS OF BUILDING EXPERTISE

In Part III, I shift the focus to adaptive forms of expertise that are the basis for creative and critical thinking skills. In Chapter 13, you will learn about problem-centered learning environments that lead to adaptive expertise. In Chapter 14, I focus on how to build mental monitoring skills called metacognition. Finally, motivation fuels the engine that drives the effort required to build expertise. In Chapters 15 and 16, I look at recent research findings on instructional strategies you can use to promote optimal motivation.

The final chapter integrates the ideas of the book by describing instructional programs I have designed based on three of the instructional architectures introduced in Chapter 2 and summarizes guidelines for building adaptive forms of expertise through exploratory learning environments that encourage critical and creative thinking.

About Pfeiffer

Pfeiffer serves the professional development and hands-on resource needs of training and human resource practitioners and gives them products to do their jobs better. We deliver proven ideas and solutions from experts in HR development and HR management, and we offer effective and customizable tools to improve workplace performance. From novice to seasoned professional, Pfeiffer is the source you can trust to make yourself and your organization more successful.

Essential Knowledge Pfeiffer produces insightful, practical, and comprehensive materials on topics that matter the most to training and HR professionals. Our Essential Knowledge resources translate the expertise of seasoned professionals into practical, how-to guidance on critical workplace issues and problems. These resources are supported by case studies, worksheets, and job aids and are frequently supplemented with CD-ROMs, websites, and other means of making the content easier to read, understand, and use.

Essential Tools Pfeiffer's Essential Tools resources save time and expense by offering proven, ready-to-use materials—including exercises, activities, games, instruments, and assessments—for use during a training or team-learning event. These resources are frequently offered in looseleaf or CD-ROM format to facilitate copying and customization of the material.

Pfeiffer also recognizes the remarkable power of new technologies in expanding the reach and effectiveness of training. While e-hype has often created whizbang solutions in search of a problem, we are dedicated to bringing convenience and enhancements to proven training solutions. All our e-tools comply with rigorous functionality standards. The most appropriate technology wrapped around essential content yields the perfect solution for today's on-the-go trainers and human resource professionals.

Essential resources for training and HR professionals

Building Expertise

Cognitive Methods for Training and Performance Improvement

Third Edition

Ruth Colvin Clark

Pfeiffer
A Wiley Imprint
www.pfeiffer.com

Published by Pfeiffer
An Imprint of Wiley
989 Market Street, San Francisco, CA 94103-1741
www.pfeiffer.com

For additional copies/bulk purchases of this book in the U.S. please contact 800-274-4434.

Pfeiffer books and products are available through most bookstores. To contact Pfeiffer directly call our Customer Care Department within the U.S. at 800-274-4434, outside the U.S. at 317-572-3985, fax 317-572-4002, or visit www.pfeiffer.com.

Pfeiffer also publishes its books in a variety of electronic formats. Some content that appears in print may not be available in electronic books.

Library of Congress Cataloging-in-Publication Data

Clark, Ruth Colvin.
    Building expertise : cognitive methods for training and performance improvement / Ruth Colvin Clark. — 3rd ed.
        p.   cm.
    Includes bibliographical references and index.
    ISBN 978-0-7879-8844-9 (cloth)
        1. Employees—Training of.   2. Learning, Psychology of.   I. Title.
HF5549.5.T7C5882   2008
658.3'124—dc22

                                                                                          2008021037

Acquiring Editor: Matthew Davis   Editor: Rebecca Taff
Director of Development: Kathleen Dolan Davies   Editorial Assistant: Lindsay Morton
Developmental Editor: Leslie Stephen   Manufacturing Supervisor: Becky Morgan
Production Editor: Dawn Kilgore

Printed in the United States of America

Printing   10 9 8 7 6 5 4 3 2 1

CONTENTS

Introduction to the Third Edition

GETTING THE MOST FROM THIS RESOURCE

Purpose

Building expertise is the central challenge of all instructional practitioners. Yet few know the psychology or the evidence underlying training methods that lead to expertise. The training field is evolving from a craft based primarily on fads and folk wisdom to a profession that integrates evidence into the design and development of its products. A professional knows not only what to do but why she is doing it and how she might adjust techniques to accommodate different learners or diverse learning outcomes. Professionals can summarize the research behind their recommendations to their stakeholders. Because everyone who has gone to school considers him- or herself a learning expert, instructional practitioners face a unique challenge to establish themselves as professionals to their clients and their learners.

In this book you will learn techniques to build expertise. But just as important, you will learn the psychological reasons and the evidence for those techniques.

Audience

If you are a facilitator, designer, developer, evaluator, or consumer of training, you can use the guidelines in this book to identify learning environments that accelerate expertise. Although most of my examples are drawn from workforce learning, I believe that educational professionals can also benefit from these guidelines.

Package Components

The heart of the book is the seventeen chapters summarized in Figure I.1. Most chapters are organized around a pivotal psychological event involved in learning. These chapters summarize the psychology and illustrate training techniques that support each learning process. You will not only read about the techniques, but review evidence for them as well as application examples. At the end of each chapter you will find some references that offer more in-depth or technical information on the chapter topic.

Glossary

A glossary provides definitions of technical terms that appear throughout the book.

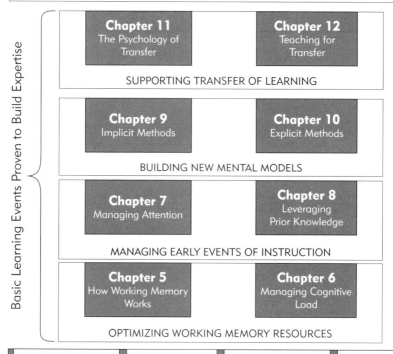

Chapter 17
Practical Applications in
Building Expertise

BUILDING EXPERTISE IN ACTION

Chapter 13
Problem-Centered
Instruction

Chapter 14
Metacognition and
Self-Regulation

Chapter 15
Motivation and
Expertise

Chapter 16
Motivating Your
Learners

PROMOTING ADAPTIVE EXPERTISE AND MOTIVATION

Basic Learning Events Proven to Build Expertise

Chapter 11
The Psychology of
Transfer

Chapter 12
Teaching for
Transfer

SUPPORTING TRANSFER OF LEARNING

Chapter 9
Implicit Methods

Chapter 10
Explicit Methods

BUILDING NEW MENTAL MODELS

Chapter 7
Managing Attention

Chapter 8
Leveraging
Prior Knowledge

MANAGING EARLY EVENTS OF INSTRUCTION

Chapter 5
How Working Memory
Works

Chapter 6
Managing Cognitive
Load

OPTIMIZING WORKING MEMORY RESOURCES

Chapter 1
Expertise in the Global
Economy

Chapter 2
Four Ingredients
of Instruction

Chapter 3
No Yellow Brick
Road

Chapter 4
The Psychology of
Building Expertise

FOUNDATIONS OF BUILDING EXPERTISE

PART ONE

Foundations of Building Expertise

HOW HAS the 21st Century global economy driven the need for adaptive forms of expertise that are the basis for innovation? What has recent research on experts from sports to medicine told us about how to efficiently grow expertise?

In Chapters 1 through 4 I lay the foundation for *Building Expertise* by summarizing recent research on expertise as well as describing the key ingredients and psychological events essential to any instructional program that supports expertise.

CHAPTER 1 TOPICS

The Value of Expertise

The Challenge of Global Expertise

What Is an Expert?

Seven Lessons Learned About Experts

1. Expertise Requires Extensive Practice
2. Expertise Is Domain Specific
3. Expertise Requires Deliberate Practice
4. Experts See with Different Eyes
5. Experts Can Get Stuck
6. Expertise Grows from Two Intelligences
7. Challenging Problems Require Diverse Expertise

1

Expertise in the Global Economy

An expert is a man who has made all the mistakes that can be made in a very narrow field

NEILS BOHR

WHAT IS AN EXPERT? How do people become experts? Is expertise a matter of talent or learning? What types of expertise are most needed in the new global economy? How can instructional professionals make use of what we know about experts to build more effective learning environments? This chapter sets the stage for the book by summarizing what we know about expert performance and why effective training programs are critical to organizations facing the competitive pressures of a growing global pool of expertise.

The Value of Expertise

If you have taken an airplane trip, consulted a medical professional, used computer systems, or attended a professional ball game or a concert, you have benefited from expertise! In fact, few of us would get through a normal week were it not for the varied expertise that provides the infrastructure for our many daily activities. This is a book about expertise—specifically how to grow and deploy expertise most effectively to achieve organizational goals.

There is a large untapped reservoir of knowledge about how novices become experts and how that transition can be facilitated through training and other workplace solutions. In fact, as I write this third edition of Building Expertise, the research on expertise has grown sufficiently to warrant a new forty-two-chapter book: Cambridge Handbook of Expertise and Expert Performance, published in 2006! Knowledge about expertise is untapped in part because much of the recent research on human learning and expertise is buried in academic resources such as the Cambridge Handbook not routinely accessed by practitioners.

Instructional professionals like you who are responsible for the growth of expertise in your organization can benefit from this research. In other words, you need expertise on expertise. My objective in this book is to summarize the research and psychology about what we currently know about growing and leveraging expertise in organizational settings.

The Challenge of Global Expertise

Workers in developed countries face increasing global competition for expertise. Uhalde and Strohl (2006) estimate as many as forty million American jobs, equivalent to nearly a third of the U.S. labor force are theoretically vulnerable to off shoring. The expanding global pool for the type of higher level skills that have historically been the province of developed nations comes from the BRIC (Brazil, Russia, India, and China) supply chain. Since the turn of the century, 1.5 billion people from China, India and countries from the former Soviet bloc have joined the global labor force. Data from a 2005 McKinsey report summarized in Figure 1.1 show young professionals from low-wage countries, including engineers, finance analysts and accountants, and

Figure 1.1. Young Professionals in the Global Talent Pool, 2005
From McKinsey, 2005

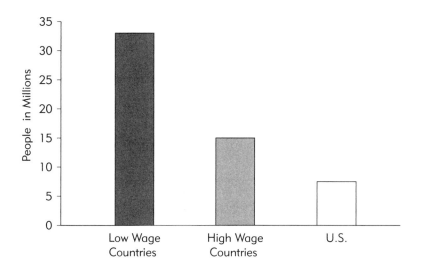

generalists with university degrees make up the largest segment in the global talent pool. And foreign skilled professionals will continue to be inexpensive for several decades to come making some forms of expertise in Western workforces less competitive.

An organization's ability to innovate becomes the competitive edge in a global economy. "The need to innovate is growing stronger as innovation comes closer to being the sole means to survive and prosper in highly competitive and globalised economies" (David & Foray, 2003, p. 22). Therefore a recurrent theme in this book is the psychology of expertise—especially adaptive expertise that is the basis for creative and critical thinking.

What Is an Expert?

According to Wikipedia (2007), an expert is "someone widely recognized as a reliable source of technique or skill whose faculty for judging or deciding rightly, justly, or wisely is accorded authority and status by the public or their peers. An expert, more generally, is a person with extensive knowledge or ability in a particular area of study". Wikipedia, one of a growing cadre of open-access software, did not exist at the writing of the second edition of this book and illustrates one way that expertise can be deployed through the Web 2.0.

Of course, expertise is not all or nothing. As one begins to learn a new set of skills, one evolves from novice through various skill levels up to expert or master performer. Table 1.1 summarizes the common labels and attributes associated with stages of expertise. As training professionals we encounter diverse levels of expertise in the course of our work. We may interview subject-matter experts who are, as the name implies, experts or even

Table 1.1. Levels of Expertise

Level	An Individual Who
Novice	Has minimal exposure to the field
Apprentice	Has completed a period of study beyond introductory level and is usually working in a domain under supervision
Journeyman	Can perform routine work unsupervised
Expert	Is highly regarded by peers; whose judgments are uncommonly accurate and reliable; whose performance shows both skill and economy of effort; and who can deal with unusual or tough cases
Master	Can teach others; a member of an elite group of experts whose judgments set regulations, standards or ideals

Based on Chi, 2006

master performers. Our learners are often at the novice or apprentice stages. Our training goals are often relatively modest in scope, perhaps to bring a novice closer to an apprentice level, or perhaps to teach a journeyman a new set of specialized skills or knowledge. As instructional professionals however, we are collectively responsible for the investment of close to $60 billion a year in the United States alone devoted to the growth of the specialized expertise that makes our organizations competitive (Industry Report, 2007).

Seven Lessons Learned About Experts

Psychologists have studied experts in a variety of domains, including sports, medicine, programming, music, and chess to see how they are different from less-skilled individuals. Here are the main lessons learned from that research:

1. Expertise Requires Extensive Practice

As you can see in Table 1.2 world-class experts start early in life and pursue their vocations through many years of prolonged and

Table 1.2. Years of Practice to Achieve World-Class Performance

Domain	Starting Age	Years to International Performance	Age of Peak Performance
Tennis	6.5	10+	18 to 20
Swimming	4.5	10	18 to 20
Piano	6	17	NA
Chess	10	14	30 to 40

Source: Ericsson, 1990

concentrated practice. While an acceptable level of performance in many tasks such as typing or tennis can be reached in a matter of a few weeks or months, high levels of expertise demand years of practice. Some of the first research focused on master-level chess players. About ten years of sustained chess practice is needed to reach master levels. In fact, from sports to music to programmers, the ten-year rule has proved pretty consistent. "Until most individuals recognize that sustained training and effort is a prerequisite for reaching expert levels of performance, they will continue to misattribute lesser achievement to the lack of natural gifts, and will thus fail to reach their own potential" (Ericsson, 2006, p. 699). In other words, while innate ability is one factor that contributes to expertise, most of us do not invest the level of practice needed to fully exploit the talents we have.

While most practice takes place on the job, as a trainer or instructional designer, you can leverage what we have learned about accelerating expertise through appropriate practice during training. For example, after twenty-five hours of study with a computer training simulator called Sherlock, learners with about two years of experience achieved a level of expertise that matched technicians with ten years of experience (Gott & Lesgold, 2000)! Acceleration of expertise can be achieved when training is designed on the basis of human psychological learning processes.

2. Expertise Is Domain Specific

Because someone is an expert chess player, will he or she be better prepared to solve a problem in physics? In general, the answer is no! Fields of expertise are very narrow. That's because expertise relies on a large body of *specific* knowledge accumulated over time in memory. Master-level chess players, for example, store over 50,000 chess plays in memory (Simon & Gilmartin, 1973).

These play patterns were acquired gradually over a ten-year period. Successful programmers solve new programming problems by drawing on specific programming strategies that have worked for them in the past.

Studies of expert performers show that concrete and specific knowledge stored in memory is the basis for expertise. Each job domain will require a unique knowledge base and a specialized educational and developmental program to build it. When it comes to high levels of expertise, there are no generic or quick fixes!

3. Expertise Requires Deliberate Practice

Although a long period of practice is needed, not everyone who invests a great deal of practice time will achieve high proficiency levels. We are all familiar with the recreational golfer who spends many hours playing, but never really moves beyond a plateau of acceptable performance. Ericsson (2006) distinguishes between *routine practice* and *deliberate practice*. For example, he found that all expert violinists spent over fifty hours a week on music activities. But the best violinists spent more time per week on activities that had been *specifically tailored* to improve their performance. Typically, their teachers identified specific areas of need and set up practice sessions for them. "The core assumption of deliberate practice is that expert performance is acquired gradually and that effective improvement of performance requires the opportunity to find suitable training tasks that the performer can master sequentially. . . . typically monitored by a teacher or coach" (Ericsson, 2006, p. 692). Deliberate practice requires good performers to concentrate on specific skills that are just beyond their current proficiency levels.

4. Experts See with Different Eyes

A profession that relies on visual discrimination such as radiology provides a salient example of seeing with different eyes.

Even experienced physicians rely on the unique expertise of the radiologist to review various forms of medical imagery and provide interpretations However, experts from all domains "see" the problems they face in their domains with different eyes than those with less experience. A programmer looking at code, a chess player viewing a mid-play board, or an orchestral conductor scanning the musical notation and hearing the symphony—all take in relevant data and represent it in ways that are unique to their expertise. As a result of their unique representations, they can choose the most appropriate strategies to solve problems or improve performance. Part of building expertise is to train the brain to "see" problems through the eyes of an expert; in other words, to build the ability to represent problems in ways that lead to effective solutions.

5. Experts Can Get Stuck

While expert performance is very powerful, expertise has its down sides. For example, based on their extensive experience, experts can be inflexible; they can have trouble adapting to new problems—problems that will not be solved by the expert's well-formed mental models. Bias is a facet of inflexibility. In presenting hematology cases or cardiology cases to medical specialists such as hematologists, cardiologists, and infectious disease specialists, Chi (2006) reports that specialists tended to generate hypotheses that corresponded to their field of expertise *whether warranted or not.*"This tendency to generate diagnoses about which they have more knowledge clearly can cause greater errors" (p. 27).

An advantage of any organization competing in a global talent pool is innovative and creative expertise. Uhalde and Strohl (2006) point to thinking and reasoning competencies including critical thinking, originality, innovation, inductive and deductive reasoning, and complex problem solving as critical to the new economy. Therefore, seeking ways to build flexible expertise that is the source of innovation is an increasingly important goal.

6. Expertise Grows from Two Intelligences

Bransford and his colleagues (2006) distinguish between *routine expertise* and *adaptive expertise*. Routine experts are very effective solving problems that are representative of problems in their domain. They are adept at "seeing" and efficiently solving the problem based on their domain-specific mental models. The medical experts mentioned in the previous paragraphs are examples of routine experts. In contrast, adaptive experts evolve their core competencies by venturing into new areas that require them to function as "intelligent novices."

Cattell's (1943, 1963) concepts of crystallized and fluid intelligence align well with the distinction between routine and adaptive expertise. *Fluid intelligence* is the basis for reasoning on novel tasks or within unfamiliar contexts; in other words, it gives rise to adaptive expertise. In contrast, *crystallized intelligence* is predicated on learned skills such as mathematics and reading and is the basis for routine expertise. "In this view, crystallized abilities are essential in the development of well-organized knowledge structures that lead to expertise, while fluidization requires that learners revise existing problem-solving strategies, assemble new ones, search for new analogies, or new perspectives" (Neitfeld, Finney, Schraw, & McCrudden, 2007, p. 511).

In a test of four dominant theories of intelligence, Nietfeld and his co-authors (2007) found that the crystallized-fluid theory of intelligence best fit their data. Important for our perspective as trainers is that both crystallized and fluid abilities can be developed. The research team suggests that initial lessons should "provide background knowledge in a direct instruction format (crystallized abilities) followed by discovery or inquiry based formats enhanced with cooperative learning projects that emphasize the abstraction, transfer, and application of important classroom concepts (fluid ability)" (p. 511).

An emphasis on innovative or creative thinking as a source of competitive edge suggests the need to encourage adaptive types of expertise or fluid intelligence through education, training and organizational policies and practices. In Part III of this book, I discuss instructional approaches that support adaptive forms of expertise.

7. Challenging Problems Require Diverse Expertise

Because expertise tends to be extremely specific and because most problems that face large organizations are complex enough to require diverse expertise, increasingly, innovation will depend on what psychologists call *distributed cognition*. One example of distributed cognition is found in work teams. Effective teams made up of multidisciplinary experts are the key to solving many challenging problems. Accomplishments based on teamwork are more the rule than the exception. For example, contrary to the myth of the lonely scientist, most modern scientific findings today are the result of research teams working collaboratively. In the medical arena, health care depends on the effective interaction of the nurse, laboratory technician, radiologist, and primary and specialty physicians.

Distributed expertise suggests that those responsible for expertise in organizations consider not only training but other vehicles for the leveraging of diverse skills. The evolution of the Web-2 with social software such as wikis opens new channels for distributed expertise in organizations. You can deploy valuable expertise throughout your organization with knowledge management techniques that use participative technology. For example, experienced sales professionals post proposal templates and examples on the corporate website. Or experienced technicians contribute to a maintenance wiki that includes troubleshooting decision trees for unusual failures as well as stories—stories indexed to specific equipment failures.

Expertise, both routine and adaptive, is an essential asset to any organization. Training and performance improvement professionals are entrusted with designing work environments that effectively build and distribute expertise in organizations. In *Building Expertise* you will learn about research-based instructional methods that lead to organizational expertise.

COMING NEXT

Four Ingredients of Instruction

We've seen that expertise is the product of mental models that develop over long periods of time, with the highest levels of expertise growing out of deliberate practice. In the next chapter, I present an overview of four key components in any training program: delivery media, communication modes, instructional methods, and design architectures. Your decisions about these components will define the success of your efforts to build expertise in your organization.

Suggested Readings

Chi, M.T.H. (2006). Two approaches to the study of experts' characteristics. In K.A. Ericsson, N. Charness, P.J. Feltovich, & R.R. Hoffman (Eds.), *The Cambridge handbook of expertise and expert performance.* New York: Cambridge University Press.

Ericsson, K.A., Charness, N., Feltovich, P.J., & Hoffman, R.R (Eds.). (2006). *The Cambridge handbook of expertise and expert performance.* New York: Cambridge University Press.

CHAPTER 2 TOPICS

Which Media Are Best for Learning?

Four Components of Learning

    What Are Communication Modes?

    What Are Instructional Methods?

    Instructional Architectures: The DNA of Learning

Three Views of Learning

    The Absorption View

    The Behavioral View

    The Constructive View

Four Instructional Architectures

    Receptive Architectures

    Directive Architectures

    Guided Discovery Architectures

    Exploratory Architectures

    Architectural Blends

2

Four Ingredients of Instruction

Overwhelming evidence has shown that learning in an online environment can be as effective as that in traditional classrooms

TALLENT-RUNNELS, THOMAS, LAN, COOPER,

AHREN, SHAW, AND LIU, 2006

IN THIS CHAPTER I introduce the four key components of all learning environments: modes, methods, media, and architectures. Communication modes include text, audio, and graphics. Instructional methods are techniques such as examples and practice exercises used to deliver content and promote learning. Media are the devices that deliver training and include instructors, books, and various types of digital technology. Finally, lessons are framed on the basis of four design architectures: receptive, directive, guided discovery, and exploratory. Each architecture reflects different views of learning and has appropriate applications depending on the learners and the training goals.

Over fifty years of media comparison research concludes that it is instructional modes, methods, and architectures – not media- that most directly influence learning. However the "best" modes, methods and architectures will depend on your learner's background knowledge as well as your learning outcome goals.

Which Media Are Best for Learning?

Which is better for learning: a face-to-face classroom, a textbook, self-study e-learning, or an online virtual classroom? For many years, we've wondered about the effectiveness of different instructional delivery *media*. With each new technology wave, enthusiasts argue that the latest is the best! What research do we have about media effectiveness?

Hall and Cushing conducted one of the first media comparison studies for the U.S. Army in 1947. They believed that film would teach better than classroom instruction (Hall & Cushing, 1947). They presented a lesson on how to calibrate a micrometer to separate groups via film, classroom instructor, or self-study using a workbook. The words and pictures in all three lesson versions were identical except that the film used moving pictures. In other words, the script used in the movie used the same words that the instructor used in the classroom. And the visuals used in the workbook were the same as in the movie, except they were still visuals. All students were tested at the end of the lesson. The results? No differences in learning!

After many years of media comparison research with outcomes similar to the Army study, we realize that the media per se do not determine instructional effectiveness. Bernard, Abrami, Lou, Borokhovski, Wade, Wozney, Wallet, Fishet, & Huang (2004) conducted a meta-analysis that incorporated over 350 experimental comparisons of learning from a face to face classroom with learning from some form of electronic distance learning. They found that, most of the effect sizes fell close to 0, indicating no practical differences in learning. However, in some situations the classroom version resulted in much better learning than the digital version and vice versa. All of us have attended traditional classroom events that were not effective. The same holds true for digitized lessons. Tallent-Runnels, Thomas, Lan, Cooper, Ahren, Shaw, and Liu (2006) conclude: "Learning in an online environment can be as effective as that in traditional classrooms. Second, students' learning in the online environment is affected by the quality of online instruction. Not surprisingly, students in well-designed and well-implemented online courses learned significantly more, and more effectively than those in online courses where teaching and learning activities were not carefully planned" (p. 116).

Four Components of Learning

What influences learning is not the delivery medium but the way the facilities of the medium are used to promote learning. Regardless of medium, learning effectiveness depends on the best use of the other three components: *modes, methods,* and *architectures.* These are the active ingredients of any instructional environment. As a former science teacher, I can't resist a chemistry metaphor. In Figure 2.1 I illustrate the modes, methods, and architectures with atoms, molecules and DNA.

Figure 2.1. A Chemistry Analogy for Modes, Methods, and Architectures
From Clark and Kwinn, 2006

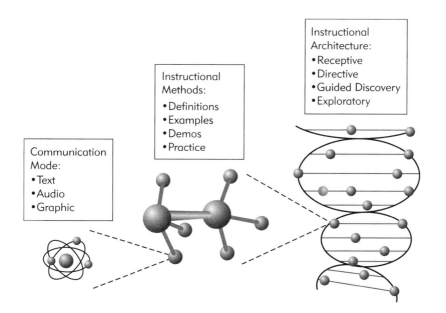

What Are Communication Modes?

No matter what delivery media you use in your training, you will communicate content and training techniques through some combination of text, audio, and graphics—still and animated. I imagine these as the atoms that are the basic building blocks of your lessons. As you present content and prepare practice opportunities, you will use words and visuals as your communication vehicles. As you will see throughout the book, we have quite a bit of research on how best to use text, audio, and visuals to promote learning.

Your selection of communication modes will depend on your delivery medium and on research on how best to use audio and visual elements to teach new knowledge and skills. Some media are limited in the modes they can handle. Books like this one, for example, are generally limited to text and a few still graphics. Computer lessons, however, can include text, audio, and both still and animated visuals. When using media that can handle multiple modes, apply the research I will review in Chapters 6 and 9 to guide your decisions.

What Are Instructional Methods?

Learning requires an active processing of lesson content so that it becomes integrated with existing knowledge already in memory. Instructional methods are techniques such as examples and practice exercises that lead to learning. Well-crafted methods support the psychological processes that mediate the transformation of lesson content into internal knowledge and skills stored in memory. For example, a useful practice exercise will guide the learner to rehearse new information in ways that will encourage its encoding into memory. Use instructional methods that support the learners' mental processes and avoid methods that disrupt learning processes. Most of the chapters in this book will show you methods to support these processes. I picture methods as the molecules of instruction—the building blocks that deliver your content and promote its active integration into memory.

Instructional Architectures: The DNA of Learning

In my chemistry metaphor, I represent architectures as the DNA of instruction—the design framework that will orchestrate how the modes and methods will be used and combined in any learning event. When instructional professionals construct a training or educational program, they usually will begin with a blueprint that illustrates the content and activities to be included in the final event. For example, they may write an outline, learning objectives, or flow charts. This planning phase is referred to as *design* and it is during this process that the instructional architecture and instructional methods are specified. Later, the blueprint is transformed into training materials in the form of workbooks, slides, or online screens. This stage is referred to as *development* and it is here that the architectures and methods are implemented. Let's take a more detailed look at three learning assumptions and four architectures that reflect those assumptions.

Three Views of Learning

Three views of learning reflect different assumptions that lead to different instructional approaches. The three views are: *absorption, behavioral,* and *constructive.*

The Absorption View

From lectures to reading assignments, I believe that the majority of learning environments reflect an absorption view of learning. In this view, learning is about assimilating information and instruction is about providing information to learners. Mayer

(2001) calls this perspective a *"transmission"* view of teaching. Why are transmission-type courses so common? I believe it's because: (1) they are the fastest and easiest to prepare, (2) they represent a familiar teaching environment that many have adopted from their educational experiences, and (3). many stakeholders and some instructional professionals lack an understanding of the active nature of learning.

The Behavioral View

A popular form of training in the mid part of the 20th Century was programmed instruction. Although the early forms of programmed learning presented in books have virtually disappeared, modern versions are prevalent in many digital training environments. Programmed instruction and its modern counterparts are designed on the assumption that learning is based on the acquisition of mental associations. In this view, learning is about making correct responses to questions, and instruction is about providing small chunks of information followed by questions and corrective feedback. In the course of making many small correct responses, learners build large chains of new knowledge.

The Constructive View

In the last part of the 20th Century, learning was again reconceptualized. In a constructive view, emphasis is on the active processes learners use to build new knowledge. This construction requires an integration of new incoming information from the environment with existing knowledge in memory. In the constructive view, learning is about active construction of new knowledge by engaging with diverse sources including instructors, training materials, and peers, and instruction is about setting up learning environments that mediate constructive activities.

Although the active construction of knowledge is commonly accepted today as the mechanism for learning, that construction can be fostered through diverse instructional environments. I characterize four different approaches to instruction as four *architectures*. Each architecture reflects different views about learning and makes different prescriptions for the design of effective learning environments. In the next section I introduce the four architectures. As you read, think about educational or training events you have experienced in your career or have designed yourself that reflect each architecture.

Four Instructional Architectures

Each of the four architectures reflects one of the different views of learning summarized above and differ regarding: (1) how lesson content is organized, (2) whether and what kind of practice is included, (3) the amount of guidance offered to learners, and (4) the opportunities for learners to select their instructional resources. I call the four architectures: *receptive, directive, guided discovery*, and *exploratory*. The major features of each are summarized in Table 2.1.

Receptive Architectures

Perhaps the oldest and still most prevalent architecture today is the receptive architecture. Often reflecting an absorption view of learning, lessons are built with a receptive architecture emphasize information delivery. The information may be in the form of words and pictures both still and animated. A good metaphor for the receptive architecture is learners as sponges and the instruction as a pitcher of water pouring out knowledge to be absorbed. In some forms of receptive instruction, such as lectures or video lessons, learners have minimal control over the pacing or sequencing of the content. In other situations such as a text assignment, learners control the pace and can select the topics of interest to them. Some examples of a receptive architecture

Table 2.1. Four Instructional Architectures

Architecture	Features	Learning Assumptions	Examples	Best Used For
Receptive	* Delivery of content/* Few or no opportunities for overt engagement	* Passive absorption of information/* Learners as sponges/* Instruction as water pitcher vessels	* A traditional lecture/* A documentary video/* A textbook	* Briefings vs. skill building/* Experienced learners/* Brief instructional events
Directive	* Bottom-up sequences/* Short lessons/* Frequent practice events/* Immediate corrective feedback/* Instructive approach/* Avoidance of errors/* Rule – Example – Practice – Feedback	* Gradual building of knowledge chains through frequent correct learner responses and feedback/* Learners as responders/* Instruction as providers of questions and feedback	* Programmed instruction/* Much procedural training such as learning new software	* Building procedural skills/* Novice learners
Guided Discovery	* Problem-centered lessons/* Opportunities to try and learn from errors/* Inductive approach/* May use collaboration and simulation	* Knowledge and skills constructed through authentic work-related experience/* Mistakes are learning opportunities/* Learning in a community of practice /* Learners as problem solvers/ * Instruction as providing relevant problems, resources, and guidance	* Problem-based learning/* Cognitive apprenticeship/* Some digital learning games	* Learners with some background knowledge/* Building strategic skills/* Building problem-solving skills
Exploratory	* Rich network of learning resources/* Effective navigational interfaces/* High levels of learner control	* Learners are self-regulated/* Learners able to define their own goals and select appropriate resources	* Courses (mostly digital) that offer high levels of learner control over content and methods/* Internet research-based learning	* Learners with relevant content knowledge/* Learners with self-regulatory skills/* Independent learning goals

include a traditional (non-interactive or didactic) lecture, an instructional video, or a reading assignment. e-Learning programs lacking interactivity known as "page turners" also embody this architecture.

Although receptive learning environments do not provide for overt engagement with the content, they can promote learning through instructional methods that support the appropriate learning processes. In Chapters 9 and 10, I will review instructional methods that promote deep learning that do and do not require explicit learner responses.

Directive Architectures

Directive architectures reflect a behavioral view of learning. They assume that learning occurs by the gradual building of skills starting from the most basic and progressing to more advanced levels in a hierarchical manner. The lessons present short topics and provide frequent opportunities for learners to respond to related questions. Immediate corrective feedback to student responses ensures formation of accurate associations. The goal is to minimize the aversive consequences of errors which are believed to lead to incorrect associations.

Directive architectures are based on instructive models of learning in which definitions or steps are followed by specific examples and practice with feedback. Programmed instruction, popular in the 1950s and 1960s, is a prime example of a directive architecture. Such lessons were originally presented in books but soon migrated to computer delivery. In programmed instruction, short content segments are followed by a question and corrective feedback. Many asynchronous e-lessons designed to teach procedures use a directive architecture.

Figure 2.2 illustrates a screen from a course that teaches the use of a new computer system to manage telephone calls. In each lesson the learner views a step-by-step demonstration followed by a

Figure 2.2. A Directive Lesson on Using a Computer System

simulation practice. If the learner makes a mistake during the practice, immediate feedback provides a hint and asks the learner to try again. Typical of directive architectures, the lesson topics present small tasks and the lessons progress from simple to complex tasks.

Guided Discovery Architectures

Guided discovery uses job-realistic problems as a context for learning. After receiving their problem or task assignment, learners typically access various sources of data to resolve problems and along the way instructional support—sometimes called scaffolding—is available to help them. Unlike the directive architecture, guided discovery offers learners opportunities to try alternatives, make mistakes, experience consequences of those mistakes, reflect on their results, and revise their approach.

The goal of guided discovery is to help learners build mental models by experiencing the results of actions taken in the context of solving realistic cases and problems. In some forms of e-learning, simulations are the basis for guided discovery lessons. Guided discovery designs are based on inductive models of learning—that is, learning from experience with specific cases and problems.

A guided discovery e-course shown in Figure 2.3 is a simulation designed to teach bank agents how to analyze creditworthiness of a commercial loan applicant. After getting an assignment to research a new loan applicant, the learner can access many sources of information, including literature on the industry, credit checks, references, and interviews with the client. In the screen shown in Figure 2.3, the learner is requesting a credit

Figure 2.3. A Guided Discovery Lesson on Assessing Loan Applicants
With permission from Moody's Analytics

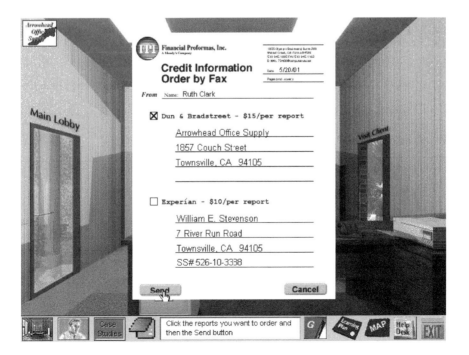

check on a simulated applicant. Coaching is available from a learning agent who provides tips and advice as needed. At any point, the learners can compare their solution path to that of an expert and make adjustments. The learners continue to collect and record data, following a structured loan approval process. When they have collected sufficient data, learners write up a loan funding recommendation with supporting justification and submit it to a virtual loan committee.

Exploratory Architectures

The exploratory design, also known as open-ended learning, offers the greatest amount of *learner control* of all four architectures. By learner control I mean freedom given to learners to set their learning goals, identify relevant resources for knowledge and skills, and monitor their own learning processes and outcomes. The role of the instruction is to provide a rich network of learning resources, including content, examples, demonstrations, and exercises, as well as other learners, all made available through effective navigational facilities. This architecture is commonly seen in Internet courses that provide multiple resources within and outside the course. The role of the learner is to select those resources most relevant to his or her work goals and current knowledge state. Exploratory architectures often incorporate collaborative structures whereby learners can exchange ideas and resources with one another in the service of a common goal. Popular Internet facilities such as Google and Wikipedia are common resources used in exploratory architectures.

Figure 2.4 illustrates a screen from a course designed on the basis of an exploratory architecture. The left-hand navigation allows learners to select from a variety of alternatives including tutorials, lab exercises, and library resources, to name a few. This example is a relatively defined exploratory course. At the other extreme, some courses allow even greater freedom. For example,

Figure 2.4. An Exploratory Course on Internet Programming

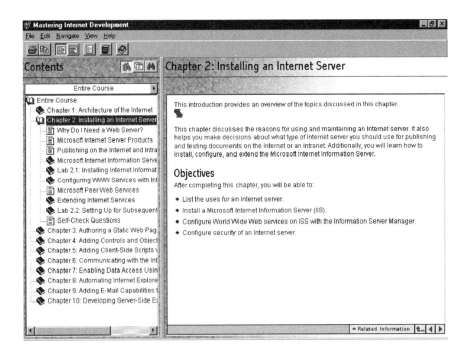

they may have no specific learning objectives and use projects brought in by participants as the learning drivers.

Architectural Blends

Most courses are a mixture of one or more of the architectures. For example, a course on medical ethics starts with a problem in the form of a case that offers an ethical dilemma. The course provides various resources for solving the problem through virtual experts and through links to American Medical Association documents. It incorporates features of both guided discovery and exploratory architectures. Either a guided discovery or an exploratory course may incorporate short tutorials that reflect a directive architecture. Or a series of lessons that are for the most part directive in design may start off with a problem scenario that provides a context for the lesson content.

As an instructional professional your job is to select the best mix of modes, methods, and architectures to achieve your instructional goals. So which modes, methods, and architectures are best? I turn to that question in the next chapter.

COMING NEXT

No Yellow Brick Road

One path to expertise is the selection of the best modes, methods, and architectures to meet your instructional goals and match your learners. In the next chapter we will see what research has to say about the best instructional components. You will see that there are few universal rules; rather, the best mix will depend on your learners' background knowledge and your instructional goals.

Suggested Readings

Clark, R.C. (2000). Four architectures of learning. *Performance Improvement, 39*, 31–38. (Available at www.Clarktraining.com).

Clark, R.E. (1994). Media will never influence learning. *Educational Technology Research and Development, 42*(2), 21–30.

Tallent-Runnels, M.K., Thomas, J.A., Lan, W. Y., Cooper, S., Ahern, T.C., Shaw, S.M., & Lee, X. (2006). Teaching courses online: A review of the research. *Review of Educational Research, 76* (1), 93–135.

CHAPTER 3 TOPICS

Instructional Components and Learning: No Yellow Brick Road

Graphics and Learning: A Journey Down the Yellow Brick Road

    Learning Benefits of Adding a Visual to Text

    Who Benefits from Visuals?

    What Kinds of Visuals Improve Learning?

Factors That Influence Learning

    Learner Differences: Prior Knowledge

    Routine vs. Non-Routine Tasks: Near and Far Transfer

    Matching Architectures to Learners and Tasks

Toward an Evidence-Based Training Profession

About the Numbers

    Statistical Significance

    Effect Sizes and Practical Significance

    Meta-Analysis: Drawing Conclusions from Multiple Experiments

3

No Yellow Brick Road

Dorothy: *Now which way do we go?*
Scarecrow: *Pardon me, this way is a very nice way. . . .*
It's pleasant down that way, too.
Of course, some people do go both ways

L. FRANK BAUM

WHAT ARE THE BEST MODES, methods, and architectures to use in a training program? In this chapter, I begin with a simple question: *Do graphics improve learning?* I review the research on this question to illustrate how different learners and different instructional goals can shape your selection of instructional components that lead to learning. I also briefly summarize the meaning of three important statistical concepts to guide your interpretations of research presented throughout the book.

Instructional Components and Learning: No Yellow Brick Road

Research on instructional modes, methods, and architectures can sometimes leave you more confused than enlightened. You read one study showing that method X improves learning, while another study finds that same method results in no effect or sometimes even a negative effect. For example, some enthusiasts recommend educational games to make learning environments engaging and motivating. Others are more cautious in recommending games. What accounts for these discrepancies in research and opinion on instructional methods?

One explanation is that we need to consider how instructional modes, methods, and architectures work psychologically. Rather than ask, *Do games improve learning?*, a better question is: *Under what conditions (for what learners and what instructional goals and what types of games) will we see improved learning from games?* The answers to these questions require research studies that evaluate how a method might work under different conditions. A given method may have different effects for different instructional goals, for different types of learners, and under different implementations. Let's look at a specific example in more detail.

Graphics and Learning: A Journey Down the Yellow Brick Road

Let's start with what seems like a simple and straightforward question: *Do graphics improve learning?* In fact, several researchers have asked this question and the answer is: It depends! The learning value of visuals depends on three factors summarized in Figure 3.1. Specifically, graphics will have different effects as a result of (1) the learners—especially how much relevant background knowledge they have, (2) the instructional environment—in this case the type of graphic, and (3) the desired learning outcomes of the training. I'll use a series of experiments on the value of graphics to illustrate these ideas.

Figure 3.1. No Yellow Brick Road to Learning Success

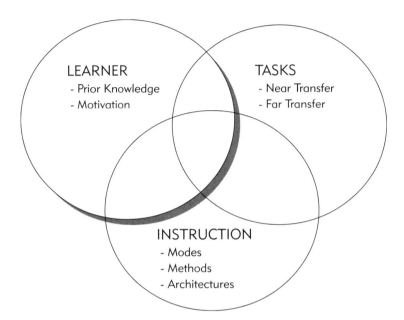

Learning Benefits of Adding a Visual to Text

We begin with a basic question: Will learning be better from a lesson that gives an explanation with words alone or from a lesson with an explanation that includes words and graphics? Mayer and his associates (2001, 2005) conducted a number of experiments in which one group of learners studied a lesson with words alone (either in print or narration), while a second group of learners studied a lesson with the same words but with the addition of visuals (still or animated). For example, two lesson versions on how a bicycle pump works were tested—one with words alone and a second with the same words plus a simple visual showing the parts and movements of the pump.

Figure 3.2. Learning Is Better from a Combination of Text and Visuals Than from Text Alone

From Clark and Mayer, 2008

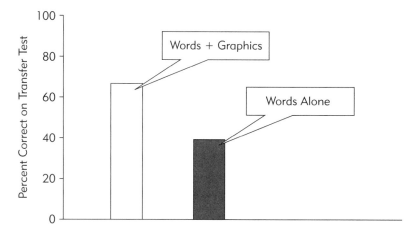

The results of these studies are shown in Figure 3.2. As you can see, adding a visual of the pump greatly improved learning. In fact, overall Mayer found that adding a relevant visual to words resulted in an 89 percent advantage in learning outcomes. Our conclusion seems straightforward: *Visuals improve learning!*

Who Benefits from Visuals?

However, additional studies showed that not all visuals improve learning for all learners. Mayer and his colleagues developed two versions of lessons on pumps, brakes, and generators: a words only and a words plus graphics version. In these experiments, however, they compared learning from two groups: learners who knew little or nothing about the lesson topics versus learners who had background knowledge. You can see the results in Figure 3.3. Learners with little knowledge about the topic were greatly helped by graphics; whereas graphics did not improve learning of learners with relevant background. Why? Most likely, learners with relevant background can actually create their own visuals mentally. As they

Figure 3.3. **Lessons with Graphics Aid Learning of Low But Not High Prior Knowledge Learners**

Based on data from Mayer and Gallini, 1990

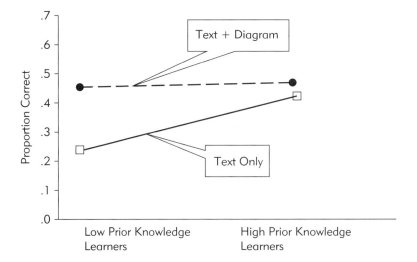

read a description of how a pump works, they know enough about pumps to form a mental image on their own. For novices however, the visual provided information they could not generate for themselves. So now we have to modify our initial conclusion to: *Visuals improve learning of individuals who are new to the lesson content but not of experienced individuals.*

What Kinds of Visuals Improve Learning?

However, additional research leads us to even more qualifications on the value of graphics. Mayer (2001) created a lesson on how lightning forms. One version (basic) included visuals and words that explained the basic process of lightning formation. To liven up this rather boring science lesson, a second version was created. The second version included everything in the first version but added some stories about lightning. For example, as shown

Figure 3.4. Do Interesting Visuals and Stories Improve Learning?

A. Basic Version

Lightning results from the
difference in electrical charges
between cloud and ground.....

B. Enhanced Version

When flying through updrafts,
An airplane ride can become
bumpy. Metal airplanes conduct
lightning very well, but they
sustain little damage because the
bolt passes right through.

Figure 3.5. Learning Is Depressed by Visuals That Are Irrelevant to
            Learning Objectives

Clark and Mayer, 2008

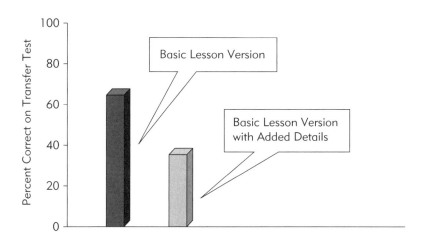

in Figure 3.4, visuals and words were added that discussed the effects of lightning on aircraft, summarized the statistics on people struck by lightning etc. Learners who were unfamiliar with the topic were randomly assigned to study one of the two versions and then take a test on lightning formation. Where was learning greater: the basic version or the 'enhanced' version that added some interesting stories and visuals?

You can see the results in Figure 3.5. Most people to whom I show this research are surprised since they thought that learning would be better from the more interesting version. It turns out that although the added visuals were related to the topic of lightning – they were irrelevant to the learning objective which was to understand the process of lightning formation. Not only did the interesting (but irrelevant) visuals not improve learning – they actually disrupted the formation of the desired mental models and consequently depressed learning! From experiments like this one we see that the type of visual makes a difference to learning. So now we have to again modify our conclusion: *Visuals relevant to the learning objective improve the learning of novices but not of experienced learners.*

To summarize the research on visuals, we see that the three factors summarized in Figure 3.1 interact. First, the relevant background knowledge of the learner will affect how they process an instructional component such as a graphic. Second, the instructional material itself—in the case of graphics—the kind of graphic (relevant or irrelevant) will shape the instructional effectiveness of the lesson. Third, the desired outcomes can make a difference as well. For example, if your goal is to teach a procedure, the impact of a given instructional method may be different than if your goal is to teach a strategic task.

In short, there are few absolute laws in learning. The answer to almost any question about the effectiveness of instructional environments is: It depends! Luckily, from our knowledge of how humans process information and from a growing body of research, we can narrow down the main factors that will determine learning.

Factors That Influence Learning

We saw in the previous section that learner background knowledge as well as the desired outcomes can influence the effectiveness of any instructional method. Let's look at these two factors in a bit more detail.

Learner Differences: Prior Knowledge

In spite of the popularity of individual differences known as *learning styles,* research points to *prior experience* as the most significant learner characteristic influencing learning. We saw in the previous section that graphics that improved the novice's learning had little effect on more experienced participants. Novices have little in the way of relevant prior knowledge in their memory. As a result, their mental processes are different from those of learners with greater background experience. Therefore, novices benefit from different instructional methods than more experienced learners.

For example, learners with relatively little background knowledge benefit from a directive architecture that provides information in small chunks and offers frequent practice opportunities. In contrast, learners with greater prior knowledge have more mental resources to draw upon during learning. They are able to manage larger chunks of information and, based on what they already know, are often able to spontaneously integrate new knowledge. Experienced learners will profit more from the guided discovery, exploratory, and receptive architectures.

Routine vs. Non-Routine Tasks: Near and Far Transfer

In addition to prior knowledge, the type of task you are teaching will influence your choice of modes, methods, and architectures.

Some tasks must be performed consistently each time and by each worker who does them. I call these routine or procedural tasks. Routine tasks are the mainstay of any organization such as a Mc-restaurant chain that must efficiently produce a consistent product. Routine tasks require a *near-transfer* performance—one based primarily on the consistent application of procedures. Some common examples of near-transfer tasks are logging into e-mail and completing a routine customer online order.

Other work environments demand strategic or *far-transfer* performance. Far-transfer tasks require the worker to use extensive judgment. Each work situation demands a different approach or solution. In fact, there are no invariant steps for all cases. The worker must tailor general guidelines to each unique situation. Sales tasks are good examples. Depending on the product, the customer, and prior history, the effective salesperson uses a different approach each time. In some situations, goals that call for innovative thinking must go beyond routine expertise. Critical thinking or creative solutions require adaptive forms of expertise that extend beyond the typical domain-specific skills of the routine expert.

While I will discuss ways to build both near- and far-transfer skills, a major emphasis of this book is on how to develop the mental models that are the basis for far-transfer work as well as for adaptive expertise.

Matching Architectures to Learners and Tasks

As shown in Chapter 2 (see, for example, Table 2.1), a directive architecture lends itself to helping novices acquire skills that lead to near-transfer procedural tasks. However, for far-transfer work leading to either routine or adaptive expertise, the guided discovery architecture is often more appropriate. For learners with high background knowledge and/or good learning management skills, I recommend an exploratory or receptive architecture.

These brief examples illustrate that is *no single path* to good instruction. There are always tradeoffs. Regardless of which modes, methods, and architectures you select, learners must actively construct an expanded knowledge base in memory. The activity may be explicit, as when learners respond to questions in a directive architecture lesson. Or the activity may be invisible, as when a learner views a relevant visual. But one way or the other, learning relies on active processing of new information.

Toward an Evidence-Based Training Profession

The goal of *Building Expertise* is to present instructional modes, methods, and architectures in terms of how they support psychological processes that mediate learning. Knowing how these training components work should help you deploy them more effectively. For example, in Chapter 6 you will see that you can best explain a complex visual such as an animation with words in audio rather than in text. You will learn the psychological reason for this principle as well as the research that supports it. As a professional, it is important that you consider evidence and psychological effectiveness when you make important decisions about your learning environments. The Educause advisory committee identified the need to establish a culture of evidence and to translate learning research into practice their number 1 and 3 priorities for higher education learning environments (Campbell & Oblinger, 2007).

It has been a struggle to establish ourselves as professionals in the training field. One reason is that everyone who has been to school considers him- or herself an expert on learning and education. Therefore, all stakeholders, including line managers, students, and subject-matter experts, assume they know how learning materials should be constructed.

Hannafin and his colleagues (1997) recommend we build our professional practice by embracing *grounded design* defined as "the systematic implementation of processes and procedures *that are rooted in established theory and research in human learning*" (p. 102, emphasis added). To the extent that you can make tradeoffs in lesson design based on their psychological effects and can justify your decisions to others, you embrace evidence-based practice. As instructional professionals who are collectively responsible for the expenditure of close to $60 billion annually (Industry Report, 2007), all of us are remiss if we cannot offer our clients best-known methods and explain the reasons for our recommendations.

In *Building Expertise* I focus on the psychological factors that support the selection of one instructional mode, method, or architecture over another. Yet I know that you can't base your training decisions on psychological factors alone; other factors will intervene—factors like time, money, expectations, and the delivery technology, to mention a few. However, I hope that as a result of this book, you will be able to make instructional decisions based on psychological processes and the research that supports them to develop the expertise on which your organization relies.

About the Numbers

Throughout *Building Expertise* you will see snapshots of experimental data such as the bar graphs I showed in Figures 3.2 and 3.5. How can you interpret this kind of data? For example, how much higher should a score be on a lesson with graphics and text compared to a lesson on text alone to be meaningful? Additionally, how much can you rely on a single experiment to guide your decisions? In this section I briefly summarize three statistical concepts you will see throughout the book: *statistical significance, effect size,* and *meta-analysis.*

Statistical Significance

Statistical significance is a measure of the probability that the outcome differences between experimental lesson A and experimental lesson B reflect a real difference and are not due to chance alone. In general, when the probability is less than .05, researchers conclude that the difference is real, that is, not due to random factors. This is called statistical significance. In most of the data I present throughout the book, I will simply write SD on the graph to indicate that it is a statistically significant difference.

Effect Sizes and Practical Significance

If you compare learning between two different lesson versions among a very large group of learners (say one hundred or more assigned to each version), even a very small difference in outcome scores will be statistically significant. But the small differences in scores may not warrant you applying the findings to your instructional decisions—especially if the better method is more expensive or cumbersome to produce.

Fortunately, we have a second statistic known as effect size that can give you better information about the practical relevance of numeric differences. An effect size tells us the amount of standard deviation difference in average scores between those taking version 1 and version 2 lessons. For example, suppose a lesson with graphics and text resulted in an average score of 90 percent, while a lesson with only text resulted in an average score of 80 percent. The results are statistically significant at .05, so we can be confident that the differences are real. Is the 10-point difference sufficient to warrant adding graphics to text? We can calculate an effect size to answer this question.

Suppose that the *standard deviation* (dispersion) among the scores is 10. To calculate the effect size, we subtract the average scores of the two groups and divide by the standard deviation. In this example,

90 minus 80 divided by 10 is 1. An effect size of 1 means that overall, if a learner takes a lesson that adds graphics to text, her average score will increase by one standard deviation. For example, if a class average is 70 percent with a standard deviation of 6 from lessons that used text alone, the average score could be expected to be 76 percent from lessons that added graphics. Had the effect size been .5, the class average would be around 73 percent from lessons with added graphics.

We have some general rules of thumb about effect size values. Overall, effect sizes of .8 and greater are considered large and offer a strong argument that you should probably implement them. Effect sizes around .5 are moderate. Effect sizes of .2 or below are too small to worry much about in a practical sense.

Meta-Analysis: Drawing Conclusions from Multiple Experiments

Any one experiment does not prove a lot. To be confident with a recommendation such as *Add Graphics to Text*, we need many research studies that include different types of content, various forms of visuals, and different ages of learners, for example. Once we get quite a few experiments on an instructional component such as graphics, how can we make sense of the data?

I feel that one of the most important recent statistical innovations for our field is the meta-analysis. A meta-analysis evaluates the effect sizes from a number of research studies and makes some generalizations about them. For example, a meta-analysis done on graphics by Mayer (2005) evaluated twenty-one experiments that compared lessons that added graphics to text to lessons with text alone. He found a median effect size of .97, which would be considered large. This median effect size gives us more confidence in our recommendation to use graphics because it falls in the large range and it is based not on a single study but on multiple experiments. As you read through the book, keep in mind that effect sizes derived from meta-analysis are more persuasive than effect sizes from any single study.

COMING NEXT

The Psychology of Building Expertise

We've seen that the best modes, methods, and architectures depend on learner prior knowledge and your instructional goals. That is because these components interact with human memory in different ways. In the next chapter, I introduce human learning psychology with an overview of our two memory systems and six learning processes that transfer content in the lesson into internal knowledge and skills in memory.

Suggested Readings

Clark, R.C., & Mayer, R.E. (2008). *e-Learning and the science of instruction* (2nd ed.). San Francisco, CA: Pfeiffer. See Chapters 2 and 3.

Clark, R.C., Nguyen, F., & Sweller, J. (2006). *Efficiency in learning.* San Francisco, CA: Pfeiffer. See Chapter 2.

CHAPTER 4 TOPICS

Two Memories for Learning

Working Memory: A Powerful Bottleneck

Long-Term Memory: A Large Capacity Repository

Working Memory and Long-Term Memory Work Together

The Transformation of Content into Knowledge and Skills

Supporting Attention

Activation of Prior Knowledge

Management of Load in Working Memory

Rehearsal in Working Memory Leading to Encoding into Long-Term Memory

Retrieval from Long-Term Memory

How Long-Term Memory Influences Learning

Metacognition and Self-Regulated Learners

Motivation and Learning

Eight Principles for Instruction

1. Optimize Motivational Beliefs
2. Activate Prior Knowledge Early in Instruction
3. Direct Attention to Important Elements in the Lesson
4. Manage Irrelevant Cognitive Load
5. Promote Encoding into Long-Term Memory
6. Use Job-Context to Promote Retrieval and Transfer of Near-Transfer Skills
7. Build Robust Mental Models to Support Far-Transfer Learning
8. Adapt Instruction to Your Learners' Metacognitive Skills and Your Instructional Goals

4

The Psychology of Building Expertise

The great poem and the deep theorem are new to every reader, and yet are his own experiences, because he himself recreates them.

JACOB BRONOWSKI

THIS CHAPTER LAYS THE FOUNDATION for the chapters to follow by presenting an overview of what we know about psychological processes during learning. I will summarize the important features of two memories involved in learning: working memory and long-term memory, as well as five stages in the psychological events that transform training content into new knowledge and skills in memory. I will also summarize eight universal principles of instruction linked to those learning processes.

Two Memories for Learning

Learning requires the active transformation of content from the environment into new knowledge and skills in memory that can be accessed when needed on the job.

Figure 4.1. Human Learning Processes

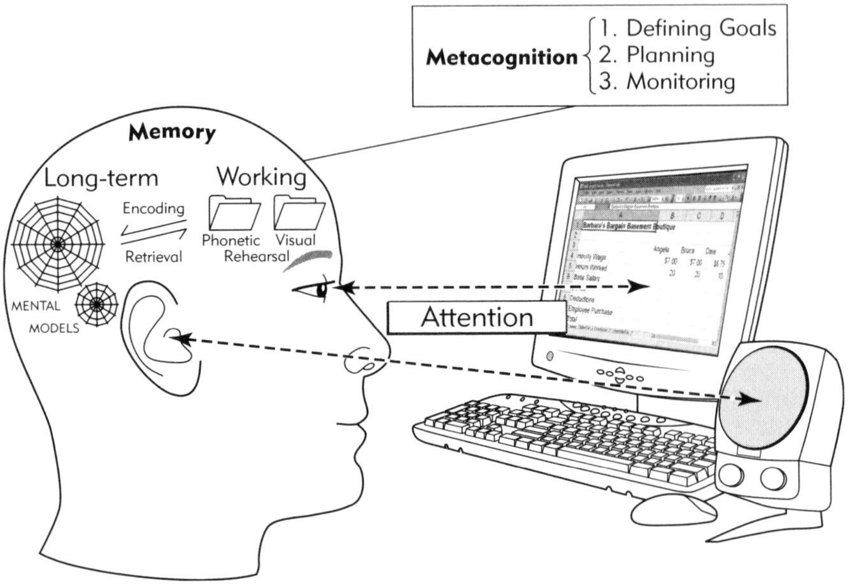

A high-level view of the process is illustrated in Figure 4.1. Current psychological learning theories include two main memory systems involved in this transformation:

- *Working memory* (WM)—also known as short-term memory—and

- *Long-term memory* (LTM)

Table 4.1 summarizes the key features of the two memories.

Working Memory: A Powerful Bottleneck

There are three major features of working memory that are important to learning: (1) capacity limits, (2) processing power, and (3) separate storage for visual and verbal information. Working memory is both the powerhouse and the bottleneck of learning. You may have heard the expression *seven plus or minus two*. This

Table 4.1. Two Memories Involved in Learning

Memory	Features
Working (Short-Term)	Center of conscious cognition
	Limited capacity
	Brief duration of new content
	Includes separate areas for processing and storage of phonetic (auditory) and visual data
Long-term	Storage but no processing of content and skills
	Large capacity for storage
	Permanent repository of knowledge
	Knowledge stored in two forms:
	Declarative – facts and concepts:
	Procedural – skills:
	Knowledge structures called schemas or mental models

refers to the capacity limits of working memory. It means that working memory can only hold a limited amount of information at one time. The original notion of a capacity limit of seven plus or minus two proposed by George Miller in the mid-1950s has actually been revised to an even more restrictive limit of around four to five chunks of information when working memory is active.

At the same time, working memory is the center of conscious thinking. It's where active processing and learning take place. Therefore the term "memory" is a bit of a misnomer while the label of "working" fits. One major role of instruction is to keep working memory from becoming overloaded so that its limited capacity can be devoted to learning processes. In the research on graphics described in Chapter 3, graphics that were interesting but irrelevant to the learning objective depressed learning, likely because working memory was overtaxed. In Chapter 6 I will discuss a number of methods you can use to avoid overload in working memory during learning.

Working memory has two storage areas—one for holding visual information such as pictures and another for holding phonetic information such as words. This is an important feature of working memory that we can also exploit in training. By making judicious use of visual and auditory modes, we can maximize learning outcomes. Chapter 6 on managing cognitive load will review ways to most effectively use the auditory and visual capacity of working memory to promote learning.

Because working memory is where learning processes occur, instructional methods such as practice exercises and graphics can be used to stimulate the kinds of processing that result in learning. Chapters 9 and 10 will describe in detail how to maximize these processes in working memory.

Long-Term Memory: A Large Capacity Repository

In contrast to working memory, *long-term memory* has a huge storage capacity. The memories that are the basis for all your knowledge and skills reside in long-term memory. Memories in long-term memory of greatest relevance to learning are of two main types—knowledge about things that are easy to articulate (called *declarative knowledge*) and knowledge of how to do things that can be difficult to articulate (called *procedural knowledge*). For example, you can easily talk about your knowledge of bicycles, such as parts of bicycles and types of bicycles. However, it is more difficult to accurately describe your procedural knowledge of how to ride a bicycle—especially how to balance so you don't fall off.

Declarative and procedural knowledge work together. For example, if you were to add 29 and 36, your procedural knowledge would activate the rule that you should start by summing the numbers in the right-most column. From your declarative knowledge, you would access the fact that 9 and 6 equal 15. Then from your procedural knowledge you would apply the rule that when the sum exceeds 9, you put the 1's value in the 1's column and carry the 10's value to the 10's column. You continue this interactive process until you have completed your goal of adding 29 and 36. Related declarative and procedural knowledge are stored in long-term memory in structures called *schemas* or mental models. These are represented as web-like structures in Figure 4.1. The primary goal of organizational training is to help learners build the best mental models to support job-relevant expertise.

Working Memory and Long-Term Memory Work Together

Working memory and long-term memory interact with each other. I mentioned above that working memory has a limited capacity of around four or five chunks. However, "chunk" is a relative term. Chunk size can vary depending on the content of long-term memory. The more knowledge stored in long-term memory, the greater the size of chunks that working memory can hold. This is why experts in a domain can process much more information more efficiently than can novices. The expert can find patterns or chunks that incorporate much more information than the novice can by representing data based on the schemas stored in long-term memory. Therefore, the expert makes much better use of her limited working memory capacity.

Automaticity is a second advantage of expertise stemming from long-term memory. Automaticity refers to any task that can be executed out of long-term memory without using the resources of working memory. Tasks become automatic through hundreds of repetitions. Anyone who has a routine work commute knows the experience of being on automatic. No attention needs to be allocated to either the driving task or the route. Automaticity allows us to bypass the limits of working memory.

However, automaticity can cause problems when the situation calls for conscious performance such as the need to respond rapidly to avoid an accident.

The interactions between LTM and WM have major consequences for the design of training. For example, novices will be much more subject to cognitive load in working memory than will experts in their skill field, and therefore novices will require different instructional methods for success in learning. We saw in our discussion of graphics that relevant visuals aid novices but do not promote learning of individuals familiar with the lesson topic. No doubt the schemas in the LTM of the more experienced individuals allow them to generate their own visual images as they read the words. In fact, many instructional methods that benefit novices but not experts serve as "schema substitutes." They provide supports for missing schemas. Once schemas are constructed, these types of supports become redundant and no longer contribute to learning.

Now that I have described the major features of WM and LTM, I turn to a summary of how content from the learning environment is stored in the form of new knowledge and skills in long-term memory.

The Transformation of Content into Knowledge and Skills

Content from the instructional environment—usually in the form of words (presented in text or audio) and pictures—enters the senses and is incorporated into existing memories already in LTM as follows:

Supporting Attention

Depending on where the learner directs her *attention,* a subset of data from the environment (external or internal) is selected for transfer into working memory. Attention is an important mental process to manage the limited capacity of working memory. Attention-focusing instructional methods should help the learner select important information in the environment for processing in working memory.

For example, a word processing lesson begins with a learning objective that tells the learner that by the end of the lesson she will be able to create and edit a document. The learning objective focuses her attention to the important content of the lesson. Later in the lesson, during the animated demonstration, an arrow draws her eye to the tool bar that contains the editing functions. Cues such as arrows are another instructional method that can support attention. Chapter 7 summarizes proven methods you can use to optimize attention during learning.

Activation of Prior Knowledge

Learning involves the integration of new content from the instruction into existing schema in long-term memory. Activating *prior knowledge* in long-term memory that is relevant to the new content will optimize this integration process. Activation of prior knowledge means that existing related knowledge (schemas) in long-term memory is moved into working memory.

In a word processing lesson, if the learners have had prior experience with word processing, the lesson might begin with questions about what kinds of editing features learners have used in other software. This activity will bring relevant prior knowledge into working memory. Alternatively, if word processing is an entirely new skill, the lesson might show handwritten versions of common edits and use these paper versions to introduce the editing functions of the software. In this way prior knowledge of a familiar task such as editing paper documents is used as a base for the new skills. Chapter 8 discusses proven methods that activate or build relevant prior knowledge.

Management of Load in Working Memory

Because the integration of new content with existing knowledge will occur primarily in working memory, it will be important to ensure that limited working memory capacity is devoted to learning activities. *Cognitive load* refers to the amount of work that is imposed on working memory. It will be important to keep irrelevant cognitive load low so that the learner can devote working memory capacity to learning. In a word processing lesson, each topic is short. During the demonstration, the animation is described by words presented in an audio format rather than a written format to maximize the visual and phonetic storage areas in working memory. These are two of many proven methods to avoid cognitive overload during learning. More methods are summarized in Chapter 6.

Rehearsal in Working Memory Leading to Encoding into Long-Term Memory

Once in working memory, content must be rehearsed in order for it to become encoded into long-term memory. *Rehearsal* refers to a processing of new content in ways that lead to its integration with prior knowledge activated from long-term memory. The more frequently information is *encoded*, the more likely it will be learned. For example, we saw previously that relevant graphics are powerful methods for learning of novices. One reason is that they stimulate *dual encoding*. Dual encoding means that when viewing an illustration, the learner encodes it visually and also verbally. Another method that promotes encoding is effective practice exercises.

To promote encoding in a word processing lesson, for example, graphics in the form of animations are used to demonstrate the editing functions. After viewing an animated demonstration, the learner is assigned a practice exercise to try out the editing functions themselves. The visuals in the demonstration, and the practice exercise will all promote encoding. Chapters 9 and 10 summarize many methods you can use to promote encoding of new content.

Retrieval from Long-Term Memory

You might think that your work is done once you have new knowledge encoded into long-term memory. But in order for new knowledge and skills to be useful when needed, *retrieval* must occur. Since working memory is the active processor, any new knowledge and skills stored in LTM must be retrieved *back into working memory* after training when needed on the job. When retrieval on the job does not occur, the result is *transfer* failure. The knowledge may be present in LTM as evidenced by a test following the training. However, at a later time, retrieval breaks down and the new skills do not transfer to the job.

Transfer of learning of procedural skills like word processing is supported by providing examples and practice exercises that are similar to the environment of the job. Therefore, in a word-processing lesson, the best demonstrations and practice will use the same screens and steps as will be used on the job. That way new skills will be stored in a form that can be readily transferred when needed later to perform similar tasks. While transfer of procedural skills such as word processing is relatively straight-forward, ensuring transfer to far-transfer tasks like sales is much more challenging. Chapters 11 and 12 summarize instructional methods to support retrieval and transfer.

How Long-Term Memory Influences Learning

The schemas already in LTM influence all of these learning events. Specifically, a well-developed schema can direct attention to information in the environment that might not be noticed otherwise. It can expand the capacity of working memory by supporting formation of larger chunks and by automating new skills that then bypass working memory. Learners who have well-developed schemas have a more extensive basis for the integration of new content than learners lacking related schemas. The interaction between the schemas in long-term memory and new content from the environment is the basis for the re-creation of knowledge in each individual. No two individuals will end up with exactly the same representation in memory from the same lesson.

Differences in schemas affect how instructional methods will influence learning processes. A more experienced learner with more related schemas already in LTM requires different instructional methods than those required by a novice. This is why some instructional architectures and methods work well for novice learners, while others are better suited for learners with greater related background. Since novices lack relevant schemas, their instruction must include methods such as graphics and examples that serve as schema substitutes. Learners with experience in the subject domain already have relevant schemas and generally won't profit from instructional methods that compensate for a lack of schemas.

Metacognition and Self-Regulated Learners

The transformation of content into knowledge and skills is monitored and adjusted by the operating system of cognition called *metacognition.* Metacognitive skills are the basis for self-regulated learning. Metacognitive processes help you to set learning goals, select effective learning techniques, monitor progress toward your learning goal, and adjust your strategies as needed. Learners of equal intelligence can have greater or lesser success in learning due to differences in metacognitive skills.

A good contrast in metacognitive skills is found in the college senior compared to the freshman. As she enters college, the freshman may begin by attending classes. But soon she discovers that attendance is not taken and there are few assignments. At the same time she is meeting new friends and enjoying freedoms of college life. If she lacks the regulating and monitoring skills of metacognition, she may find herself cramming for midterms two or three days prior to the exams. In contrast, the senior has learned a repertoire of metacognitive skills, including defining the goal of the class, setting up study schedules, and monitoring herself for comprehension failures.

You can design lessons that compensate for poor metacognitive skills by using instructional methods that support monitoring and adjusting. An example is a course that includes frequent diagnostic quizzes accompanied by recommendations for additional practice. In contrast, learners who already have good metacognitive skills can make these determinations themselves and are best left to their own devices to plan and adjust their learning processes.

Metacognitive skills play a major role during learning and also during problem solving on the job. Chapter 14 summarizes the research on how to build metacognitive skills in learners and how to provide metacognitive support in your instructional materials.

Motivation and Learning

All of these psychological learning processes are fueled by *motivation*. Motivation is any factor that drives the selection of learning options and the main elements of *self-regulation,* including goal setting, effort invested, and responses to learning outcomes—to give up or to persist. Motivation relies on of a set of beliefs— beliefs about yourself, about the learning goals and content, and about the outcomes from a learning event. Enabling beliefs include self-confidence, a positive value in the learning outcome, and goals that focus on self-improvement rather than on competition with others. Enabling beliefs result in a greater likelihood of selecting a learning event and persisting to achieve learning goals. Chapters 15 and 16 summarize research on the various belief systems that underpin motivation, along with suggestions for instructional methods that promote enabling beliefs.

Eight Principles for Instruction

Based on this overview of learning processes as well as empirical research on what is needed to support learning, a handful of principles, well applied, can make the difference between learning success and learning failure. Each of these eight overarching principles is discussed in detail in chapters to come:

1. Optimize Motivational Beliefs

Because motivation is needed to initiate and persist to achieve a learning goal, it is important to make the relevance of the instruction obvious and to build learner confidence during early stages of learning. Techniques to make relevance clear and to build learner confidence can be initiated even before the training starts and should be evident in the first few minutes of a learning event.

2. Activate Prior Knowledge Early in Instruction

Because learning relies on the integration of new content into existing knowledge in long-term memory, techniques that activate knowledge in LTM relevant to the new information improve learning. Chapter 8 summarizes techniques proven to work well for learners who have relevant prior knowledge as well as for learners who lack related knowledge or skills.

3. Direct Attention to Important Elements in the Lesson

Because working memory capacity is limited, it is important that learners use their attention to select those aspects of the lesson that are related to the learning goal. The training environment can help learners selectively attend to what is important by adding cues such as behavioral objectives and by avoiding distractions that cause learners to divide their attention.

4. Manage Irrelevant Cognitive Load

As a consequence of the capacity limits of working memory, management of cognitive load is important in any training program.

The more novice the learners and the more complex the new knowledge and skills, the more important load management becomes. Novice learners who are studying complex topics will have to deal with high mental load, especially if it is new content. However, good instruction can help learners manage that load by using effective instructional methods that minimize irrelevant load and maximize productive load. Load management methods are discussed in Chapter 6.

5. Promote Encoding into Long-Term Memory

The integration of new information with existing knowledge in long-term memory relies on rehearsal processes in working memory that result in encoding. In Chapters 9 and 10 I discuss *implicit* and *explicit* methods that promote active processing of new information in ways that result in deep learning. Implicit methods such as relevant graphics do not require overt behavioral activity on the part of the learner. They work because they prompt mental activity such as dual encoding via formation of visual and verbal codes. Explicit methods such as practice exercises do require behavioral responses from learners and stimulate encoding through mental activity that accompanies external processing of new information.

6. Use Job-Context to Promote Retrieval and Transfer of Near-Transfer Skills

Near-transfer tasks also called procedures are best trained by emulating the job environment during training. For example, when learning new software skills, demonstrations and practice on the actual software or on simulations will encode the best retrieval cues to support transfer later.

7. Build Robust Mental Models to Support Far-Transfer Learning

Unlike near-transfer skills, *far transfer* requires the learner to respond differently to various job situations. Therefore, there will be no single set of environmental cues that will stimulate retrieval. Instead, you need to build a flexible mental model that will help workers respond in different ways depending on job circumstances. This is accomplished by using instructional methods that lead to deeper understanding, as described in Chapter 10.

8. Adapt Instruction to Your Learners' Metacognitive Skills and Your Instructional Goals

You can compensate for learners' low metacognitive skills by incorporating metacognitive supports in the training. For instance, include frequent quizzes with feedback and diagnostic advice to help learners assess their weaknesses. For learners with high metacognitive skills, a better approach is to allow them high learner control, since they already have well-developed goal-setting and monitoring skills. In some situations you may want to develop metacognitive skills in your learners. This is especially relevant if you are training far-transfer skills that involve problem solving, such as troubleshooting or assessing a bank loan applicant. To build metacognitive skills, you can use examples, practice, and feedback that focuses not only on the *outcomes* of solving a problem but also on *the process* of solving a problem.

Each of these eight principles will be described in detail in the chapters to follow. By understanding these principles you will be able to adapt instructional methods most appropriate for the background skills of your learners and for the job performance outcomes required.

COMING NEXT

How Working Memory Works

This chapter concludes Part I, an introduction to the basic concepts to be discussed in the remaining sections of the book. The chapters in Part II will describe each of the main events of learning summarized in this chapter and give guidelines and examples of how to support those events.

The next two chapters focus on working memory, which is the center of all learning processes. The features of working memory that I briefly summarized in this chapter are described in greater detail in Chapter 5. Read Chapter 5 if you are interested in the experiments that established the key features of working memory. Otherwise, skip to Chapter 6 to learn how to use instructional components that manage cognitive load in working memory. Because working memory is where all conscious cognitive processing, including learning, takes place, it's important that you apply instructional methods that both compensate for its weaknesses and exploit its strengths as you design and deliver training programs.

Suggested Readings

Clark, R.C., & Mayer, R.E. (2008). *e-Learning and the science of instruction* (2nd ed.). San Francisco, CA: Pfeiffer. See Chapter 2.

Clark, R.C., Nguyen, F., & Sweller, J. (2006). *Efficiency in learning*. San Francisco, CA: Pfeiffer. See Chapter 2.

Mayer, R.E. (Ed.) (2005). *The Cambridge handbook of multimedia learning*. New York: Cambridge University Press. See Chapter 1(Introduction to Multimedia Learning by Richard Mayer), Chapter 2 (Implications of Cognitive Load theory for Multimedia Learning by John Sweller), and Chapter 3 (Cognitive Theory of Multimedia Learning by Richard Mayer).

Schraw, G. (2006). Knowledge: Structures and processes. In P.A. Alexander & P.H. Winne (Eds.), *Handbook of educational psychology* (2nd ed.). Mahwah, NJ: Lawrence Erlbaum Associates.

Chapter 17
Practical Applications in Building Expertise

BUILDING EXPERTISE IN ACTION

Chapter 13
Problem-Centered Instruction

Chapter 14
Metacognition and Self-Regulation

Chapter 15
Motivation and Expertise

Chapter 16
Motivating Your Learners

PROMOTING ADAPTIVE EXPERTISE AND MOTIVATION

Chapter 11
The Psychology of Transfer

Chapter 12
Teaching for Transfer

SUPPORTING TRANSFER OF LEARNING

Chapter 9
Implicit Methods

Chapter 10
Explicit Methods

BUILDING NEW MENTAL MODELS

Chapter 7
Managing Attention

Chapter 8
Leveraging Prior Knowledge

MANAGING EARLY EVENTS OF INSTRUCTION

Chapter 5
How Working Memory Works

Chapter 6
Managing Cognitive Load

OPTIMIZING WORKING MEMORY RESOURCES

Basic Learning Events Proven to Build Expertise

Chapter 1
Expertise in the Global Economy

Chapter 2
Four Ingredients of Instruction

Chapter 3
No Yellow Brick Road

Chapter 4
The Psychology of Building Expertise

FOUNDATIONS OF BUILDING EXPERTISE

Basic Learning Events Proven to Build Expertise

EFFECTIVE INSTRUCTION requires that instructional modes, methods, and architectures align with human psychological events of learning, including managing load in working memory, supporting attention, activating prior knowledge, helping learners build new mental models, and supporting retrieval to ensure learning transfer.

Part II is the heart of this book, with eight chapters that focus on the core events of learning and instructional strategies proven to promote these events. Chapters 5 and 11 focus on the psychological basis of these events. Chapters 6 through 10 and 12 describe the evidence and give examples of proven training methods you can use to promote these learning processes.

CHAPTER 5 TOPICS

Working Memory: The Center of Learning

New Content Has a Short Shelf Life in Working Memory

Chess, Chunking, and Capacity Limits of Working Memory

    Recalling a Scrambled Chess Board

    Working Memory Capacity Is Limited

    Seven Plus or Minus Two Revised

    Are Experts Smarter?

    Experts Often Overload Learners

What Happens When Working Memory Is Overloaded?

Automaticity: A Working Memory Bypass

    Automaticity and Expertise

Visual and Auditory Components in Working Memory

    Multiple Components of Working Memory

Why Is Working Memory So Limited?

Working Memory and Performance

5

How Working Memory Works

All instruction requiring learners to deal with novel information must be processed by a structure that is minute in capacity and that retains the new information for no more than a few seconds. These limitations should be a central consideration of instructional design.

JOHN SWELLER, "IMPLICATIONS OF
COGNITIVE LOAD THEORY," 2005

THIS CHAPTER DESCRIBES the features of working memory that influence learning and reviews the classic research studies that revealed those features. It summarizes findings that demonstrate:

- The volatility of unrehearsed content in working memory

- The capacity limits of working memory

- The relationship between working memory capacity and prior knowledge in long-term memory

- The effect of information load on working memory processing efficiency

- How automaticity circumvents working memory limits

- The audio and visual components of working memory

Working Memory: The Center of Learning

In Chapter 4 I gave a brief overview of the main features of working memory. I devote a lot of attention to working memory in *Building Expertise* because it is so central to learning. As illustrated in Figure 5.1, it is in working memory that learning occurs through the integration of new content from lessons with activated memories from long term memory.

Instructional modes, methods, and architectures optimize learning when they interact with working memory by:

1. Managing the limited capacity of working memory in order to devote scarce resources to productive learning processes

2. Stimulating learner processing of new content in ways that promote its integration with existing knowledge.

Figure 5.1. Working Memory Is the Brain's Learning Center

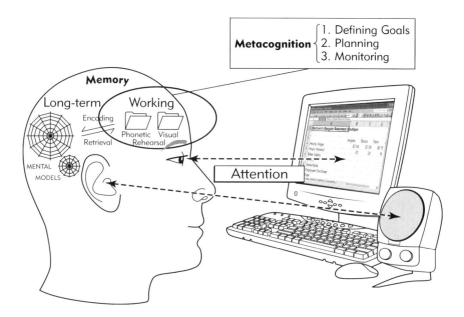

Chapters 6 and 7 describe instructional methods you can use to manage load, and Chapters 9 and 10 summarize ways to promote rehearsals that lead to processing of new content. This chapter digs into the details of how working memory works and includes brief summaries of the research used to derive these features of working memory. In this chapter I answer the following questions:

- How long does new information last in working memory?

- How much information can working memory hold?

- How does prior knowledge in long-term memory affect working memory capacity?

- What happens when working memory capacity is filled?

- How does automaticity help us bypass the limits of working memory?

- What are the subcomponents of working memory?

If you are more interested in instructional applications to manage cognitive load than the psychology of working memory, by pass this chapter and go to Chapter 6.

New Content Has a Short Shelf Life in Working Memory

Suppose you hear a small amount of information such as three letters and do not have the opportunity to process the letters because your working memory is immediately tied up with a second assignment? How long will the letters last in working memory? In a classic experiment designed to answer this question, subjects were given three letters and asked immediately to count backwards by threes from a given number (Peterson & Peterson, 1959). For example, you hear the letters MWP and the number 657 and you immediately start to count: 654, 651,

648, 645, 642, 639, and so on. Counting backwards by 3s is a
task designed to prevent the subjects from rehearsals that result
in encoding into long-term memory. After a period of time
counting backwards, you are asked to recall the letters you heard
initially. In the experiment, the amount of time spent counting varied from three to eighteen seconds and the percentage of
recall accuracy of the letters was averaged for each time period.

Figure 5.2 shows a typical result. If rehearsal is successfully
blocked, the letters are mostly unavailable from working memory within about twelve seconds. Therefore we see that, in the
absence of rehearsal, the shelf life of information in working
memory is very brief.

Think about a time you were told a telephone number and
had to walk into the next room to get your cell phone. If you
did not store the number externally by writing it down or keep

**Figure 5.2. Recall of Information Decreases Rapidly When Rehearsal
Is Blocked**

Adapted from Peterson and Peterson, 1959

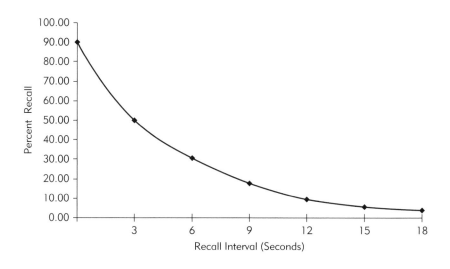

the number alive in working memory by repeating it, you would most likely forget it by the time you retrieved your phone.

Chess, Chunking, and Capacity Limits of Working Memory

Imagine you were shown a mid-play chess board for a few seconds and then asked to reconstruct it from memory. How many times would you need to refer back to the board in order to accurately reconstruct it?

This was the experiment that Chase and Simon (1973) conducted with two different groups: novices and master-level chess players. This research is one of the first experiments to systematically compare the performance of novices with the performance of experts. Each subject had a brief time to study a mid-play chessboard and then reconstruct that board from memory. The experimenters measured the number of times each individual needed to refer back to the chess board in order to accurately reconstruct all twenty-four pieces. Who needed to refer back more times: the novices or the experts?

You won't be surprised to see in Figure 5.3 that novice chess players needed to refer back to the board many more times than did master players. On average, master players were able to reconstruct all pieces with about four glances back to the board, while novices needed to look back seven or more times. Why did experts have better recall? Is it because they have superior memories? Or could it relate to their prior experience? This question led Chase and Simon to part two of the experiment.

Recalling a Scrambled Chess Board

In part two, they repeated the experiment but replaced the mid-play chessboard with a chessboard on which the pieces were randomly placed. The experiment was then conducted as described

---

Figure 5.3. Expert Memory for Board Pieces Was Better than Novice Memory
Adapted from Chase and Simon, 1973

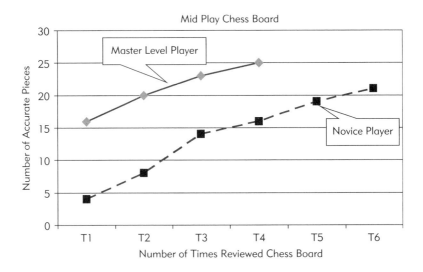

above—novices and master players were asked to reconstruct the board after a brief exposure to it. Now what do you think are the results? Would master players still have an edge? Would they be more or less the same? Or might novices do better than the master players? If superior memory capacity accounted for the better performance of master chess players, they should still do better than novices with the random board. However, if prior experience accounted for their better performance, then with a meaningless board, they would lose their advantage.

The results were somewhat surprising! As you can see in Figure 5.4, master players did worse than novices!

Working Memory Capacity Is Limited

What can we learn from this experiment? First, the capacity of working memory is limited. A single glance at a board with twenty-four pieces overloads working memory capacity. One of

Figure 5.4. Expert Memory for a Random Board Is Worse Than Novice Memory

Adapted from Chase and Simon, 1973

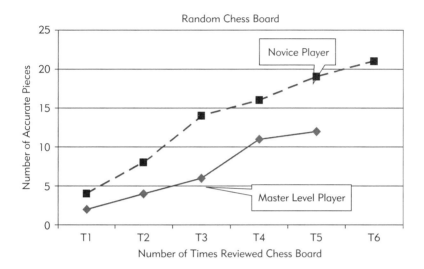

the birth events of cognitive psychology was the publication in 1956 of George Miller's famous paper describing working memory capacity as seven plus or minus two chunks of information (Miller, 1956).

But what is a chunk? As we see in the chess experiment, chunk size is relative to the prior experience of the individual. Here we see the interaction between working memory and long-term memory. The chessboard holds about twenty-four individual chunks of information for the novice chess player because each piece represents a single chunk. However, the master player clusters individual pieces into larger chunks and labels these chunks with familiar play pattern terms. These patterns have been abstracted from many games into schemas in long-term memory. The experts use these schemas to support a top-down process whereby they efficiently represent the chessboard. In other words, when viewing a mid-play board, the expert uses his existing prior knowledge to seek out familiar patterns.

The typical chess master is estimated to have stored around 50,000 play patterns in long-term memory (Simon & Gilmartin, 1973). When reviewing a mid-play board, chess masters scan it for those common play patterns and chunk the individual pieces accordingly. Thus, while a mid-play board contains approximately nine to eleven chunks for an expert, it contains twenty-four chunks for a novice. When the board lost meaning—that is, when the pieces were placed on the board in a random pattern—expert performance was disrupted. In trying to interpret a world that lost its meaning, cognitive processes crumbled. Since the board never had meaning for the novices, their memory for a scrambled board was no different than for the mid-play board.

Seven Plus or Minus Two Revised

Until recently, the capacity of working memory has been considered to fall in the range of seven plus or minus two chunks of information. However, 21st Century Cognitive Load Theory suggests that the limit is actually much smaller. According to Sweller working memory "can probably process in the sense of combine, contrast, or manipulate no more than about two to four elements" (Sweller, 2005, p. 21).

Are Experts Smarter?

The chess research is the first of many studies demonstrating that the performance of experts is based on a large repository of well-organized and very specific acquired knowledge. As I mentioned in Chapter 1, this knowledge is accumulated gradually over years of practice—generally around ten years to reach the highest levels of expertise. While we cannot completely eliminate the effects of aptitude on expert performance, focused and tailored practice is essential to build the knowledge in long-term memory that is the basis for expertise.

A major difference between experts and novices is not that experts have a greater working memory capacity than novices. Rather, it is that they are able to use their limited capacity to greater advantage because they can bring larger chunks of information into it. As a legacy of their greater experience, they use their schemas in long-term memory to efficiently represent and solve problems. This increased virtual mental capacity is one of the keys to expert performance.

Experts Often Overload Learners

Frequently, trainers are subject-matter experts. While their expert knowledge is usually valuable, when it comes to teaching others, it can raise a barrier. Unless experts can shift into the psychological shoes of the novice, they inadvertently impose too much working memory load on their learners. They will present large amounts of information and fail to explain underlying knowledge that is second-nature to them. They fail to sequence and chunk information in order to accommodate the cognitive limits of learners who are novices. Chapters 6 and 7 describe a number of instructional methods that can be used to manage cognitive load in instruction.

What Happens When Working Memory is Overloaded?

Figure 5.5 shows a letter transformation experiment adapted from one reported by Hamilton and others (1977). You might want to try it yourself to get a feeling for how it works.

As you can see, the task involves mental work requiring you to perform letter transpositions and at the same time to hold

Figure 5.5. A Memory Load Experiment
Adapted from Hamilton, Hockey, and Rejman, 1977

Instructions:

1. Start with the first letter in the list and mentally add four letters to it.
2. Hold that answer in memory.
3. Go to the next letter and mentally add four letters to it.
4. Continue until all the letters in that problem have been transposed and then write down your answer.

JFI + 4 =
BTFM + 4 =
EOLMV + 4 =
SBNCKO + 4 =

intermediate products as you work through each problem. It's a bit like solving 897 times 87 in your head. For just a few letters, it's a doable task. However when you get to four- or five-letter problems, having to do the mental work and the same time to remember the intermediate products from the previous letters becomes increasingly difficult. For example, if solving the problem LSEP, you begin by adding four letters to the L, arriving at P and storing P in memory. Then you go to the S, add four letters and arrive at W. Now you are holding P and W in memory. By the time you get to the fourth letter, P, you are now holding three letters in working memory while transforming the P. In plotting the amount of time needed to transpose a letter as a function of the number of intermediate letters held in working memory, you will find that your processing time slows dramatically. And the rate of slowing is not linear. It's a pretty steep curve. Holding information as small as three letters actually imposes enough load on working memory to considerably slow down its processing. Furthermore, as the memory load increases, so does your frustration as you attempt to process more letters.

Since learning requires active rehearsal of new content in working memory, the instructional environment must preserve the limited capacity of working memory for this rehearsal process. We see from this experiment that imposing even a small memory load on working memory inhibits processing and can lead to negative consequences both for learning and for motivation. Therefore, one of your goals as an instructional professional is to free limited working memory capacity for productive learning processes.

Automaticity: A Working Memory Bypass

Any task, be it a physical task such as driving a car or a mental task such as reading, that is repeated literally hundreds of times becomes hardwired in long-term memory and does not require working memory resources for execution. We call this phenomenon *automaticity*. For example, most of us take a standard route for our daily commute to work. We typically find ourselves on automatic regarding both the driving mechanics and the route. We do not need to devote many working memory resources to this activity. When we can perform one or more tasks on automatic, our cognitive system is freed up for *parallel processing,* more commonly known as multi-tasking. In other words, we can devote working memory resources to completing one task while we perform the others automatically. This works fine until the primary task demands our working memory resources.

For example, you are driving along an expressway on a routine trip and talking on your hands-free cell phone. Suddenly a large box drops out of a truck about thirty yards ahead of you. You must immediately switch your working memory resources from the conversation to the driving task. All too often people do not make this switch quickly enough to avert an accident. Thus we see that automaticity is a dual-edged sword. It affords us greater working memory capacity, but can create problems when environmental changes require allocation of resources back to the automated task. Recent accidents caused by text messaging while driving underscore the limits of our memory systems when multi-tasking.

Automaticity and Expertise

Through years of practice, experts have accumulated large reservoirs of automated knowledge and skills stored in long-term memory. Many skills that have become automated take the form of tacit knowledge. In other words, it is very difficult for an expert to clearly and completely articulate automated knowledge. While automaticity gives experts an edge in performance, it can be a detriment when they serve as instructors or subject-matter experts. That's because experts have only limited conscious access to the strategies they use to solve problems or perform tasks. Therefore, when explaining their techniques in a training session, they tend to leave out important steps. For example, six computer programming experts worked a series of debugging tasks and described their problem-solving processes. However, no single expert was able to describe more than 53 percent of his problem-solving steps as recorded on videotape (Chao & Salvendy, 1994). Feldon (2007) suggests that "a critical reexamination of the expert's role as a direct source of knowledge for instruction is necessary" (p. 102). I recommend that, when working with subject-matter experts to define knowledge and skills as part of your job analysis, you do not rely on interviews alone. Instead, consider a knowledge elicitation technique that defines knowledge and skills in the context of job performance.

Visual and Auditory Components in Working Memory

Suppose someone reads you a list of numbers such as 8, 3, 6, 2, 9, 1, 7, 5, 4. When the person stops reading, you are asked to repeat those numbers back. Each time the person reads a new list of numbers, he adds a digit. Eventually the list is too long for you to accurately recall all of the digits. The number of items that you can successfully recall is called a *digit span*. Most people have a digit span of around seven plus or minus two due to the limited capacity of working memory.

Now suppose you are assigned a secondary task to perform during the digit span task. The secondary task asks you to trace a dot moving on a computer screen with a mouse. The dot moves pretty fast—fast enough to require your concentration. This type of study is called a *dual task experiment*. How will a visual scanning task affect your digit span? Figure 5.6 shows data from this

Figure 5.6. Decrease in Digit Span with a Secondary Visual Task in Three Populations

Based on data from Baddeley and Logie, 1999

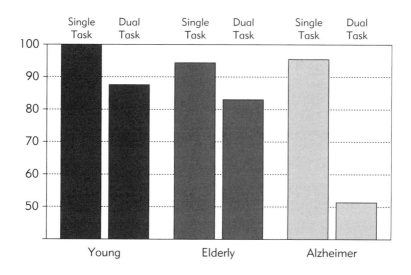

experiment (Baddeley & Logie, 1999). The graph shows the decline in digit span under dual task conditions for each of three groups: young, elderly, and individuals with Alzheimer's. As you can see, on average young people experience a digit span decline of approximately 10 percent under dual task conditions. In other words, a visual task does not adversely impact an auditory task. What does this tell us about working memory?

Multiple Components of Working Memory

Research such as the dual task experiments reveals that working memory includes three components: an executive component that is responsible for integration and rehearsal of content and two subcomponents responsible for processing and storage of visual-spatial and auditory data respectively (Baddeley & Logie, 1999). Therefore, in dual task assignments that call on the visual and the auditory components of working memory, the workload is distributed between those two sub-processing systems. This is why most people maintain a high digit span when doing a visual tracking task. However, what if you were asked to repeat back words read into your left ear and numbers read into your right ear? This would be a much greater challenge because both tasks call on resources in the phonetic center. In Chapter 6 I will summarize some instructional methods you can use to manage cognitive load by dividing content across the visual and the auditory components of working memory.

Why Is Working Memory So Limited?

Sweller (2005) proposes that the limits of working memory have evolved as a safety mechanism to guard against adverse consequences of trying out too many alternatives at once. He suggests that, when learning new skills or solving new problems, being able to hold and process too many elements in working memory in a trial-and-error manner would pose a major barrier to success. The number of combinations of solution steps would be so great that a workable solution may never be found. "A cognitive architecture structured to test the relative effectiveness of millions of possibilities is likely to be unworkable. As a consequence, and paradoxically, a somewhat smaller working memory is likely to be more efficient than a larger one. We may have evolved with a limited working memory because a slightly larger, or worse, unlimited working memory may be counterproductive" (pp. 22–23).

Working Memory and Performance

Although my primary focus in *Building Expertise* is on accommodating working memory during learning, the limits of working memory have implications for design of work environments. For example, computer interfaces and control panels can balance input in the visual and auditory centers of working memory by effectively using both modalities. Or web screens can provide memory support and thus eliminate paging back and forth among screens. I will mention some workplace performance issues to consider in the chapters to follow.

COMING NEXT

Managing Cognitive Load

Now that you have reviewed the details of how working memory works, you can see that it's important to manage those fragile resources so that learning can take place. Chapter 6 on managing load and Chapter 7 on supporting attention summarize a number of instructional methods you can use to optimize the limits of working memory during learning.

WORKING MEMORY FEATURES

To recap, the major features of working memory and the research that supports these are

- ☐ Limited capacity of seven plus or minus two chunks; two to four elements when simultaneously processing information. No one recalled all twenty-four pieces of the chess board on a single try.

- ☐ Chunk size is a function of prior knowledge. Master chess players needed to refer back to the mid-play chessboard fewer times than did novice players.

- ☐ Because of their schemas in long-term memory, experts can process more efficiently by bringing larger information chunks into working memory

- ☐ Rapid decay of new data that enters working memory if processing in working memory is blocked. Within about twelve seconds, even small amounts of new information are lost if they are not rehearsed.

- ☐ When working memory fills, processing slows. It's hard to solve a four-letter transposition problem when you have to hold more than three letters in memory at the same time.

- ☐ Automaticity leads to a working memory bypass. Any task per- formed hundreds of times becomes hardwired into long-term memory allowing dual processing. Dual processing can be a hazard when the primary task requires working memory resources.

- ☐ Automaticity leads to tacit knowledge that may hinder experts when they attempt to articulate how they solve a problem or complete a complex task. Secondary methods to elicit knowledge and skills from experts may provide a fuller and more accurate set of skills.

- ☐ Working memory has separate systems for storing/processing audi- tory and visual information. If a dual task assignment calls on these separate components, performance does not decline dramatically.

Recommended Readings

Feldon, D.F. (2007). The implications of research on expertise for curriculum and pedagogy. *Educational Psychology Review, 19,* 91–110.

Morrison, R.G. (2005). Thinking in working memory. In K.J. Holyoak& R.G. Morrison (Eds), *The Cambridge handbook of thinking and reasoning.* New York: Cambridge University Press.

Sweller, J. (2005). Implications of cognitive load theory for multimedia learning. In R.E. Mayer (Ed.). *The Cambridge handbook of multimedia learning.* New York: Cambridge University Press.

Sweller, J., van Merrienboer, J.J.G., & Paas, F.G.W.C. (1998). Cognitive architecture and instructional design. *Educational Psychology Review, 10* (3), 251–296.

CHAPTER 6 TOPICS

The Cognitive Load Management Principle
> What Is Cognitive Load?
> Factors That Affect Cognitive Load
> Productive vs. Irrelevant Cognitive Load

Methods That Bypass Working Memory
> External Memory Support
> Internal Memory Support: Building Automaticity

Methods That Minimize Content
> Write Concisely
> Omit Unnecessary Technical Details
> Omit Unnecessary Audio, Including Music
> Omit Tangential Stories and Visuals
> Avoid Redundant Modes
> Minimize Animations

Methods to Impose Content Gradually
> Teach Relevant Concepts First
> Segment Lessons
> Let Learners Pace Themselves

Methods to Minimize Unproductive Mental Work
> Replace Some Practice with Worked Examples
> Represent Spatial Content with Visuals

Methods to Maximize Working Memory Capacity
> Describe Visuals with Audio Narration

6

Managing Cognitive Load

Instructional designs that ignore working memory limitations are likely to be random in their effectiveness.

JOHN SWELLER, "IMPLICATIONS OF COGNITIVE
LOAD THEORY," 2005

IN THIS CHAPTER I describe instructional methods you can use to optimize cognitive load in learning environments and in the workplace. I organize these methods based on how they work psychologically:

- Methods such as job aids to by-pass working memory

- Methods such as concise writing to minimize content

- Methods such as chunking and sequencing to impose content gradually

- Methods such as worked examples to minimize unproductive mental work

- Methods to maximize working memory capacity with judicious use of visual and audio modalities

The Cognitive Load Management Principle

Working memory is a paradoxical resource, because it's both the bottleneck and the engine of learning. As discussed in Chapters 4 and 5, working memory is where conscious thought and learning occur. At the same time, its capacity to hold information is very limited. These dual properties of working memory are the foundation for the *Cognitive Load Management Principle* of instructional design:

Cognitive Load Management Principle: Manage cognitive load in the design of instructional materials and activities so that limited cognitive resources can be devoted to learning processes.

What Is Cognitive Load?

Cognitive load is the amount of work imposed on working memory. John Sweller, the originator of modern cognitive load theory, summarizes his rationale as follows: "The implications of working memory limitations on instructional design can hardly be over estimated. All conscious cognitive activity learners engage in occurs in a structure whose limitations seem to preclude all but the most basic processes. Anything beyond the simplest cognitive activities appears to overwhelm working memory. Prima facie, any instructional design that flouts or merely ignores working memory limitations inevitably is deficient" (Sweller, van Merrienboer, & Paas, 1998, 252–253).

Factors That Affect Cognitive Load

The amount of cognitive load imposed during any given lesson will depend on (1) the complexity of the lesson content, (2) the related experience of your learners, (3) the rate and control of presentation of information, and (4) the instructional modes and methods used to teach the content. Table 6.1 summarizes how each of these factors affect cognitive load.

A lecture that rapidly presents a great deal of complex information without the support of visuals, examples, or questions is likely to impose high load on novice learners. In contrast, a multimedia presentation of the same information that uses graphics explained by audio and allows learners to control

Table 6.1. Factors Influencing Cognitive Load

Factor	Influence
Complexity of content	Content and instructional goals of greater complexity will impose higher cognitive load. When goals and content complexity are high, it is important to apply instructional techniques that reduce cognitive load.
Experience	Learners with greater experience in a domain will not require as much cognitive load support as novices because they already possess many related mental models in long-term memory.
Presentation rate and control	When content is presented to learners at a fast rate that they cannot control such as a video presentation, the amount of cognitive load is higher than in learner-controlled media such as self-paced e-learning or a book.
Instructional modes and methods	Instructional modes and methods can impose unproductive types of cognitive load as well as useful forms of cognitive load. For example, in most cases, describing a complex visual with text imposes irrelevant cognitive load, compared with describing the visual with audio narration.

the rate of presentation will impose less load. In both of these learning environments, the content is complex and learners are unfamiliar with it. Therefore, there is a high potential for overload. However, instructional techniques in the multimedia lesson have mitigated this threat by optimizing limited working memory capacity. When learners are new to the content and the content is complex, trainers and designers can maximize learning by using load reduction techniques. Conversely, when working with relatively simple content or with experienced learners, such as in an intermediate course, you need not worry as much about instructional techniques to reduce cognitive load.

Productive vs. Irrelevant Cognitive Load

Not all cognitive load is bad. In fact, learning demands load imposed by tackling tasks that promote the learning objectives. An ideal amount of effective load falls just beyond the competency limits of the learner so that she is challenged to invest mental effort in the learning tasks. For example, entering the correct formula in a spreadsheet to achieve a desired calculation can provide productive load for someone learning how to use electronic spreadsheets. If cognitive load is too low, the learner can respond without investing effort, and learning is minimal. If cognitive load is too high, the learner is overwhelmed, and learning is disrupted. Your challenge is to define learning tasks that impose the right amount of productive load and at the same time minimize irrelevant sources of cognitive load. For example, you might assign a spreadsheet task that uses a simple formula for the first exercise to impose the right amount of productive load and provide a memory support that summarizes formula operators and formats to minimize irrelevant cognitive load.

In this chapter, I will focus primarily on how to reduce irrelevant cognitive load so that learners can allocate limited working memory capacity to the learning tasks. I have grouped methods to minimize irrelevant load into the following categories based on how they are likely to interact with working memory:

1. Allow content to bypass working memory

2. Weed out unneeded content

3. Impose essential content gradually

4. Minimize wasted mental work

5. Maximize working memory sub-system capacity

Methods That Bypass Working Memory

Since working memory can probably hold only two or three chunks while processing information, any methods that allow content to be stored and accessed *outside of working memory* will reduce load. Storage outside working memory can be in two places: externally in the environment or internally in long-term memory.

External Memory Support

In this section I summarize methods you can use to provide memory support in the external environmental including job aids, reference-based training, and memory support in the training interface.

Job Aids. A *job aid* is an external memory resource that can be easily accessed on the job. Job aids can be as simple as a reference card listing software codes or as complex as online wizards that offer guidance tailored to individual user requests or profiles. It's a good idea to introduce job aids during training so that learners become familiar with them during practice exercises. This approach will promote their use on the job. Have you ever cringed when you read the notice: "Some Assembly Required"? Products that require assembly typically include job aids—many of dubious quality. Job aids such as assembly instructions intended to be self-explanatory should be especially well designed since they serve as training substitutes.

When planning job aids, first identify job tasks that rely on substantive amounts of factual or procedural information. Second, ask yourself which tasks could be supported by a working aid in a timeframe and location that will not compromise job outcomes. In some settings, job aids are not feasible because the worker must respond quickly. For example, a train engineer must be able to respond to track signals so quickly that access to a reference would jeopardize safety. In other situations, the work environment may preclude the use of a job aid, such as in a clean room in a manufacturing plant. When you are ready to develop the job aid, apply some of the layout guidelines regarding visuals and text summarized later in this chapter and the next.

Reference-Based Training. In reference-based training, rather than spending time on direct teaching of procedural steps and facts, the learner completes practice assignments with the aid of a reference guide that presents procedural steps and factual information. Reference-based training is an approach often used in software training. The reference guide may be packaged in a paper manual or may be accessed online. The training manual is designed to "wrap" around the reference guide. It includes lessons that present objectives, teach relevant concepts, and pose case studies for learners to resolve by using the reference guide. To manage productive cognitive load, carefully sequence case studies to introduce learners initially to a few simple skills and gradually incorporate greater complexity.

The goal of reference-based training is to familiarize learners with the reference materials during training so that they will use them back on the job. In most situations, the training manual serves its main role during the class and will not be used much afterward. Figures 6.1 and 6.2 show a page from a software reference guide and a page from the training manual that accompanies it.

Figure 6.1. Reference Materials for Software Procedure

How to Adjust the Account

Step	Action	Example
1.	Assign the appropriate type code based on the reason for the adjustment.	BNR, CTO, LTM, etc.
2.	Use the table below to determine the XXX entry format. **IF adjusting / THEN enter the type code (space) and the** a single call — item number. Example: DAK 14 sequential calls on the same TEM screen — item numbers separated by a dash. Example: DAK 14-19 Non-sequential calls on the same TEM screen. — item numbers separated by a comma. Example: DAK 14, 17, 19 Note: If adjusting calls on multiple pages use [F11] to page forward, then use the above table for formatting.	
3.	Press [F9] the ASUM key. Result: Page 2 of the ASUM screen will appear.	

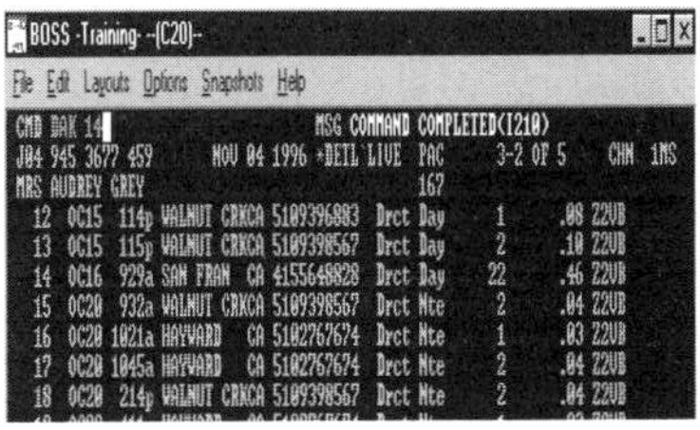

Figure 6.2. Training Materials for Software Procedure

Lesson 6: Making Customer Adjustments

Objective:

You will use customer scenarios and the TEM System to adjust the account with no errors.

Scenario:

Ms. Jones has called in requesting a refund on her last month's billing since she moved. Her account number is 222-33-5555. You will need to access her account to verify her request and make the adjustment.

Use your reference manual to access the appropriate policy and procedure.

Memory Support Embedded in the Training or Work Interface. In the beginning stages of learning, embed memory support for facts or procedural steps into the instructional interface. For example, a virtual classroom session focuses on how to construct formulas in Excel. On the first practice assignment, the instructor places a memory aid in a box on the spreadsheet. The memory aid summarizes the formatting requirements for an Excel formula. Having visual access to this memory jogger will aid the learner during the first few practice exercises. If it is important that the worker can respond without reference, the memory aid should be removed after the first few practice sessions. Pop-ups are another common embedded memory aid used in asynchronous online training and on web pages intended for solo use. When the learner rolls the cursor over a relevant portion of the interface, a box with a few words appears with important factual information. For example, a pop-up box on an online form asking the user to input a new password may summarize the parameters of a legal password.

Internal Memory Support: Building Automaticity

The instructional methods suggested in the previous paragraph involve packaging factual and procedural information in external sources such as paper checklists or online wizards. Another strategy for bypassing working memory is to automate knowledge and skills in long-term memory. In Chapter 5, I summarized the cognitive process of automaticity in which knowledge and skills become "hard-wired" into long-term memory. Automaticity occurs naturally for both cognitive and motor skills that are repeated many times. Driving to work is a common situation in which both the mechanics of driving and the route become automatic over time. Once knowledge and skills are automated in long-term memory, they can be applied without using working memory resources.

In many cases, the most cost-effective and painless way to build automaticity is to let it evolve naturally over time on the job. As the new hire repeatedly performs tasks, those tasks will naturally become automatic. In some situations, however, an automatic response is required the first time the task is performed. For example, a train operator must respond quickly and accurately to a track signal. Or baggage inspectors must quickly and accurately identify weapons during airport screening. The requirement of a quick response precludes use of a job aid. In situations that require accurate responses without a job aid, automatic interpretation of and response to environmental cues must be developed during training.

The execution of complex cognitive tasks such as reading relies on layers of automated knowledge that will support the final performance. As a result of automatic decoding skills, an expert reader like you can scan paragraphs and quickly abstract meaning. Therefore, effective learning of complex cognitive skills will depend on automation of prerequisite skills that support the final performance. This automation can be accomplished by inserting additional task practice sessions throughout training or by assigning on-the-job work periods in-between training sessions to give learners time to automate the foundational skills needed for higher-level performance.

Drill and Practice. When you need to build automaticity during training, the best method is extensive repetitive practice known as drill and practice. Drill and practice was traditionally imposed with flash cards to learn basic skills such as word recognition or math facts. Computers offer an updated route to drill and practice. Computers can measure both the accuracy of response and response time. During early practice stages, accuracy increases but response times remain slow. During later stages, as the skill automates, response time falls dramatically. The combination of high accuracy and quick response is a signal that the learner has automated his or her skills. To make drill and practice more interesting, it can be embedded in an online game context. For example, train engineers must click on the correct engine control when a given signal appears on the screen. Points are awarded based on accuracy and time to respond. The learner can see progress over time plotted on the game interface.

Methods That Minimize Content

When you can't by-pass working memory, consider minimizing the total amount of content imposed on learners. Most trainers have heard the expression "nice to know versus need to know." In this section, I recommend taking a minimalist approach to your total content and your explanations of that content. The theme of this section is: **Less Is Usually More!**

Write Concisely

Learning is often better when fewer words are used to present content. My guideline is to use only the number of words needed to clearly and concisely present the content; avoid unnecessary elaboration of ideas. Mayer, Bove, Bryman, Mars, and Tapangco (1996) created two versions of a lesson on how lightning forms. The standard version included six hundred words and five captioned illustrations. A concise version included a summary of eighty words taken from the standard version and used as captions for the five illustrations. In three separate experiments, students who read the summary performed better on tests of retention and transfer than students who read the whole passage. Figure 6.3 shows the results from one of the experiments in this study.

Omit Unnecessary Technical Details

Often subject-matter experts want to present many details about the content. First, they are usually enthusiastic about the topic.

Figure 6.3. Learning Is Better When Non-Essential Text Is Excluded
From Clark and Mayer, 2008

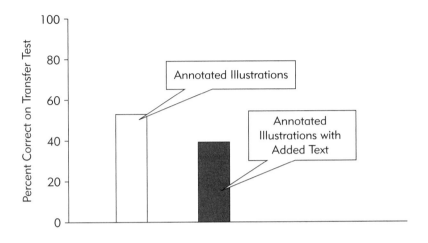

And second, as subject-matter experts, they fail to realize the cognitive overload that novices might experience when subjected to those details. Research has shown that, when it comes to technical detail, less is often more. Mayer and Jackson (2005) compared learning from a multimedia lesson on how ocean waves work in a concise format with a second lesson version that added technical information. In the embellished version, words and graphics were added about computational details such as how to apply formulas related to ocean waves. The expanded versions depressed learning. Mayer and Jackson (2005) conclude that novice learners need to first form a qualitative model of phenomena such as how waves form. Adding quantitative information during the early learning stages may have overloaded learners.

Omit Unnecessary Audio, Including Music

Some multimedia courses add audio in the form of background music or environmental sounds related to the content. For example, a lesson on ammunition safety includes bomb and bullet explosions on a screen describing the energy contained in ammunitions. A different lesson on product knowledge includes some lively background music to add an upbeat motivational theme. Many believe that the MTV and video game generation is accustomed to high-intensity multimedia and will profit from rich media. However, experiments with college-age learners in which background music, environmental sounds, or both music and sounds were added to a narrated multimedia lesson found that learning was 61 to 149 percent better in the *absence of unnecessary audio* (Moreno & Mayer, 2000). The average effect size was 1.66, which is very high.

Many workers intuitively realize that their productivity declines when trying to think deeply in noisy working spaces. Randy Stoltz, a financial planner, escapes a noisy work space by routinely taking his laptop to a local public library to find a quiet working space: "I need peace and quiet and no distractions" (p. D-1, Gibbons, 2007). Seeking a quiet refuge is supported by research demonstrating the potentially negative effects of unnecessary audio on performance. Kenz and Hugge (2002) found that reading comprehension is better in a quiet background. Ransdell and Gilroy (2001) reported that writing fluency is better when music—vocal or instrumental—is omitted.

Overall, the data suggest that learning or work that relies on deep thinking is better in the absence of extraneous auditory information. Of course, in some cases, audio in the form of sounds is essential to learning. For example, students are learning to discriminate certain types of sounds such as when listening to lung or heart sounds. In these cases, the sounds are not extraneous; they are essential lesson content. Also, you may want to add a short musical selection to the opening seconds of an e-learning course as a motivational element. We have no evidence that shows any negative effects from brief opening background music.

Omit Tangential Stories and Visuals

In an effort to spice up technical lessons, it's common practice to add stories or graphics that are related to the general topic but not essential to the learning objective. For example, in a lesson on database construction, the authors added visuals and examples from news stories of database abuses that led to violations of information privacy. Mayer (2005) has tested a number of lessons in which extra words or graphics in the form of interesting facts or stories were added to a base lesson. For example, in a lesson on how lightning forms, he added information on how lightning affects airplanes, the susceptibility of golfers to lightning strikes, and a story of a football player struck by lightning. In ten of eleven experimental comparisons Mayer found a large positive effect size for the lessons that *omitted* the extra materials. The median effect size was 1.32, which is a very large effect.

Avoid Redundant Modes

In Chapter 2, I introduced four key elements of instruction: modes, methods, architectures, and media. Modes refer to the visual or audio expressions of content and include text, audio narration of words, and graphics. By a redundant mode, I refer to a duplication of information in two modes. For example, a complex visual may be explained with words in audio, words in text, or both. Presenting explanations of a visual in text and audio narration of that text is an example of redundancy.

A number of experiments compared lessons in which visuals were explained with audio alone or with audio and on-screen text that repeats the words in the audio narration. Learners in the audio-alone versions scored between 43 and 69 percent higher with an effect size greater than 1, which is a large effect (Clark & Mayer, 2008).

Figure 6.4. Overloading of Visual Channel with Graphics Explained with Words in Audio and Redundant Written Text

From Clark and Mayer, 2008

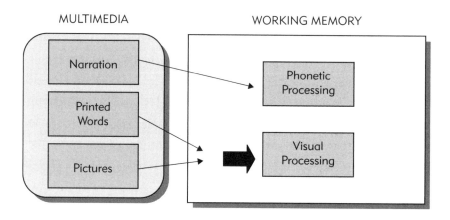

As illustrated in Figure 6.4, redundant modes depress learning by overloading minimal working memory capacity with two visual inputs (a diagram and on-screen text) and a single audio input (narration). In addition, learners may waste cognitive resources by expending mental effort to synchronize the audio narration rate to their own reading pace.

Minimize Animations

Multimedia animations are very popular in e-learning. First, they have a "gee-whiz" effect that shows off the unique capabilities of digital instructional environments. Second, they seem like a logical way to present content that involves motion. For example, animations are typically used to demonstrate step-by-step procedures or to illustrate "how it works" processes involving equipment. Animations are generally popular and seem like a logical choice for illustrating content that involves changes in time or space. So why not use animation?

In spite of these popular incentives to use animation, a number of research studies failed to find that learning was better from an animation than from a series of static frames depicting the same material. For example, Mayer, Hegarty, Mayer, and Campbell (2005) compared four lessons dealing with formation of lightning, formation of ocean waves, how hydraulic brakes work, and how toilet tanks work. One group of learners viewed a narrated multimedia lesson that used animations to illustrate the changes. A second group viewed a series of static frames in which the words were presented in text. In all four lessons, the illustrations and text groups learned as much or more than the animations and narration groups with a median effect size of .57, which is moderate.

We don't yet know why still frames can be more effective. Perhaps as learners view a series of static frames, they engage in a mental animation process that imposes productive cognitive load. In a comparison of learning an immunology process from a version with animated graphics and a version with still graphics, learners who viewed the stills navigated through nine still frames an average of thirty-four times (Schar & Zimmermann, 2007). Apparently the learners were constructing their own mental animations as they moved among the visuals. Ironically, static displays that might on the surface seem passive led to greater mental activity. In contrast, learners may assume a more passive state when viewing an animated version. Additionally, the amount of visual and auditory information in the animations that are often displayed at a pace outside the control of the viewer may overload working memory capacity.

Notice that all of the experimental lessons focused on "how it works" content. It may be that animations are more effective for some types of content such as "how to do it" than for others such as "how it works." We will need to wait for more research that reveals when animations are most useful for learning. Meanwhile, if budget or technical constraints preclude animations, you can likely accomplish as much if not more learning with a series of still frames.

Methods to Impose Content Gradually

Even when you follow the previous guidelines to minimize your content, you are still likely to be left with quite a bit to teach. In this section I summarize some research-proven ways to sequence and segment that content so that learners receive it in chunks—rather than all at once.

Teach Relevant Concepts First

When you have to teach a task or process, there are typically a number of concepts associated with that content. For example, when teaching how to construct a formula for an Excel spreadsheet calculation, some related concepts include spreadsheet cells, cell naming conventions, and formula formats, including operators. Here I offer the following sequencing guideline: **Start the lesson by teaching and practicing the key concepts followed by teaching and practicing the task steps or process stages.** For instance, in the Excel lesson, first teach about cells and cell-naming conventions, followed by formula formats. Then teach the task of constructing and entering a formula to achieve a desired calculation.

What evidence do we have for this sequencing guideline? Mayer, Mathias, and Wetzell (2002) constructed two versions of a course on how a car's braking system works. One version included a one-minute narrated animation with the following script: "*When the driver steps on a car's brake pedal, a piston moves forward on the master cylinder. The piston forces brake fluid out of the master cylinder, and through the tubes to the wheel cylinders. In the wheel cylinders, the increase in fluid pressure makes a smaller set of pistons move. Those smaller pistons activate the brake shoes. When the brake shoes press against the drum, both the drum and the wheel stop or slow down."* A second lesson version preceded this explanation with a summary of each major part of the braking system. The learner could view the brake pedal or the piston and click on it to see how it moved. In three separate experiments, the versions that sequenced the concepts first resulted in much better learning with a median effect size of .9, which is large.

We need more evidence to support this sequencing guideline and to tell us the conditions under which it applies. However, based on what we know so far, break out key concepts and teach them prior to the steps or stages of the task or process to manage the amount of content learners receive at one time.

Segment Lessons

Another way to manage the amount of content learners receive in one lesson is to **keep lessons short.** This guideline is especially important in e-learning settings, where learner attention easily drifts. Exact lesson lengths will vary based on your instructional goals, your learning audience, and practical constraints. As a rule of thumb, I recommend that asynchronous e-lessons be limited to approximately three to five minutes each, and instructor-led lessons that include periodic learning activities not exceed periods of approximately sixty to ninety minutes. To apply this principle to this book, in this edition, I broke up lengthy chapters into two or more shorter, focused chapters. For example, what in this edition appears in Chapters 1 and 2 originally was a single chapter.

Let Learners Pace Themselves

We saw previously in this chapter that animations can depress learning. Lessons that "play" independently of learner control, such as a video lesson or an extended animation, can quickly overload working memory capacity. It is always better to present small content segments and allow the learners to move through those segments at their own pace. e-Learning controls should always include the opportunity to move forward and backward, and to replay short segments. Mayer and Chandler (2001) compared learning from two lesson versions on how lightning forms. In a continuous version a narrated animated segment played for 2.5 minutes. A second version presented the same content in sixteen segments of about ten seconds each with a continue button in the bottom right corner of each screen. In several studies of this type using different content, better learning occurred from the learner-paced lessons with a median effect size of about 1, which is high. Based on evidence to date, I recommend learner control of pacing through short content segments.

Methods to Minimize Unproductive Mental Work

In the previous sections, we have reviewed techniques you can use to bypass working memory or to limit the amount of content imposed on working memory at any one time. In this section, I turn to quite different instructional strategies, strategies that will minimize working memory processes that do not contribute to learning.

Replace Some Practice with Worked Examples

We've all heard the expression "practice makes perfect." However, we have a great deal of research showing that practice is not always the most efficient route to learning. If you think back to your high school math class, you often had homework assignments in which one or two examples were followed by twenty or more practice problems. Sweller and Cooper (1985) found that learning could be much more efficient (faster and better) when learners reviewed examples in place of some of the practice problems.

A worked example is a step-by-step demonstration of how to solve a problem or complete a task. By studying a worked example, the learner can build a mental model of how to solve that type of problem in a manner that requires less mental effort than directly solving the problem herself. Sweller and Cooper compared training time, training errors, test time, and test errors from two groups of learners. Both groups completed a short lesson on solving algebra problems. One group was then assigned to an all-problem version that assigned them eight algebra problems. A second group used a different lesson version in which a worked example was followed by a practice exercise four times. Therefore, both groups were exposed to the same number of problems; one in the form of practice and the other in the form of mixed examples and practice. As you can see in Table 6.2, it's no surprise that those studying the worked examples finished their lessons much faster. However, as you can see from the data, they also had fewer errors during learning and on the test.

Table 6.2. Worked Example Problem Pairs Are More Efficient for Learning

Outcome	Worked-Example-Practice	All Practice
Training Time (Sec.)	32.0	185.5
Training Errors	0	2.73
Test Time	43.6	78.1
Test Errors	.18	.36

From Sweller and Cooper, 1985

The so-called *Worked Examples Effect* is perhaps one of the better researched yet still underutilized cognitive load guidelines available to practitioners today. Since the early experiments such as the one described above, we have learned a great deal more about the best ways to design and position worked examples for learning. I'll review guidelines and evidence from these studies in upcoming chapters.

Represent Spatial Content with Visuals

We began this chapter discussing the benefits of job aids. However, to be effective a job aid must be well designed. Take a look at the assembly directions in Figure 6.5. One version presents the directions in text and the other in diagrams. Which would lead to more effective performance? You are probably not surprised to learn that the text instructions resulted in much longer performance times. Marcus, Cooper, and Sweller (1996) found that assembly of parallel resister combinations like those shown in Figure 6.5 took more than twice as long to complete when using text instructions as opposed to when using the diagram.

The parallel connections are relatively complex. They involve three resistors of three different values and four connections that need to be made in a complex sequence. When reading textual directions like these, the performer needs to translate the words into a spatial representation in order to complete the task. You can short-cut this unproductive mental work by representing this type of content with figures and diagrams rather than with words. This guideline applies primarily to relatively complex content. When performers made single series connections that involved connecting one resistor to another in a simple chain, either text or visual instructions resulted in equivalent performance.

Figure 6.5. Use a Graphic to Display Complex Spatial Content
From Marcus, Cooper, and Sweller, 1996

Text Format:

Using the resistors supplied, make the following connections:

• Connect one end of an 8 ohm resistor to one end of a 3 ohm resistor, and connect the other end of the 8 ohm resistor to the other end of the 3 ohm resistor

• Connect one end of the 3 ohm resistor to one end of a 5 ohm resistor, and connect the other end of the 3 ohm resistor to the other end of the 5 ohm resistor.

Diagrammatic Format:

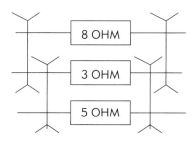

Methods to Maximize Working Memory Capacity

In previous sections, I have summarized methods you can use to bypass working memory, to impose content on working memory gradually, and to minimize the amount of unproductive mental work imposed on working memory. Now I present a guideline related to most productive use of the visual and phonetic subsystems of working memory.

Describe Visuals with Audio Narration

In Chapter 5, I described two major subsystems for memory storage in working memory. One subsystem stores phonetic or auditory inputs, while the second subsystem stores visual information.

One way to extend the limited capacity of working memory is to balance your content across both these subsystems. Based on a number of experiments, instructional scientists have derived the *Modality Principle.*

Modality Principle: Describe complex visuals with words in audio narration rather than with on-screen text.

Of all of the various cognitive load principles I've described in this chapter, the Modality Principle has the strongest evidence. Many experiments have shown that audio descriptions of complex visuals are more effective. In one meta- analysis, Mayer (2005) identified twenty-one experimental comparisons of learning from lessons using printed text and graphics versus learning from lessons using narration and graphics. The experimental lessons included a variety of topics including mathematics, electrical engineering, environment science, and aircraft maintenance, as well as explanations of how brakes work, how lightning storms develop, and how an electric motor works. The median effect size was nearly 1 in favor of audio narration. A second meta-analysis by Ginns (2005) also found strong evidence for the modality effect with an average effect size of .72. In addition to the many laboratory studies, the modality principle has also been demonstrated to apply to learning in classroom settings (Harskamp, Mayer, & Suhre, 2007). Because the Modality Effect has been observed with learners of different ages and with different types of content, we can apply it with considerable confidence.

Like all instructional guidelines, this one has its limitations. In some cases, presenting words in audio imposes more cognitive load than presenting the words in text. Second-language learners, for example, are likely to benefit from text so they can read and review the content at a rate comfortable to them. Also, content that should remain accessible to learners over time should be presented with on-screen text. A typical example is directions for a practice exercise. As the learner works the exercise, she may need to refer back to the directions several times. Finally, when there is no visual, or when the visual is simple or the learners are experienced with the visual, the Modality Principle will have less effect.

There is much more to say about cognitive load and in fact, with John Sweller and Frank Nguyen I wrote an entire book on this topic called *Efficiency in Learning*. I recommend it along with other resources listed at the end of the chapter to readers who would like more in depth discussion.

GUIDELINES FOR MANAGING COGNITIVE LOAD

To recap, in this chapter I have summarized a number of instructional methods that are effective because they reduce the amount of irrelevant work imposed on working memory. The techniques include:

☐ Methods to Bypass Working Memory

- Job aids
- Reference-based training
- Memory aids in the training interface
- Drill and practice

☐ Methods to Minimize Content

- Concise writing
- Eliminate unnecessary audio
- Cut unrelated stories and visuals
- Avoid redundant modes
- Minimize animations

☐ Methods to Impose Content Gradually

- Teach relevant concepts before steps or stages
- Segment lessons into bite size pieces
- Allow learners to control their pace

☐ Methods to Minimize Unproductive Mental Work

- Replace some practice with worked examples
- Represent spatial content with visuals

☐ Methods to Maximize Working Memory Capacity

- Describe visuals with audio narration

COMING NEXT

Managing Attention

A topic closely related to management of cognitive load involves supporting learner attention. Because working memory is limited in capacity, it is important that learners focus their limited cognitive resources on the essential elements of the learning environment. In the next chapter I will review a number of techniques you can use to help learners focus attention and avoid divided attention during learning.

Recommended Resources

Clark, R.C., Nguyen, F., & Sweller, J (2006). *Efficiency in learning.* San Francisco, CA: Pfeiffer.

Clark, R.C., & Mayer, R.E. (2008). *e-Learning and the science of instruction* (2nd ed.). San Francisco, CA: Pfeiffer.

Schnotz, W., & Kurschner, C. (2007). A reconsideration of cognitive load theory. *Educational Psychology Review, 19,* 469–508.

Sweller, J. (2005). Implications of cognitive load theory for multimedia learning. In R.E. Mayer (Ed.), *The Cambridge handbook of multimedia learning.* New York: Cambridge University Press.

CHAPTER 7 TOPICS

The High Price of Attention Failure

The Attention Principle
What Is Attention?
Strengthen and Focus the Beam: A Flashlight Analogy

Instructional Methods to Support Attention
Attention During Learning

Optimizing Attentional Capacity in the Classroom
Manage the Physical Environment
Manage Fatigue
Promote Accountability and Engagement
Competency-Based Instructional Models
Questions
Instructor Contact
Pacing

Methods to Focus Attention
Research on Selective Attention

Methods to Support Selective Attention
Incorporate Cues in Visuals and Text
Use Signaling Techniques in the Classroom
Focus Goals to Direct Attention
Insert Questions During Learning Events
Include Learning Objectives with Achievement Criteria

What Is Divided Attention?
Research on Divided Attention

Methods to Minimize Divided Attention
Integrate Related Visuals and Words on Pages and Screens
Integrate Instruction in the Same Medium

7

Managing Attention

I sometimes worry about my short attention span,
but not for very long.

HERB CAEN

I N THIS CHAPTER, I summarize the role of attention in learning and describe three classes of instructional methods you can use to optimize and direct learner attention:

- Methods to optimize attentional capacity
- Methods to support selective attention including cueing and goal setting, and
- Methods to avoid divided attention among information displays

The High Price of Attention Failure

The following headlines alert us to the damaging effects of widespread attention failure:

- BlackBerry causes pileup on freeway: WA ready to take action
- Bill banning iPods and cell phones on New York City streets coming

- Woman falls on subway track while text messaging
- Speed cameras to trap mobile phone users at the wheel
- Listening, hands-free, distracting to drivers

Of course, not all attention lapses have severe consequences. Most simply exert their toll in lost productivity and inefficiency. Spira (2005) reports that unnecessary interruptions consume 28 percent of a knowledge worker's day, which translates into $28 billion in the United States alone! Savvy workers like Randy Stoltz, a financial planner whose work demands concentration, are escaping the distractions of the office by taking their laptops to quiet retreats such as public libraries. As Stoltz put it: "I need peace and quiet and no distractions" (Gibbons, 2007, p. D1).

Because working memory is such a powerful problem solver and thinker, we tend to overlook the severe limits described in Chapters 5 and 6. One remedy is to support attention during learning and in the workplace.

The Attention Principle

Attention is the gateway to our brains. That's why gaining and sustaining attention is an early and ongoing central consideration in any learning event. The critical role of attention in managing limited working memory capacity is the rationale for my *Attention Support Principle:*

Attention Support Principle: Manage attention in the design of instructional environments in ways that (1) optimize attention capacity, (2) direct attention to important instructional content, and (3) minimize divided attention in order to devote limited cognitive resources to learning.

What Is Attention?

Sternberg (1996) defines attention as "the phenomenon by which we actively process a limited amount of information from the enormous amount of information available through our senses, our stored memories, and our other cognitive processes" (p. 69). Experienced trainers are quite familiar with attention focus and attention loss in their learners. And we have all experienced loss of attention enough to have an intuitive sense of what attention is. However, describing exactly how attention works has proved elusive to psychologists. To account for contradictory results from experiments on attention, Hidi (1995) proposes two attentions—early and late. The *early attention* is at least partially preconscious and is responsible for automatic detection of relevant features in the environment as well as determination of importance. The *late attention* is responsible for focused effort devoted to learning.

Although there is disagreement on exactly how attention works, there is consensus that attention is one of the first stages in the processing of information in working memory that leads to learning. In other words, without attention on the right things, nothing much is going to happen.

Strengthen and Focus the Beam: A Flashlight Analogy

I find that a capacity view and a selection view of attention offer useful perspectives. A flashlight provides a good analogy. A flashlight is powered by a battery that influences the strength of the light beam. As the capacity of the battery wanes, the beam is less intense. However, whatever capacity is available can be allocated in different ways, depending on how you aim and focus the beam. You will see more if you aim your flashlight at a specific object than if you try to split the beam among several objects. The best performance will come from a flashlight that has a high battery charge (capacity) and directs the beam fully onto a single important object (selective attention), rather than dividing it among two or more objects (divided attention). In this chapter, I will focus on methods to optimize capacity as well as methods to focus that capacity on important elements of the learning environment.

Instructional Methods to Support Attention

Table 7.1. summarizes techniques related to the capacity and focusing mechanisms of attention.

Instructional methods that optimize capacity include physical and motivational factors that influence learner arousal. Assuming optimal capacity, the learning environment needs to focus learner attention on what is relevant to the goals of the training. There are two sides to focusing techniques: selective attention and divided attention. Your goal is to maximize *selective attention* and minimize *divided attention.* Selective attention methods, also called signals, are of two major types: cueing and goal setting. In contrast, divided attention refers to how effectively we can allocate our limited mental resources to several things at once and thus succeed at multitasking. Since our working memory capacity is limited, your goals as an instructional professional are

Table 7.1. Instructional Strategies to Manage Attention

Optimize Capacity	Focus Attention	
	Support Selective Attention	Minimize Divided Attention
Physiological Techniques	Cueing Techniques	Page and Screen Contiguity
Motivational Techniques	Goal-Setting Techniques	Media Contiguity

to support selective attention and minimize divided attention originating from the suboptimal display and delivery of instructional messages.

Attention During Learning

As I mentioned in Chapter 3, there are always several factors that influence any psychological learning process. Attention during learning is influenced by (1) layout and features of the instructional materials and learning environment, (2) learner background knowledge, goals, and metacognitive skills, and (3) assignments during learning, such as questions. For example, the need for attention support is much greater when your learners have limited knowledge of the content and are learning complex materials that do not include assignments such as practice exercises. Under these conditions, use one or more of the techniques described in this chapter. In contrast, if the content is simple or your learners are advanced, adding attention-support methods may not improve learning outcomes.

Optimizing Attentional Capacity in the Classroom

The capacity view suggests that our attention levels vary depending on our physical state of arousal. Arousal can be affected by various physiological factors, including fatigue, drugs, and anxiety. While the instructor may have limited impact over learners' physiological state, she can influence arousal during training as follows:

- Optimize the physical elements of the environment (temperature, ventilation, light, food)

- Manage fatigue by interspersing breaks, adding variety, and injecting activities throughout the instruction

- Make learners accountable for outcomes in ways that optimize the effects of stress

Manage the Physical Environment

Experienced instructors are "picky" about the instructional environment. In my seminars, I focus on factors that alleviate fatigue and reduce distractions. For example, I prefer to keep the room temperature a little cool (not so cold as to be uncomfortable) and to maintain fresh air circulation. Because I'm often in a setting where I cannot easily control the temperature, such as a hotel meeting room, I advise participants to bring sweaters or jackets. A lack of lighting in the training environment can, over time, isolate participants from the instructor and from each other. I avoid dimming lights—doing so only when showing something that displays best with reduced lighting. Instructors have different preferences about what kinds of food to provide. I have found that most participants in classroom training enjoy beverages and snacks available throughout the training event.

Manage Fatigue

Learning is hard work. Even after as little as twenty minutes of intensive learning, attention batteries can deplete. The instructional designer and the trainer can manage fatigue by reducing the length of more intense learning periods and by pumping energy into the system periodically. All too often, learners are required to sit passively for lengthy presentations. Attention soon wanders. Instead, in conjunction with a lecture or reading assignment, learners can complete an exercise or collaborate in a discussion or case study. Although fatigue management depends on the instructor in classroom situations, the course design can also make a difference. Build in variety in media, activities, and participant movement as you plan the choreography of your learning event.

Promote Accountability and Engagement

There is an inverse bell-shaped relationship between anxiety and achievement. When little is demanded of us, often we invest little effort. Low levels of stress result in minimal effort and attention. In contrast, too much demand can be paralyzing. The middle road is best. To aim for the top of the curve, the instructional environment should provide moderate challenge without over-stressing participants. To optimize accountability and engagement in your training consider the use of:

- Competency-based instructional models
- Questions
- Instructor contact
- A lively pace in the classroom

Competency-Based Instructional Models

Many training events make no demands of the individual participant. Even though some exercises and discussions may be included, there is no requirement that individual participants demonstrate acquisition of new knowledge or skills. When you are deploying training that supports important operational goals, I recommend that you build accountability by requiring learners to demonstrate application of new knowledge and skills. A certification program is one approach. In my Instructional Design Certification program, after class, participants are required to complete a project in the workplace and submit it as evidence of competency. For example, after taking a performance assessment class, each participant has a month to conduct an assessment at his or her work site and submit a report to the instructor.

Of course, competency demonstrations—be they tests, testimonials of others, or portfolios of work, require additional instructional and administrative resources. The competency evaluation instrument, such as a test or a project checklist, must be developed. Also, coaching resources may be needed to guide participants during projects. Resources must be allocated to evaluate the demonstration and keep records of accomplishments. Finally, policies and provisions must be made for passing criteria and for individuals who fail to demonstrate competencies.

Commercial certification programs have become popular and in many cases require only attendance at a training event. I believe a meaningful certification should incorporate a tangible demonstration of competency. For more information on certification see *Performance-Based Certification* by Judith Hale.

Questions

I recommend the use of directed questions or discussions throughout any instructor-led event. These are especially useful during virtual classroom sessions when learners can drop out both mentally and physically by minimizing the screen and turning to e-mail, cell phones, or other distractions. Frequent directed questions will sustain attention. Specifically, I recommend asking a question, pausing, and then calling on someone to respond. I also usually call on individuals to respond to practice exercises—but only after they have had time to work the practice and to discuss their responses with peers in the class.

Questions need not be all "knowledge" questions with correct or incorrect answers. Instructors can also include "What do you think?" and "How does this work in your organization?" types of questions. Likewise, questions need not all be instructor to participant. Questions can be raised by the instructor or a participant and responses can be among participants in pairs or in small groups.

Instructor Contact

Research shows that when learners have contact with the instructor while doing individual work, their engagement rates increase by around 10 percent. Rosenshine and Stevens (1986) observe that "Teachers moving around and interacting with students during seatwork is also an illustration of the 'active teaching' which was successful" (p. 387). In general, keep contacts relatively brief—one to three minutes in most cases. Longer contacts reduce the amount of time you can spend with other participants. If during these process checks you identify participants who need more help, arrange a separate instructional opportunity for them. If you find a number of participants struggling, that's an indicator to stop individual work and clear up general misconceptions.

In large group workshops, I always wander around the room during practice assignments to see whether anyone needs help and to judge progress. A secondary benefit of my room tour is to focus attention to the assigned task. Some individuals, seeking to escape accountability in a large group setting, pick up their pencils and get to work as I roam the room. My physical proximity alone stimulates attention.

Pacing

Too much lag time invites loss of attention. Research on pacing suggests that a relatively rapid rate leads to best learning (Anderson & Torrey, 1995). On the other hand, if the content is complex, pacing should be slowed to manage cognitive load. In a review of teacher behaviors most consistently associated with learning, Brophy and Good (1986) recommend that "It is important not only to maximize content coverage by pacing the students briskly through the curriculum, but also to see that they make continuous progress all along the way" (p. 360). Finding the perfect balance for everyone in a face-to-face setting is just about impossible due to individual differences in learning rates. The instructor's best bet is to set a brisk pace and at the same time keep in touch with learners to verify understanding with exercises and questions.

I have found that the common technique of pausing and asking: "Does anyone have a question?" is usually *not* productive.

Instead, pause for a practice exercise or brief participant discussion that requires learners to apply new knowledge and skills. During the activity, the participants and instructor can verify understanding and learner questions will surface.

Methods to Focus Attention

Help learners focus on what is important during instruction by using techniques that direct attention and by avoiding situations that lead to divided attention. We will look at directing attention in this section.

Research on Selective Attention

Imagine someone reading aloud two different articles simultaneously—one into your left ear and another into your right ear. If you are asked to repeat back aloud what is being read into your left ear as it is being read, how much would you be able to assimilate from the right ear? This was the type of experiment done during early research on attention. Asking participants to restate the message read into the left ear is called *shadowing* and is used to focus attention to that ear. After the reading, researchers evaluated how much was recalled from the right or unshadowed ear. They found that, although people could successfully recall the attended message (shadowed message), little of the unattended message was consciously recalled (Cherry, 1953). Even if the same word was repeated many times in the unattended message, most subjects were unaware of it. The shadowing experiments indicate that humans are good at filtering out distractions when they are specifically focusing on one aspect of the environment. However, little of what occurs in the unattended elements is consciously absorbed. In instruction, you can use both cueing and goal-setting techniques to guide learners to selectively attend to what is most important in the training.

Methods to Support Selective Attention

Cueing and goal focusing are two excellent techniques to support selective attention. *Cueing* refers to any of a number of physical techniques applied to pages or screens or vocal variety that direct the learner's eyes and ears to important content. *Goal focusing* refers to techniques that convey the intended outcomes of the instructional event to the learner and thereby guide the learner's focus of attention.

Incorporate Cues in Visuals and Text

A *cue*, also called a *signal*, is any technique used to make some elements of the content more salient than other elements. You can see a common example in Figure 7.1 taken from an animated narration of how to perform a computer procedure.

Figure 7.1. Use On-Screen Cueing to Direct Attention to Elements of the Screen

With permission from RELATE Corporation

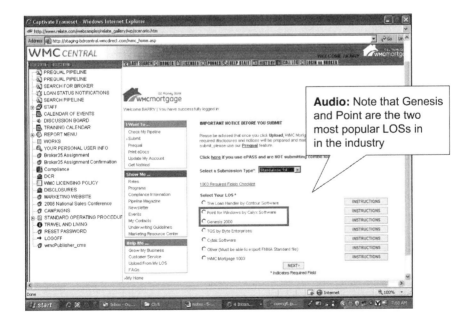

As the narrator describes the different items on the screen, a red square surrounds them. Research has shown that, especially in fast-paced complex media such as animations, cues are essential to learning. Using a multimedia animation of the circulatory system, de Koning and his colleagues (2007) found that cueing of one process (heart valve functionality) improved comprehension and inference learning not only of the cued valve process but of other related processes as well. The research team concludes: "By guiding attention to the relevant aspects in the animation, working memory resources can be allocated more efficiently" (p. 740).

In addition to geometric cues such as circles or arrows, signals can be textual or auditory. For example, compare the unsignaled with the signaled versions of the passage on airplane lift in Figures 7.2 and 7.3. As you can see, the signaled version includes text added immediately following the first paragraph that previews the remaining content. In addition, bolded section heads have been added and individual words have been bolded or italicized. An auditory version would use vocal emphasis to signal the words that appear in bold or italics. Do textual signals like these improve learning?

Mautone and Mayer (2001) compared learning from signaled and unsignaled full versions of the airplane lift passages in three different formats: a text version, an audio version, and an animation-audio version that included narrated visuals. All three signaled versions resulted in significantly better learning. Learning was between 48 percent and 44 percent better in the signaled versions with moderate effect sizes around .7.

Mayer (2005) summarizes his *Signaling Principle:*

Signaling Principle: "People learn more deeply from a multimedia message when cues are added that highlight the organization of the essential material" (p. 184).

Figure 7.2. Initial Paragraphs from Unsignaled Text Version

From Mautone and Mayer, 2001

Airplane Flight–The Principles of Lift

What is needed to cause an aircraft that is heavier than air to climb into the air and stay there? An aerodynamic principle formulated by Daniel Bernouille in 1738 helps explain it. Bernouille's Principle explains how upward forces, called lift, act on the plane when it moves through the air.

A cross-section of a bird's wing, a boomerang, and a Stealth bomber all share a shape similar to that of an airplane wing. The upper surface of the wing is curved more than the bottom surface. The surface on the top of the wing is longer than on the bottom. This is called an airfoil.

In order to achieve lift, air must flow over the wing. The wingspan of a 747 is more than 200 feet; that's taller than a 14-story building. When the airplane moves forward, its wings cut through the air. As the air moves across the wing, it will push against it in all directions, perpendicular to the surface of the wing.

Figure 7.3. Initial Paragraphs from Signaled Text Version

From Mautone and Mayer, 2001

Airplane Flight –The Principles of Lift

What is needed to cause an aircraft which is heavier than air to climb into the air and stay there? An aerodynamic principle formulated by Daniel Bernouille in 1738 helps explain it. Bernouille's Principle explains how upward forces, called lift, act on the plane when it moves through the air.

New Organizer

To understand how lift works, you need to focus on differences between The top and bottom of an airplane's wing. First, how the top of the wing is shaped differently than the bottom; second, how quickly *air flows* across The top surface, compared to across the bottom surface; and third, how the *air pressure* on top of the wing compares to that on the bottom of the wing.

Section Heads

Wing Shape: Curved Upper Surface Is Longer

A cross-section of a bird's wing, a boomerang, and a Stealth bomber all share a shape similar to that of an airplane wing. The upper surface of the wing is curved more than the bottom surface. The surface on the **top** of the wing is *longer* than on the **bottom**. This is called an airfoil.

Bold, Italics

Air Flow: Air Moves Faster Across Top of Wing

In order to achieve lift, air must flow over the wing. The wingspan of a 747 is more than 200 feet; that's taller than a 14-story building. When the airplane moves forward, its wings cut through the air.

He explains that signals are effective because they direct "the learner's attention toward essential material, thereby enabling the learner to ignore extraneous material and use all available cognitive capacity to process essential material" (p. 187).

Signals are most useful when the text structure is complex. These findings are in line with what we know about cognitive load and learner experience. Any strategy designed to reduce cognitive load will be most effective when the content is complex and/or learners are novice.

Use Signaling Techniques in the Classroom

Signals in classroom presentations or audio narration include preview summaries, pointer words, and shifts in vocal emphasis and timing given to headings and important words. In reviewing teacher behaviors that are associated with improved learning, Brophy and Good (1986) recommend that: "Achievement is maximized when teachers not only actively present material, but structure it by…outlining the content and signaling transitions between lesson parts; calling attention to main ideas; summarizing subparts of the lesson as it proceeds" (p. 362).

A relevant study compared learning from taped lectures with and without signals when learners did and did not take notes. Best learning was found among learners who took notes from signaled content and worst learning among learners who took notes from unsignaled content (Rickards, Fajen, Sullivan, & Gillespie, 1997). Taking notes while listening demands cognitive resources from working memory and will debilitate learning unless signals are added as cognitive aids.

Focus Goals to Direct Attention

In the previous section, we focused on physical mechanisms such as circles, arrows, bolding, and addition of organizing text to direct learner's attention. In this section, I describe an alternative route. By helping learners assume appropriate goals during learning, attention can be directed to the most relevant aspects of a lesson. As we will see in Chapter 15, goal setting is one of the proven mechanisms that mediate optimal learner motivation. Goals are effective because they direct attention. Two common techniques for goal focusing are the use of questions and learning objectives.

Insert Questions During Learning Events

Research conducted in the 1970s reported that questions included with reading assignments increased learning of the text material that was questioned, but not text material that was not questioned (called incidental information). Similar results have been reported in the use of classroom questions. The effect of questions on learning has been revisited recently with an emphasis on how questions interact with human thinking processes. Van den Broek, Risden, Tzeng, Trabasso, and Brasche (2001) measured the effects of questions placed during and at the end of text on learning of readers of different ages. Specifically, students from fourth, seventh and tenth grades and college read short stories that included one of the following: (1) questions interspersed throughout the story, (2) questions placed at the end of the story, or (3) no questions. After reading and answering the questions, following a brief pause, learners were asked to recall what they had read. The study assessed overall recall and compared recall of questioned information versus unquestioned information for the different ages and question locations.

Not surprisingly, older students recalled more from the stories. However, the results showed that questions had different effects depending on the age of the readers and on the placement of the questions.

Figure 7.4. Placement of Questions and Age of Learner Influences Learning
Based on data from Van den Broek, Risden, Tzeng, Trabasso, and Brasche, 2001

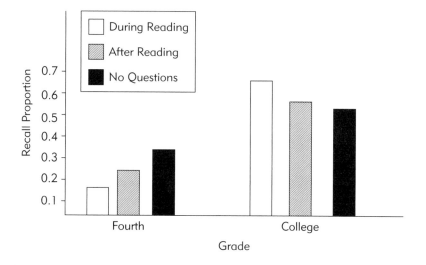

Grade

As shown in Figure 7.4, younger readers who received questions recalled less than younger readers with no questions. The texts in which questions were distributed throughout the story were especially harmful for young readers because they drew mental resources away from the reading task that required all their attention. The opposite pattern was seen among college students for whom questions increased recall. Questions distributed throughout the story resulted in the best recall for the college readers. The research team proposes that questions caused divided attention among younger readers by taking resources away from the reading tasks. Questions, especially questions that interrupted the reading of the story, depressed learning because reading requires the full attention of unskilled readers. In contrast, older readers, for whom reading is an automatic skill, benefited from questions that directed greater attention to important story information. Consistent with earlier research, information that was questioned was recalled better than information that was not included in questions. Further, the specific text information that learners gave in their responses was remembered much better than textual information that was not included.

The authors conclude: "Our findings suggest that questioning can be used to direct the attention of students to specific information and to prompt them to encode specific connections. However, teachers should be careful in using questions to enhance comprehension until students reach an adequate level of reading proficiency. . . . Questions during reading are likely to have more profound effects—for better or for worse—than questions after reading" (p. 527). This research is enlightening not only as it relates to support of attention but as an example of a study that illustrates how a given technique (questions) affects learning differently due to the cognitive processes it either enhances or diminishes. By understanding how specific instructional methods interact with human cognitive processes, you can more skillfully adjust your use of instructional methods for specific learners and training topics.

A recent study by McCrudden and colleagues (2005) confirms the value of preceding a reading with questions that will help focus attention by giving learners specific goals. With specific goals in mind, readers can more readily sort through the text, discriminating between relevant and irrelevant content. In this research, all readers were instructed to read a passage on space travel carefully in preparation for a test. Before reading, three different conditions were applied. One-third of the readers were given questions related to a physiology theme in the passages, one-third of the readers were given questions related to a different theme in the passages, and one-third were not given any questions. For example, before reading a passage on space travel, learners assigned to the physiology theme were asked "Why does the potential for kidney stones become greater in space?"

Analysis of content recalled on the test showed that text segments related to the particular questions asked were better recalled than those that were not related. Apparently, questions focused greater attention to content that was the focus of the questions.

These studies measured recall of text ideas rather than application. We will have to await further research showing that not only recall but also application learning benefits from questions. Meanwhile, a simple and inexpensive strategy to help focus learner attention is placement of relevant questions within a lesson or reading assignment.

Include Learning Objectives with Achievement Criteria

A *learning objective* is a statement of what the learner will do after the lesson or module to demonstrate they have understood the content or acquired the skill. Learning objectives are one of the most common instructional methods seen universally in workforce training materials. Is there any value to their use? What are the psychological benefits of learning objectives?

Reading times and eye movements were compared among readers who were given goals prior to reading with readers who were not given goals. Readers who were given goals had a lower overall reading time than those who were not. When reading background information that was not included in the goals, reading was rapid. However, when encountering goal-relevant information, readers switched to an inspection style of reading in which they rescanned lines and took longer times to read. Readers who spent more time on the goal-specific text segments had better recall of that information than of background information (Rothkopf & Billington, 1979). These results support the positive effects of learning objectives to help direct attention to elements of the instruction that are most relevant. Similar results have been reported in comparison of learning from computer lessons that included and excluded learning objectives (Cavalier & Klein, 1998).

Research on motivation that I will review in Chapter 15 indicates that learners' attention should be focused on their own progress over time, rather than on how their performance compares with others. When participants are competing with others for grades, their attention is focused on social goals, that is, looking good, rather than strategies that will lead to improvement over time. Therefore, establish a learning environment that requires all learners to evaluate their individual progress in meeting the criteria of a learning objective and minimizes comparisons with other participants.

SUPPORTING SELECTIVE ATTENTION: SUMMARY OF TECHNIQUES

- [ ] Use physical devices such as circles or arrows to direct attention to graphic elements in complex visual displays; especially when they are narrated.

- [ ] Use text effects such as topic headers, bolding, and italics.

- [ ] Use vocal emphasis and pauses to signal important content in audio segments.

- [ ] Use questions and learning objectives to help learners adopt goals related to the most relevant portions of an instructional environment.

What Is Divided Attention?

In the previous section I summarized various signaling techniques you can use to point the learners' attention to the most relevant content in the lesson. Now I turn to the other side of the attention coin—techniques to minimize divided attention during learning.

Research on Divided Attention

While the selective attention research set up tasks that required subjects to concentrate on one source of information (the shadowed words), in divided attention experiments, learners are asked to attend to two or more simultaneous events in the environment. Psychologists call these *dual tasking experiments.* I described dual tasking experiments in Chapter 5. In a dual tasking experiment, subjects are usually assigned a primary task that is the central focus of their attention and at the same time a lower-level secondary task. For example, subjects might be asked to study a lesson and respond to a periodic auditory tone with a key press. Alternatively, they might be asked to listen to a list of numbers for later recall and at the same time trace a moving dot on a computer screen with the mouse. Success at divided attention tasks depends on three factors:

1. *Modality of inputs or outputs.* When the inputs are directed to the same sensory modality, such as one into the left ear and one into the right ear, attention to both is poor. In contrast, when asked to attend simultaneously to a visual stimulus such as a moving dot on a screen and an auditory stimulus such as someone reading into one ear, performance is better. This is because attention capacity can be allocated separately between the visual and auditory processing centers in working memory, as discussed in Chapter 6.

2. *Difficulty of the task.* If one task is relatively simple, humans are pretty good at multi-tasking. This is because they can allocate working memory capacity to several mental events.

3. *Experience of the performer.* If individuals receive a great deal of practice in dual task performance, their results improve dramatically. In one study, individuals were asked to read text for meaning and take dictation on different text read aloud at the same time (Spelke, 1976). At first, their performance was poor on both tasks. However, after many practice sessions, they dramatically improved their performance. In fact, eventually they

became as proficient on both tasks as on each task alone. Part of the improvement probably reflected automatization of one or more of the tasks. Once automated, a task does not require any working memory capacity allowing for multitasking.

Methods to Minimize Divided Attention

At the beginning of this chapter, I shared some recent headlines regarding the dangers of text messaging and similar distractions while driving. We might get by with some multi-tasking when neither task requires complete attention. However, when two tasks compete for limited resources and safety demands total attention to one of them, consequences of multi-tasking failures can be severe. During instruction, I recommend that you keep divided attention to a minimum so that maximum cognitive resources can be allocated to the instructional goals. In the following sections, I summarize techniques you can use to avoid divided attention.

Integrate Related Visuals and Words on Pages and Screens

It's a common experience to read some text that discusses a visual that is located on the back of the page of the text. Neither the text nor the visual is completely understandable alone. You feel annoyed as you flip the pages back and forth to mentally connect the words and the graphics. This annoyance is your working memory complaining about the use of scarce processing resources to integrate information located in distant places. Split attention is a very common experience during learning that can easily be avoided. According to Mayer (2005), "The format of much instruction is determined by tradition, economic factors, or the whim of the instructor. Cognitive factors are rarely considered resulting in instructional designs in which split-attention is common" (p. 145).

To avoid split attention, integrate words and visuals on pages or on screens. Mayer (2005) proposes his *Spatial Contiguity Principle* as follows:

Spatial Contiguity Principle: "Students learn better when corresponding words and pictures are presented near rather than far from each other on the page or screen" (p. 141).

Figure 7.5. Text Separated from Visual Leads to Split Attention
From Tindall-Ford, Chandler, and Sweller, 1997

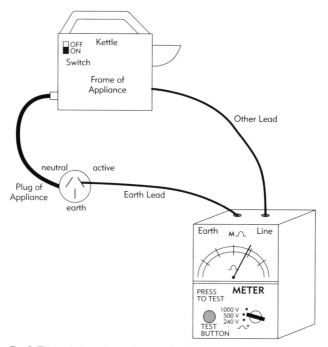

Test 2: The insulation resistance between the electrical element and the frame.

1. Set the meter to read 500 V.
2. Make sure the appliance's switch is "on."
3. Place the earth lead on the active pin of the appliance's plug.
4. Place the other lead on the frame of the appliance.
5. Press the test button.
6. Read the resistance from the meter. The required result is a reading of at least one M Ω.
7. Remove the earth lead from the active pin and place it on the neutral pin.
8. Press the test button again.
9. Read the resistance. A reading of at least one M Ω is again required.

Contiguity refers to the integration of mutually referring information on screens or pages. Think of the concept of contiguity as in *Arizona and Utah are contiguous states.*

John Sweller, who originated much of modern cognitive load theory, compared learning from two versions of a lesson on how to conduct an electrical test (Tindall-Ford, Chandler, & Sweller, 1997). You can compare these versions in Figures 7.5 and 7.6. Notice that the visuals and words are basically the same.

Figure 7.6. Text Integrated into Visual Reduces Split Attention
From Tindall-Ford, Chandler, and Sweller, 1997

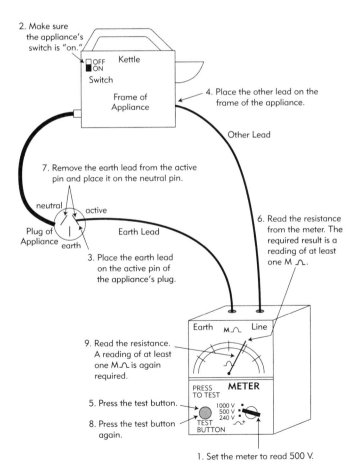

However, in Figure 7.5, the words are located under the visual rather than integrated into the visual as in Figure 7.6. The research team found that learning was nearly double among learners who studied the integrated version.

Clark and Mayer (2008) review many common violations of split attention in e-learning. These include:

- Placing explanatory text at the bottom of a screen that includes a related visual in the middle of the screen
- Displaying a visual at the top of a screen with explanatory text viewed by scrolling down the screen
- Displaying directions or feedback to a practice exercise separately from the data needed to complete the exercise
- Failing to manage use of response options in synchronous e-learning tools; for example, participants type irrelevant messages into the chat window during an instructional sequence

In most cases, the remedies for split attention are relatively simple and require designers to use various devices to integrate content on screens and pages. Different media will affect your approach to minimizing divided attention. For example, in this chapter I eliminated three visuals included in the first draft because books can successfully integrate only limited numbers of text and visuals. In contrast, in e-learning, I typically place a visual in a predominant location on the screen and position descriptive text close to the visual. Sometimes I need to use lines to link text phrases to the relevant portions of an online visual as an additional device to connect words to graphic elements.

Integrate Instruction in the Same Medium

Divided attention can also result from the separation of related elements across media. For example, some software training courses include some instructional elements on a computer screen and other related elements in a paper manual. The learner is required to look at the workbook, locate the appropriate step, then look at the screen and locate the appropriate portion of screen to apply the step. Instead of splitting instruction across media, all the instruction should be integrated into a single medium such as the computer.

Cerpa, Chandler, and Sweller (1996) compared learning spreadsheet tasks of low and high complexity from a traditional manual plus computer with learning from a computer-based training format in which the instruction was contained within the computer. As you can see in Figure 7.7, on skills of high complexity (that imposed the greatest amount of mental load), learning was better in the integrated computer version than in the manual plus computer versions. The research team concludes: "The computer-based training package used in these studies

---

Figure 7.7. Integrated Media Leads to Better Learning of High Complexity Skills

Based on data from Cerpa, Chandler, and Sweller, 1996

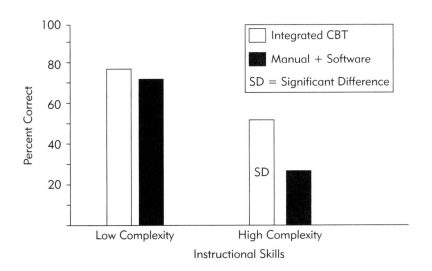

GUIDELINES FOR MANAGING ATTENTION

To recap, throughout this chapter I have offered instructional methods that optimize limited mental resources by attention-management techniques. The techniques include:

☐ Methods to Optimize Attentional Capacity

- Manage the physical environment

- Manage fatigue

- Promote accountability and engagement with

  - Competency-based instructional models

  - Questions

  - Instructor contact

  - A lively delivery pace in the classroom

☐ Methods to Support Selective Attention

- Use physical devices such as circles, arrows or highlighting, to direct attention to graphic elements in complex visual displays; such as animations

- Use text effects such as topic headers, bolding, and italics

- Use vocal emphasis and pauses to signal important content in audio segments

- Use questions and learning objectives to help learners adopt goals related to the most relevant portions of an instructional environment

☐ Methods to Avoid Divided Attention

- Place text close to visuals it describes on pages or screens

- Keep related instruction in a single medium rather than divided between two separate media such as workbook and computer

was an effective learning tool not because an electronic form of delivery was used but because it physically integrated disparate sources of information and reduced the extraneous load on working memory" (p. 364).

Leveraging Prior Knowledge

The point of focusing attention is to free limited memory capacity for the integration of new content from the training environment with existing knowledge in long-term memory. To ensure successful integration, instructional methods can be used to activate relevant prior knowledge in long-term memory or to build a knowledge base for learners lacking any background. These techniques bring related knowledge into working memory at the start of the lesson to mediate its integration with new lesson content. Chapter 8 reviews research-proven strategies that effectively exploit prior knowledge during learning.

Recommended Readings

Clark, R.C., & Mayer, R.E. (2008). Chapter 4: Applying the contiguity principle. In *e-Learning and the science of instruction* (2nd ed.). San Francisco, CA: Pfeiffer.

Clark, R.C., Nguyen, F., & Sweller, J (2006). Chapter 4: Focus attention and avoid split attention. In *Efficiency in learning*. San Francisco, CA: Pfeiffer.

8

Leveraging Prior Knowledge

Prior knowledge has a large influence on student performance,
explaining up to 81 percent of the variance in post-test scores.

DOCHY, SEGERS, AND BUEHL, 1999

IN **THIS CHAPTER,** I describe the role of prior knowledge in learning and summarize some instructional methods proven to make the most of learner prior knowledge. I recommend the following three approaches to be applied prior to presenting the main lesson content:

- For learners likely to have prior knowledge related to your lesson content, use methods to activate it.

- For learners unlikely to have relevant prior knowledge related to your lesson content, use methods that will supplement prior knowledge.

- For all learners, minimize the disruptive effects of activating inappropriate prior knowledge.

The Prior Knowledge Principle

Event three in Gagne's seven events of instruction is *activate prior learning* (Gagne, 1985). A meta-analysis of factors positively associated with school learning advises that "students' prior knowledge and level of understanding must be taken into account" (Wang, Haertel, & Walberg, 1993, p. 278). As I discussed in Chapter 4, learning involves the integration of new content from the lesson with existing schemas in long-term memory. This integration occurs in working memory and is bootstrapped by any method that brings relevant prior knowledge into conscious awareness in working memory.

In this chapter, I'll review instructional methods summarized in Figure 8.1 that activate existing prior knowledge or that compensate for lack of prior knowledge by providing a pre-instructional knowledge base. I will also review some instructional techniques to be avoided because they activate the wrong prior knowledge and subsequently depress learning. Since new content needs to be integrated into existing memory structures, it is important that relevant prior knowledge becomes available in working memory when new content enters the cognitive system. Therefore all methods designed to active prior knowledge

---

Figure 8.1. Instructional Methods to Exploit Prior Knowledge

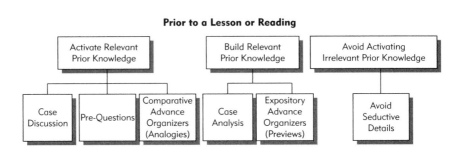

must be sequenced prior to the presentation of the main lesson content!

The critical role of prior knowledge in construction of new knowledge is the rationale for the *Prior Knowledge Principle.*

Prior Knowledge Principle: Be sure there is a knowledge base in working memory for integrating new content by: (1) activating appropriate prior knowledge, (2) compensating for missing prior knowledge, and (3) minimizing the activation of irrelevant prior knowledge.

If relevant prior knowledge already exists in long-term memory, the integration of new lesson content will be optimized when that pre-existing knowledge is brought into working memory. This is what is meant by activation of prior knowledge. In some situations, however, the learner may have little or no related prior knowledge. In those cases, before presenting the main content of the lesson, provide instructional resources and assignments that help learners build related knowledge. Third, some lessons start off with vignettes that are intended to add drama and stimulate emotional interest but that actually activate the wrong prior knowledge and subsequently depress learning. Avoid these types of introductory devices.

Methods to Activate Prior Knowledge

Three pre-learning techniques proven to activate prior knowledge are:

1. Group discussion of a problem related to the content of the lesson

2. Pre-work assignments such as responding to pre-questions prior to learning

3. Presentation of a comparative advance organizer

Problem-Based Learning

Problem-based learning is a type of collaborative learning in which a small group of five to seven learners begins their learning with a problem discussion. The lesson follows a structured process, including identifying potential solutions to or causes of the problem, defining learning issues, conducting individual research on the learning issues, and reconvening to resolve the problem. While problem-based learning has been most prominently used in the context of medical education, a number of other educational domains have also embraced this technique. In fact, problem-based learning has proven so popular that I devote all of Chapter 13 to it.

Problem Discussions Activate Prior Knowledge. How does the discussion of a problem facilitate learning? Schmidt and Moust (2000) used a problem-based learning format in which two groups of learners discussed two different problems. One group discussed the following problem: *A red blood cell is put in pure water under a microscope. The cell swells and eventually bursts. Another blood cell is added to an aqueous saline solution. It shrinks. Explain these phenomena.* The other group discussed a problem about the factors that affect airplane takeoff. After the group discussions, all learners read a text about osmosis and diffusion. The group that discussed the red blood cell problem remembered almost twice as much information included in the text as the group that discussed airplanes. All of the students were familiar with the topic of osmosis from their high school work. The group that activated their prior knowledge through discussion of the red blood cell problem learned more from the reading than the group that discussed an unrelated problem. The authors of the research study conclude: "This demonstrates that problem analysis in a small group indeed has a strong activating effect on prior knowledge" (p. 30).

How Important Is the Group Discussion in Activating Prior Knowledge? You might wonder whether the group discussion is needed to activate prior knowledge. How would problem-based learning compare with other techniques that could activate prior knowledge? For example, what if a learner read the red blood cell problem on their own and wrote out their thoughts? Or what if an individual learner simply responded to some questions regarding osmosis? How would these methods of activating prior knowledge compare to the problem-based learning format? In other words, how important is the group discussion in activating prior knowledge?

Schmidt and Moust (2000) compared three different activities designed to activate prior knowledge about osmosis. One group of learners discussed the red blood cell problem, as described previously. In the second test group, each learner read the red cell problem alone and then wrote down ideas about the problem. Students in the third group worked individually to recall as much as they could about osmosis without reading a problem. All learners then read the osmosis text and were tested. The problem discussion group recalled the most information, followed by the group that read the problem and wrote down ideas. Group three that did not read the problem recalled the least. The authors conclude that a combination of reviewing a problem *and* discussing it in a small group have independent positive effects, compared with asking individuals to recall what they know. "Group discussion had, in particular, a considerable effect, suggesting that elaboration on prior knowledge and learning from each other, even before new information is acquired, are potent means to facilitate understanding of problem-relevant information" (Schmidt & Moust, 2000, p. 31).

Because of the popularity of problem-based learning, there has been considerable research on its effectiveness. In addition to activating prior knowledge, there are a number of other benefits, especially motivational benefits to instruction that is rooted in job-relevant problems. In Chapter 13 I review the features of, evidence for, and design of problem-based lessons.

Asking and Answering Pre-Questions

In the previous chapter, we saw that questions can help focus learner attention to relevant material in the text. Another value of pre-questions is activating prior knowledge. A review of experiments that tested questioning techniques to promote use of prior knowledge suggests that either providing learners with relevant pre-questions (and requiring them to respond to them) or asking learners to generate and answer their own pre-questions improves learning by activation of prior knowledge (Pressley, Wood, Woloshyn, Martin, King, & Menke, 1992). As an example, Pressley and his colleagues compared the learning of three groups. Individual students in one group attempted to answer twenty-three pre-questions related to the lesson content based on their prior knowledge. Individuals in the second group also worked with the twenty-three questions. However, rather than answer them, they analyzed the questions for meaningfulness. This group actively processed the questions but not in a way that would activate prior knowledge. A third group had no pre-questions. After reading a chapter of university-level text, all learners were tested via short-answer questions. Those who had attempted to answer and justify responses to pre-questions learned the most. Even learners in that group who gave incorrect responses to the pre-questions showed better outcomes than those in the other two groups.

An alternative approach is to ask students to generate their own pre-questions. This has the advantage of producing questions that will access each learner's prior knowledge. This strategy improves learning provided that learners construct thoughtful rather than low-level questions. The research team suggests: "By constructing questions, students are likely to activate prior knowledge or experience relevant to the task at hand. Attempting to respond to self-generated questions should also stimulate prior knowledge" (Pressley, Wood, Woloshyn, Martin, King, & Menke, 1992, p. 105).

Other pre-study activities may also prove effective routes to activation of prior knowledge. For example Gurlitt, Renkl, Motes, and Hauser (2006) asked learners to identify the relationships among concepts in a concept map by drawing lines among the listed concepts and indicating whether the relationships were positive or negative by labeling the lines. Most of the research on prior knowledge has measured recall or comprehension of a text reading following question-answering activities. We need more research that evaluates the effectiveness of various types of pre-work assignments (not just questions) that precede diverse instructional environments (not just text readings).

Comparative Advance Organizers

In 1968 Ausubel introduced the concept of *advance organizers* as instructional presentations appearing early in a lesson that "provide ideational scaffolding for the stable incorporation and retention of more detailed and differentiated material that follows" (p. 148). Mayer and Wittrock (2006) define an advance organizer as "material presented before a lesson that is intended to promote learning by helping the learner relate the new material to existing knowledge" (p. 293). In other words, an advance organizer is information delivered in words or pictures prior to the lesson content that either activates relevant prior knowledge or provides prior knowledge that the learner can use to integrate the new information included in the lesson.

You can choose from two types of advance organizers—those that activate preexisting prior knowledge (*comparative organizers*) and those that provide new knowledge to serve as a base for integration of new lesson content (*expository organizers*). I will discuss the comparative organizers in this section and the expository type in the next.

Ausubel's comparative organizer was a brief textual comparison of the relationships between Christianity and Buddhism prior to a lengthy reading on Buddhism. Learning from the Buddhism text was compared between those who read the advance organizer comparing Christianity and Buddhism and those who read about an unrelated topic. The group assigned the comparative organizer recalled more of the text (Ausubel & Youssef, 1963).

A comparative organizer includes information that is familiar to the learner (for example, Christianity) and that links aspects of that familiar information to new information (for example, Buddhism) to be presented in the lesson. An important feature of the comparative organizer is the use of analogy to activate prior knowledge that is related to the lesson content.

To help learners recall and apply basic principles of how radar works, Mayer provided the diagram shown in Figure 8.2 to learners before they read the detailed lesson. Note that the diagram provides a high-level text and visual summary of the principle of radar using concrete familiar imagery. The image and text were intended to draw from learner's prior familiarity with how a ball bounces off an object. When comparing learning of groups that studied the same lesson with and without the diagram, the recall and application scores of the diagram group were much higher (Mayer, 1983).

What Are the Features of an Effective Advance Organizer?

An effective organizer should be concrete and provide a link between elements of the organizer and relevant concepts in the lesson.

Figure 8.2. A Graphic Comparative Advance Organizer

From Mayer, 1983

There are five steps in radar.

1. Transmission: A pulse travels from an antenna.

2. Reflection: The pulse bounces off a remote object.

3. Reception: The pulse returns to the receiver.

4. Measurement: The difference between the time out and the
      time back tells the total time traveled.

5. Conversion: The time can be converted to a measure of distance,
      since the pulse travels at a constant speed.

When developing a concrete organizer use either an illustration as in the radar example or specific and concrete language. For example, in Chapter 2 I used a chemical analogy of atoms, molecules, and DNA to illustrate the relationships among instructional modes, methods, and architectures.

You also need to consider the relationships between existing prior knowledge of the audience with the key ideas to be communicated in the lesson. A good advance organizer for a specialized learning audience may not work well for a more general audience. For example, Kloster and Winne (1989) compared learning from different types of organizers. They required learners to process the organizers by matching each paragraph of text to the relevant part of the organizer. Based on these matches (which were correct or incorrect), each student was scored for their effective use of the organizer. A higher score indicated that the learner accurately linked the textual information to the organizer. Kloster and Winne (1989) found that learning was better from students with higher matching scores. In other words, learners who correctly linked the organizer to its corresponding text segment, learned more. The researchers conclude: "True advance organizers promote learning conditionally, the condition being whether the organizers are used appropriately and accurately. A student's ability to link information in the advance organizer correctly with new information is critical" (p. 14). Therefore, to be effective, an organizer must (1) call on the prior knowledge in your learning audience and (2) be processed by the learners.

Methods to Compensate for Limited Prior Knowledge

The instructional methods described in the preceding sections focused on techniques that improve learning by activating relevant prior knowledge the learner already has stored in long-term memory. Alternatively, you can compensate for lack of relevant prior knowledge by providing a knowledge base through some type of preview activity. As an example, read the following text in and rate its meaningfulness on a 0 to 7 scale with 7 being high:

> "If the balloons popped, the sound would not be able to carry since everything would be too far away from the correct floor. A closed window would also prevent the sound from carrying since most buildings tend to be well-insulated. Since the whole operation depends on a steady

flow of electricity, a break in the middle of the wire would also cause problems. Of course, the fellow could shout, but the human voice is not loud enough to carry that far. It is clear that the best situation would involve less distance. With face-to-face contact, the least number of things could go wrong."

(Bransford and Johnson, 1972)

After you complete your rating, look at the diagram in Figure 8.3 - on the next page. The illustration provides a context for interpreting the balloon story. In a research study, readers rated the understandability of the text under three conditions. One group, like you, did not have access to the illustration. A second group read the text, looked at the illustration, and then rated the text. The third group looked at the illustration *first*, read the text, and then rated the text. Only the third group rated the text as high in meaning (Bransford & Johnson, 1972). Even though both groups two and three had access to the same information e.g. the diagram and the text, only the group that saw the diagram *prior to* reading the text found that it was helpful. That's because the illustration provided a context that was actively used during reading to make sense of the text. In essence, the "serenade" picture provided the prior knowledge needed to interpret the text.

In this section, I focus on ways to provide learners with relevant information prior to presenting the lesson content. These instructional methods are recommended primarily for situations in which learners are likely to have little or no relevant prior knowledge to activate. In fact, research has demonstrated that many of these methods work well for novice learners but not for learners with experience in the subject domain. I discuss two proven strategies to accomplish this goal: pre-lesson case analysis assignments and expository advance organizers.

Figure 8.3. A Graphic Serenade Context for the Balloon Story
Adapted from Bransford and Johnson, 1972

Pre-Lesson Case Analysis

Assigning a pre-lesson analysis of several case studies related to the lesson content results in better transfer learning than pre-lesson assignments that require learners to simply read cases (Bransford, Barron, Pea, Meltzoff, Kuhl, Bell, Stevens, Schwartz, Vye, Reeves, Roschelle, & Sabelli, 2006; Schwartz & Bransford, 1998). The researchers propose that having an opportunity to analyze several cases related to the principles of a lesson will create a new knowledge structure that helps learners to meaningfully integrate new content. I summarize the design of their experiment in Figure 8.4. Their lessons focused on two topics from learning psychology: how schema influence thinking (the schema case) and

Figure 8.4. Schwartz and Bransford's Experiment: Analyzing a Case vs. Reading a Case to Build Prior Knowledge

Adapted from Schwartz and Bransford, 1998

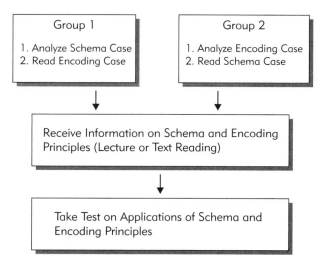

how context (such as the serenade graphic shown in Figure 8.3) influence encoding of new information (the encoding case). I will refer to the content as the schema and the encoding principles, respectively. Prior to a lecture (or reading a text) on the psychological principles of schema and encoding, each participant analyzed the case related to one set of principles (schema or encoding) and read the case related to the other set of principles (encoding or schema). In the case analysis assignments, learners were presented the case data and asked to diagram and comment on important patterns they saw in the data. In case reading assignments, learners read the same cases as the analysis cases, except that the cases did not present the data. After analyzing cases on one topic and reading cases on another topic, all learners were presented with information on both topics. The follow up-tests required learners to make predictions about situations

Figure 8.5. Learning Was Better from Pre-Work Case Analysis Than from Pre-Work Case Reading

Adapted from Schwartz and Bransford, 1998

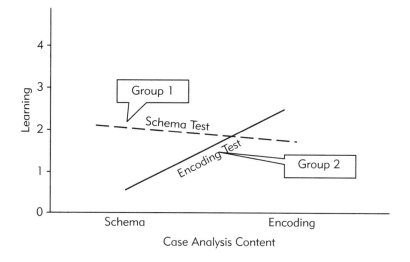

that had NOT been presented in the lesson but that related to applications of one of the two principles taught.

As you can see in Figure 8.5, learners who analyzed the schema cases and read the encoding cases did better on the schema test questions than on the encoding questions. The reverse was true for learners who analyzed the encoding cases and read the schema cases. The authors conclude: "The results indicate that teaching by telling (either through a lecture or through reading) can play a significant role in deepening students understanding *if the students have had a chance to acquire appropriate prior knowledge.* In these studies, contrasting cases helped the students generate this prior knowledge." (Schwartz & Bransford, 1998, p. 504, emphasis added).

When to Use Pre-Lesson Case Assignments

In the Schwartz and Bransford research, several factors led to improved learning: (1) several cases were used that provided slightly different perspectives on a principle, (2) learners were actively engaged by an analysis assignment prior to the lesson, (3) the follow-up lesson did not incorporate active processing opportunities such as practice activities; rather it delivered relevant information to the learners either in a lecture or through a textual reading, and (4) the lesson content was far transfer rather than procedural. The authors title their article "A Time for Telling" to focus attention to ways to improve learning from receptive environments. We don't know whether case analysis assignments undertaken prior to a directive architecture lesson with plenty of practice would be as effective.

Cases assigned for analysis should be aligned to the goals of the instruction and should offer learners opportunities to build prior knowledge based on different perspectives on a theme. Cases could either be summaries of different experiments or situations related to the lesson theme or they could be different perspectives on the same case to show contrasting view points. Either way, assignments that lead to deep processing of cases ensure building of relevant knowledge structures.

Expository Advance Organizers

Previously in this chapter, I discussed the use of comparative advance organizers to activate prior knowledge. I summarized Ausubel's use of an organizer that compared features of Buddhism to features of Christianity. However, what if the learners do not have a prior knowledge base that would be helpful? For example, what if they were atheists? If learners were not familiar with Christianity, rather than a comparative organizer, an expository advance organizer might use visuals and text to present a preview of the main premises and beliefs of Buddhism. Thus, advance organizers can be designed to build a relevant knowledge base prior to exposure to new lesson content.

The serenade graphic shown in Figure 8.3 is an example of this type of advance organizer. The graphic contains new information that provides a context for understanding the related text. Expository advance organizers are essentially previews of the lesson information delivered in a succinct form prior to the main content of the lesson.

Types of Expository Organizers. Expository organizers assume a number of forms. Outlines or previews placed prior to the lesson are common examples. In other situations, direct instruction that gives definitions or descriptions of important new lesson concepts provides an important knowledge base. For example Mayer, Mathias, and Wetzell (2002) prepared a lesson on how pumps or brakes worked. Some students were assigned a pre-lesson orientation that labeled each part of the pump or braking system and showed how each individual part moved. Pre-lessons were delivered by print hard copy, multimedia, and physical models. Learners who received an orientation to the key concepts prior to the lesson (but not after the lesson) scored higher. Since only the materials provided *before* the main lesson improved performance, most likely they served to augment prior knowledge. Mayer recommends a *Pre-Training Principle* to orient learners to important lesson concepts. (Clark & Mayer, 2007).

Site maps are another form of preview for Internet lessons and reference sites. Shapiro (2005) found that a site map improved learning more than a learning goal. Rouet and Potelle (2005) tested the effectiveness of several different site map layouts including linear alphabetic, networked, and hierarchical as shown in Figure 8.6. The format made no difference to high prior knowledge users who likely did not need any form of preview. However, the hierarchical structure was best for novices.

Figure 8.6. Three Site Map Layouts

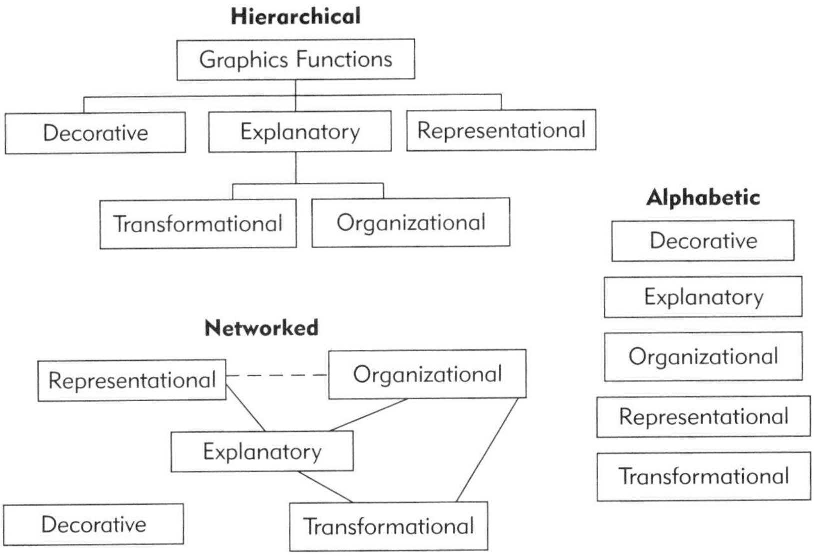

Avoid Activating Inappropriate Prior Knowledge

Since the late 1980s we've known about the harmful effects of interesting tidbits added to lessons to stimulate emotional interest. For example, a lesson on quality control might begin with short textual or video segments that describe the high costs of product recalls or that show serious consequences such as accidents resulting from product failures. While these additions are related to the topic of quality control, they are not directly relevant to building knowledge and skills needed to monitor and improve quality. Because of their harmful effects on learning, these types of additions are called *seductive details* (Garner, Gillingham, & White, 1989).

Mayer (2005) has documented the negative effects of seductive text and seductive video inserted into science lessons. In a multimedia lesson on lightning formation, he included either text or video that illustrated what happened when people were struck by lightning. Readers enjoyed the inserts. They rated them as interesting and entertaining. However, in comparisons of learning from materials with and without the seductive details, both retention and transfer were significantly better when the details were omitted. In six experiments, lessons that *omitted* seductive details showed an average gain of 105 percent with an effect size of 1.66, which is considered very high. Mayer refers to the negative effects of emotionally arousing materials as a **Coherence Effect** (Clark & Mayer, 2008; Mayer, 2005).

The Psychological Effects of Seductive Details

How do seductive details harm learning? One possibility is that they distract the learner by drawing attention away from important information to irrelevant information. Another possibility is that they interfere with the organization of new incoming information. A third possibility is that they activate the wrong prior knowledge, which disrupts integration of new content with existing memories.

To distinguish among these possibilities, Harp and Mayer (1998) used three different techniques to combat the adverse impact of seductive details. To one lesson they added highlighting of the important content. The highlighting should help the learners to focus on what is important in the lesson and thus minimize the distracting influence of seductive details. To another lesson, they added preview sentences and numbering of the steps involved in the scientific processes being explained. These methods were used to make the organization of the information explicit and thus minimize the adverse effect of seductive details on the organizing process. In a third version, they adjusted the position of the seductive details—placing them either all at the beginning or all at the end of the lesson. If the negative effects of seductive details are due to activation of inappropriate prior knowledge, placing irrelevant materials at the beginning

**Figure 8.7. The Effects of Seductive Details Combined
              with Countermeasures**

From Harp and Mayer, 1998

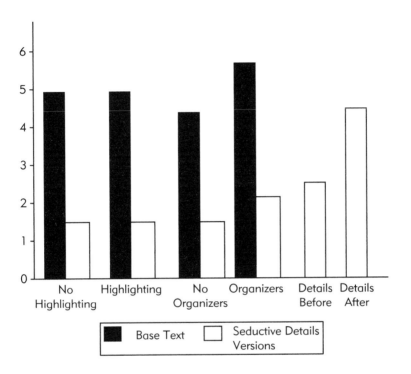

of the lesson should result in poorer learning than placing them at the end. Figure 8.7 shows the results of these lesson versions. As you can see, all versions that omitted seductive details (represented by the black bars) resulted in much better learning. Among lessons with seductive details, only the third set of revisions (represented by the right white bars) that varied the placement of seductive details made a difference. Placing details at the start of the lesson was very damaging, whereas placing them at the end of the lesson had minimal impact. The authors conclude that it is likely that seductive details activate inappropriate prior knowledge. Therefore, either seductive details should be omitted or they should be placed after the main body of the lesson (Harp & Mayer, 1998).

Some readers have interpreted this research as a caution to never use stories in training. Actually, this is not true. The issue is not about using stories but rather about selecting stories that are related directly to the learning objective. Stories add interest—one source of motivation. And, being concrete, they tend to be memorable. My recommendation is to include stories but to use care in your selection and sequencing of stories to avoid activation of inappropriate prior knowledge.

When to Use Prior Knowledge Methods

The yellow brick road metaphor described in Chapter 3 suggests that we always ask the question: *Under what conditions will any given instructional method apply?* Understanding the psychological mechanisms for instructional methods will help answer this question and improve your ability to use them effectively.

Research conducted on advance organizers (and many other instructional methods) has yielded conflicting results. In some studies they helped, and in other studies there was no effect. One reason is that the conditions under which advance organizers have been tested varied, and therefore sometimes they were helpful and sometimes not. When should you consider the use of methods such as advance organizers to activate prior knowledge? Here are some guidelines.

1. *Do your learners have considerable prior knowledge that is directly related to the new information to be taught?* If the answer is yes, they may not need any additional support to activate prior knowledge. Several research studies have shown that novice learners benefit more from instructional interventions that support their cognitive processes where as those with more experience require relatively little external processing support (Clark, Nguyen, & Sweller, 2006).

2. *Do your learners have some prior knowledge related to the new information to be taught?* If the answer is yes, begin your lesson with some activity designed to activate the learner's prior knowledge. A small group discussion of a problem relevant to the information to be presented is one approach. Design a short problem related to the new knowledge to be presented that is clearly worded but includes sufficient ambiguity to stimulate discussions and different ideas about the causes of the problem. See Chapter 13 for more details on problem-based instruction. Alternatively, design a concrete organizer to activate relevant prior knowledge. For example, Mayer (1983) used a bouncing ball as an analogical preview of how radar works.

3. *Can you build prior knowledge in your learners?* If your learners are not likely to have much relevant prior knowledge, then consider some form of preview. For receptive learning environments, assign pre-work that will lead to development of somewhat detailed relevant concepts. Schwartz and Bransford (1998) assigned learners to analyze contrasting cases to build related knowledge. Alternative techniques include an outline, a pre-lesson that explains key concepts, or an organizing graphic such as a hierarchical site map that provides a high-level overview of the concepts and principles to be presented.

4. *Do your lessons include seductive text or graphics prior to the main lesson content?* If yes, these should either be deleted or moved to the end of the lesson. Experiments on lessons with seductive details show that they disrupt the integration of new information with existing knowledge because they activate inappropriate knowledge structures.

5. *Are your instructional goals near transfer (procedural) or far transfer (application of concepts or problem solving)?* From

Buddhism to radar, all of the research discussed in this chapter involves content that is relatively conceptual and requires the building of a mental model for learning. It is possible that lessons that include concepts and principles are more likely to benefit from activation of prior knowledge than lessons with strictly procedural goals.

GUIDELINES FOR ACTIVATING PRIOR KNOWLEDGE

Although activation of prior knowledge has a relatively long history in instructional psychology, there has been remarkably little research on what types of pre-lesson methods are most effective for different learners and for different instructional goals. This is an area ripe for new research. To recap lessons learned from the research we do have, apply the following guidelines:

☐ Place the organizer or activity prior to the presentation of the major instructional content.

☐ Plan some type of activity with the organizer to ensure processing of it.

☐ Design the organizer or activity keeping in mind your learners' experience and the nature of the content to be learned.

- For learners with relevant background knowledge:
  - Assign case problem discussions
  - Assign pre-learning activities
  - Include comparative advance organizers

- For learners unlikely to have relevant prior knowledge:
  - Assign contrasting cases for analysis
  - Provide previews such as outlines or site maps
  - Include expository advance organizers

☐ Avoid using seductive visuals or text early in the lesson.

COMING NEXT

Helping Learners Build Mental Models: Implicit Methods

If you have successfully managed cognitive load, directed attention to relevant portions of the lesson, and activated prior knowledge, you are ready to help learners encode the new lesson content. The goal of encoding is to build new mental models in long-term memory by integrating new lesson content with existing knowledge. Encoding is the result of rehearsal processes in working memory. The next two chapters discuss two roads you can take to help learners build the right mental models. Chapter 9 describes implicit instructional methods that do not require overt behavioral activity, while Chapter 10 deals with practice methods that foster explicit activity on the part of learners.

Recommended Readings

Harp, S.F., & Mayer, R.E. (1998). How seductive details do their damage: A theory of cognitive interest in science learning. *Journal of Educational Psychology, 90*(3), 414–434.

Mayer, R.E., & Wittrock, M.C. (2006). Problem solving. In P.A. Alexander& P.H. Winne (Eds.), *Handbook of educational psychology* (2nd ed.). Mahwah, NJ: Lawrence Erlbaum Associates. See section on Schema-Activation Methods on page 293 and following.

Schwartz, D.L., & Bransford, J.D. (1998). A time for telling. *Cognition and Instruction, 16*(4), 475–522.

CHAPTER 9 TOPICS

The Building Mental Models Principle
What Are Mental Models?

How Learners Construct Mental Models

Explicit and Implicit Encoding Methods

Implicit Methods to Build Mental Models

Use Graphics to Build Mental Models
What Kinds of Graphics Are Most Effective?

How Graphics Build Mental Models

Personalize Your Learning Environment
Use Conversational Language to Personalize Learning

Evidence for Conversational Language

Use On-Screen Agents in Multimedia
to Personalize Learning

Features of Agents That Matter

Include Deep-Level Learning Agent Dialogs
Can Interactive Environments Be Replaced with Dialogs?

Provide Examples and Encourage Their Processing
Maximizing Learning from Examples

Provide Effective Analogies
What Makes Analogies Effective?

Include Process Content in Your Instruction

Offer Cognitive Support for Novice Learners
Evidence That Graphics Benefit Novices

The Expertise Reversal Effect

9

Helping Learners Build Mental Models: Implicit Methods

Activity may help promote meaningful learning, but instead of behavioral activity per se, the kind of activity that really promotes meaningful learning is cognitive activity.

MAYER, 2004

IN THIS CHAPTER and the next, I describe instructional methods you can use to help learners build accurate mental models. In this chapter, I focus on implicit instructional methods that do not involve overt learner activity. Implicit methods work by promoting mental rehearsals in the absence of external behavioral responses. Implicit methods that are proven to promote learning include:

- Relevant Graphics
- Personalized Instruction
- Agent Question Dialogs
- Examples and Self-Explanation Training
- Analogies
- Teaching Process Content

The Building Mental Models Principle

From the sage on the stage to the guide on the side. Shifting the emphasis from teaching to learning is one of the major contributions of educational psychology in the last decades of the 20th Century. Previous models of instruction viewed learning as a relatively passive process in which learners absorbed new information from the environment or formed associations by correctly responding to questions. In contrast, a constructive perspective emphasizes active building processes. And the action is on the part of the learner, not the instructor. The instructor's role is to create a learning environment that enables learner construction and application of the most appropriate mental models to support expert performance.

New knowledge and skills entering working memory must be integrated into existing prior knowledge in long-term memory to build new mental models. Experts not only have more knowledge related to their domain, but also their knowledge is organized more effectively. Good learning environments optimize opportunities for building mental models that support expertise. This constructive nature of learning is the basis for the *Building Mental Models Principle* of instructional design:

Building Mental Models Principle: Provide learners with an instructional environment that promotes their active construction of new mental models.

What Are Mental Models?

Let's begin by reviewing four mental models of how blood circulates through the human heart. The following four blood circulation models were derived by Chi, DeLeeuw, Chiu, and LaVancher (1994) from student drawings and descriptions: no loop, ebb and flow, single loop, and double loop. The no loop model is a primitive flawed model of blood flow as a very general notion that blood flows from the heart to the body but does not return. An ebb and flow model puts the heart into the picture and assumes that blood travels to and from the heart by way of the same vessels. The single loop model recognizes that blood flows out from the heart and is returned to the heart through the lungs. However, it envisions a single path whereby blood leaves the heart, flows throughout the body and returns first to the lungs and then to the heart in a direct path. The correct double loop model recognizes the blood leaves the left ventricle, flows to the body, returns to the right atrium, flows to the right ventricle and then to the lungs where it is oxygenated. Oxygen-rich blood is then returned to the left atrium, flows to the left ventricle, and then to the body. It is the job of the instructional professional to correct inaccurate or incomplete mental models such as the ebb and flow model to help learners build complete and valid mental models.

Mental models are memory structures (also called *schemas*), stored in long-term memory that are the basis for expertise. Good mental models enable you to distinguish and generalize concepts, to solve problems, to make predictions, and to interpret situations. I distinguish between two types of mental models:

1. *Simple mental models* that support cognitive operations such as discrimination and generalization of concepts and performing routine procedures. For example, as an instructional professional you may be able to distinguish between an effective and ineffective learning objective. Or you may have a mental model for logging into your computer.

2. *Complex mental models* that support problem solving—both routine and novel. For example, as an instructional professional you may have designed and developed

**Figure 9.1. Mental Models in Long-Term Memory Are the Basis
         for Expertise**

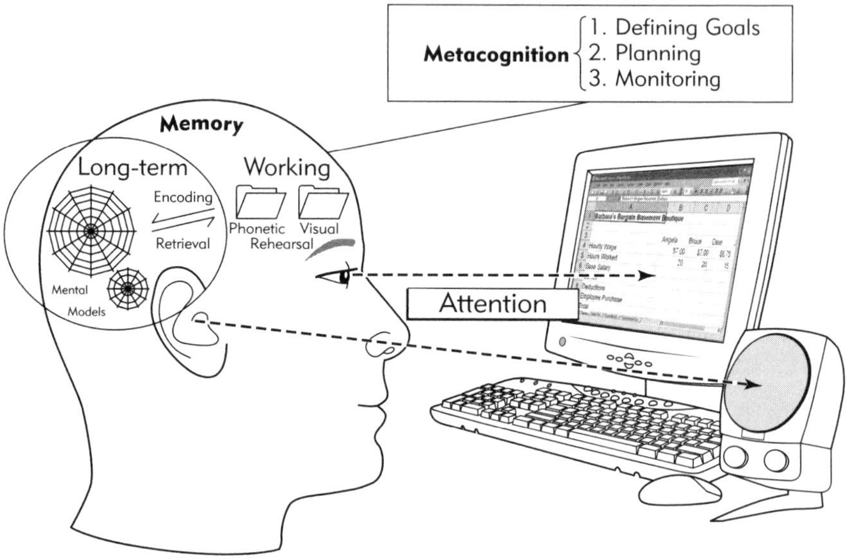

e-learning courses. Alternatively a medical professional is involved in diagnosis of an unusual condition. Figure 9.1 illustrates the focus of this chapter and the next on mental models in long-term memory.

In Chapter 8 you had the opportunity to rate the ambiguous text that accompanied the serenade diagram illustrated in Figure 8.3. Only individuals who viewed the diagram *before* reading the text were able to interpret the text. The serenade picture provides the context to make the text meaningful. In a similar way, mental models provide context to interpret our environment. The mental models in long-term memory enable us to make sense of what we experience, whether we are going to a restaurant or looking at the symbols used in our career field such as musical notes, mathematical equations, schematic drawings, or Arabic scripts. Mental models also provide a basis for making predictions and solving problems. We know that experts are more effective than novices at solving problems in their specialty fields. We also know that this expertise is based on specific knowledge—knowledge accumulated over years of experience in a career field.

How Learners Construct Mental Models

As new information enters through the eyes and ears into working memory, it must be processed or it will disappear. Mental models are constructed by the integration of new knowledge into existing schemas in long-term memory. First, appropriate prior knowledge must be activated (as described in Chapter 8) and second, the new information entering working memory must be transformed in a way that it is integrated into the activated prior knowledge. Successful integration results in encoding of new knowledge and skills into long-term memory. Information can be encoded in multiple ways and times. In general, the more ways and the more times that new information is encoded, the better the learning. Effective instructional methods lead to encodings that support the learning goal.

Explicit and Implicit Encoding Methods

Two types of instructional methods that promote encoding are *explicit* and *implicit*. Explicit encoding methods promote overt learner engagement with new information in ways that are congruent with the instructional goal. Practice exercises are an example. I use the term explicit encoding methods because they stimulate visible learner activity. I discuss explicit encoding methods in Chapter 10.

In contrast, implicit encoding methods promote learning in ways that do not involve *overt* learner activity. For example, viewing a relevant graphic that corresponds with text promotes

Table 9.1. Implicit vs. Explicit Methods for Building Mental Models

Method	Description	Examples
Implicit	Training techniques that promote mental processing with no behavioral activity on the part of the learner	Graphics or personalized writing
Explicit	Training techniques that involve overt behavioral activity on the part of the learner to build mental models	Practice exercises; Argumentation; Instructor questions

learning by stimulating the formation of more than one memory code—one visual and one verbal. The learner's activity is mental and she may not even be aware of the encoding going on. Both explicit and implicit methods rely on active mental processing. The distinction is that the explicit methods stimulate behavioral activity that leads to mental activity, while the implicit methods promote mental processes directly. Table 9.1 summarizes these two paths to building mental models.

Both implicit and explicit encoding processes can originate from the instructional environment or from the learner. For example, the instructor may assign several practice problems to the learners or the learners may ask questions of themselves. Both will stimulate encoding. Alternatively, the lesson may provide graphic representations of content or the learners may formulate their own images while reading text. Both will stimulate encoding.

While well-designed behavioral activity can promote learning, excessive or inappropriate activities can increase unproductive cognitive load thus precluding effective encoding. In contrast, receptive learning environments can integrate implicit encoding methods to prompt mental processing. Craig and his colleagues (2006) refer to computer-based learning environments in which learners are essentially observers as opportunities for *vicarious learning*. They ask the question: "How can computer-based instruction be designed to support knowledge acquisition processes when learners cannot physically interact with, or control the content of that which they are attempting to master?" (p. 566). In this chapter, we look at what research tells us about this question.

Implicit Methods to Build Mental Models

In the remainder of this chapter, I will review guidelines, evidence, and examples of instructional methods proven to improve learning in the absence of behavioral activity. These include incorporation of (1) relevant visuals, (2) conversational language and learning agents, (3) agent question dialogs, (4) examples and training in self-explanations, (5) analogies, and (6) process content.

Use Graphics to Build Mental Models

There is consistent evidence that people learn more deeply from words and pictures than from words alone. Clark and Mayer (2008) summarize eleven different studies in which learning was compared from animation and narration to narration alone or from text and illustrations to text alone. The experimental lessons taught scientific and mechanical processes, including how lightning works, how a car's braking system works, how pumps work. Figures 9.2 and 9.3 show a text-only and a text-plus-visual example from one of these studies. As you can see, the same words are used in both versions. The graphic version however adds a simple line drawing to the text.

Mayer and his colleagues found that, in eleven studies, students who received a multimedia lesson consisting of words and pictures performed better on a transfer test than students who received the same information with words alone. Across the eleven

Figure 9.2. How a Bicycle Pump Works Explained with Words Alone

From Mayer, 2001

HOW A BICYCLE PUMP WORKS

"As the rod is pulled out, air passes through the piston and fills the area between the piston and the outlet valve. As the rod is pushed in, the inlet valve closes and the piston forces air through the outlet valve."

Figure 9.3. How a Bicycle Pumps Works Explained with Words and Graphics

From Mayer, 2001

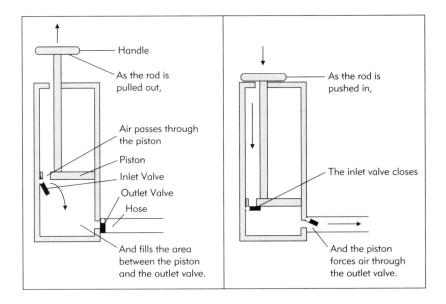

studies, people who learned from words and graphics produced between 55 to 121 percent more correct solutions than people who learned from words alone. Across all studies, a median percentage gain of 89 percent was achieved with an effect size of 1.5, which is large. These consistent and significant gains in learning are the basis for Mayer's *Multimedia Principle.*

> **Multimedia Principle:** People learn more deeply from words and graphics than from words alone.

The benefits of visuals and text over text alone have been shown in several recent experiments. Butcher (2006) compared learning of mental models of how blood flows through the heart from text alone, text plus a simple schematic cut-away diagram of the heart, and text plus a more complex anatomically correct cut-away diagram of the heart. In two experiments, she found that both diagram versions resulted in better mental models and higher general knowledge scores than text only versions. The results from experiment 2 are shown in Figure 9.4. Although both of the diagrams resulted in better learning than text alone, the simpler schematic visual proved more effective than the complex visual.

Brunye and his colleagues (2006) compared learning an eighteen-step assembly task from instructions presented in a

---

Figure 9.4. Improvements in Mental Models and General Knowledge Are Greatest When Graphics Are Included

Based on data from Butcher, 2006

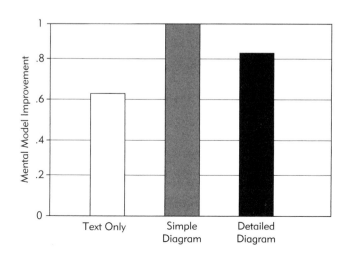

visual only format, text only, and text plus visual format. They found that both recall of the steps as well as accuracy in identifying the correct sequence of steps was better among those who studied the text and visual, rather than the text alone or the visual alone. This research extends the research of Mayer and of Butcher to procedural content that involves spatial relationships.

Brewer, Harvey, and Semmler (2004) compared judicial self-defense instructions presented to two mock juries composed of ninety legally untrained adults and ninety law students in three formats: audio instructions recorded by a judge, audio plus visual in which animations of key concepts and a flow chart were added to illustrate the key elements of self-defense, and an audio plus version that included the judge's instructions, plus the information shown in the visuals presented in an auditory format. Learning was assessed by a verdict question, a recognition multiple-choice test, a recall test, and a transfer scenario test to assess self-defense comprehension. As you can see in Figure 9.5, learning

---

Figure 9.5. Visuals Lead to Better Jury Comprehension of Legal Concepts by Novices

Based on data from Brewer, Harvey, and Semmler, 2004

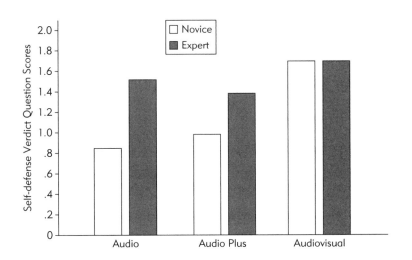

of the novices (but not the legal students) was greatly improved by the addition of visuals. If you compare the results from the audiovisual versions between the legal novices and experts, you will see that the visuals boosted the novices to the same performance level as the experts. This illustrates the potential of a visual to substitute for an expert mental model. The research team concludes: "First, very poor comprehension was shown by a community sample of jury-eligible participants when provided with a judge's verbal instructions. Second, the audiovisual format produced a marked improvement in comprehension" (p. 773).

What Kinds of Graphics Are Most Effective?

In Chapter 8 we saw that visuals that may be related to the instructional topic but irrelevant to the learning objective can depress learning by distracting learners and wasting limited working memory resources. For example, a visual of an airplane struck by lightning in a lesson on lightning formation resulted in poorer learning than a lesson that omitted the visual. In Chapter 6, I also mentioned that, at least in some situations, a series of static visuals is better for learning than animations. In the heart circulation study described in this chapter, we saw that a simpler schematic diagram was generally more effective than a more detailed realistic diagram of the heart. Therefore, we have several indications that the content and format of a graphic influence its effectiveness.

Clark and Lyons (2004) describe a taxonomy of visuals summarized in Table 9.2. Reviews of visuals included in school texts showed the vast majority served no useful instructional purpose (Mayer, Sims, & Tajika, 1995; Woodward, 1993). Most fell into the decorative category. Decorative graphics are visuals placed in a lesson for aesthetic value or to add humor. Although I have not seen research on the types of visuals present in workplace learning, my guess is that, in e-learning especially, you will find an over-reliance on decorative graphics.

Table 9.2. A Summary of Graphic Types

Type	Description	Examples
Decorative	Visuals added for aesthetic appeal or for humor	1. A person riding a bicycle in a lesson on how a bicycle pump works 2. Baseball-related icons as a game theme in a lesson on product knowledge
Representative	Visuals that illustrate the appearance of an object	1. A photograph of equipment in a maintenance lesson 2. A screen capture in Figure 2.2
Organizational	Visuals that show qualitative relationships among content	1. A matrix such as this table 2. A concept map 3. A tree diagram
Transformational	Visuals that illustrate changes in time or over space	1. An animated demonstration of a computer procedure 2. A video of how volcanoes erupt 3. A time-lapse animation of seed germination
Interpretive	Visuals that make intangible phenomena visible and concrete	1. Drawings of molecular structures 2. A series of diagrams with arrows to illustrate the flow of blood through the heart 3. Pictures that show how data is transformed and transmitted through the Internet

In general, you can best help learners build accurate mental models by providing relatively simple renditions of explanatory visuals. *Explanatory visuals* illustrate the relationships stated in the text of a lesson. Clark and Lyons (2004) describe four main types of explanatory visuals: organizational, relational, transformational, and interpretive. *Organizational visuals* such as tree charts or concept maps show qualitative relationships among topics in a lesson. *Relational visuals* summarize quantitative relationships and take the form of bar charts, pie charts, and other graphs. *Transformational visuals* show changes in time or space. For example, in a lesson on Excel, the instructor narrates a step-by-step demonstration of how to enter a formula into a spreadsheet. As the instructor performs a step, the visual changes to reflect the software responses. *Interpretive visuals* help learners build mental models of abstract or invisible processes. These are especially useful in building knowledge of technical or scientific processes and principles. For example, in Figure 9.6 from a science simulation, the learner can see the effects of temperature differences on movement of molecules and on the relational graphs under the molecule diagrams.

How Graphics Build Mental Models

Relevant graphics help learners build accurate mental models through a process called *dual encoding* (Paivio, 1986). According to dual encoding, adding a relevant visual to text improves learning by providing two memory traces. The words offer one view of the content and the visual offers a second complimentary view.

Previously in this chapter, I summarized research showing the benefits of an explanatory visual of the human heart when building an accurate mental model (double loop circulation model) (Butcher, 2006). To dig a little deeper into how visuals

Figure 9.6. A Science Simulation That Uses Interpretive and Relational Visuals

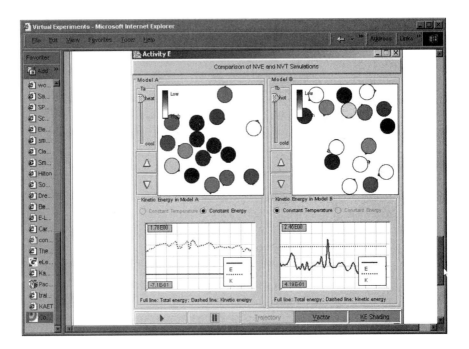

helped learning, Butcher asked all learners to provide verbal self-explanations as they were reviewing the lesson material. She then analyzed those self-explanations to compare the mental processes of those studying text alone with the mental processes of those studying text plus graphics. In comparing inference errors, she found an average of twenty-two errors among those reviewing text only, compared to an average of nine among those reviewing text and graphics. In comparing the types of statements made by learners, she found that inferences that connected individual lesson ideas (called integration inferences) were much more common in the lessons with visuals. The generation of integration inferences leads to a correct mental model of how the heart works. Learners who formed the correct double-loop model of the circulatory system generated significantly more integration inferences than those who formed one of the incorrect models. The author concludes: "Results from self-explaining suggested that the simplified diagrams were beneficial because they promoted generation of important inferences during learning. Thus, diagrams may be most useful when they have been designed to highlight the essential relationships necessary to understand the situation described in the learning materials" (p. 194).

In summary, to promote more and more accurate mental models, include explanatory visuals that illustrate the relationships described in the text or narration in your training materials. As we have discussed, an effective explanatory visual is often simple; detailed three-dimensional or animated visuals may not contribute to learning and in fact may depress learning.

Personalize Your Learning Environment

Have you even been caught "half-listening"? You are engaged in a conversation, but your mind is elsewhere. Suddenly your conversational partner asks you a question and you realize you have not really heard much of what he was saying. All of us feel a sense of embarrassment in these situations. That is because humans are social beings with cooperative behaviors serving as a basis for survival since prehistoric times. Humans are programmed to attend to social interactions and to process them deeply to comprehend and respond to the messages sent to us. Recent research shows that, as trainers, we can capitalize on this convention by engaging learners in a social experience, even in the absence of an instructor. In this section, I review proven guidelines on the use of language and on-screen learning agents to create a social learning environment.

Use Conversational Language to Personalize Learning

Clark and Mayer (2008) recommend the use of conversational language and learning agents to implement what Mayer (2005, p. 201) calls a *Personalization Principle* of learning:

Personalization Principle: "People learn more deeply when the words in a multimedia presentation are in conversational style rather than formal style."

Take a minute to compare the e-learning screens in Figure 9.7 and 9.8. Note the small character in the bottom left corner of Figure 9.7 whose dialog is quite conversational. In contrast, the introductory screen in Figure 9.8 does not include a character and the text is impersonal. Research on discourse processing shows that people work harder to understand material when they feel they are in a conversation with a partner, rather than simply receiving information. Therefore, using conversational style as well as a learning agent in your lessons conveys the idea that learners should work hard to understand what their conversational partners are saying.

Evidence for Conversational Language

Moreno and Mayer (2000b, 2004) conducted five research comparisons using a computer-based educational game on botany. In some versions the words were quite formal. For example, the lesson stated: *"This program is about what type of plants survive on different planets. For each planet, a plant will be designed. The goal is to learn what type of roots, stems, and leaves allow the plant to survive in each environment."* A more conversational version included the following script: *"You are about to start a journey where you will be visiting different planets. For each planet, you will need to*

Figure 9.7. An Informal Introduction Uses an Agent and Conversational Language

From *e-Learning and the Science of Instruction* CD

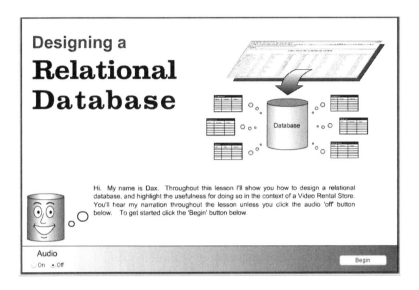

Figure 9.8. A Formal Introduction Omits the Agent and Drops First- and Second-Person Language

From *e-Learning and the Science of Instruction* CD.

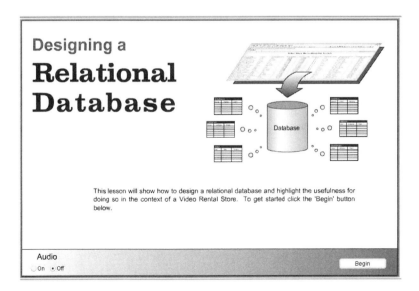

design a plant. Your mission is to learn what type of roots, stems, and leaves will allow your plant to survive in each environment." As you can see, the conversational version addressed the learner directly using the second person.

In five out of five studies, students who learned with personalized text performed better on subsequent transfer tests than students who learned with formal text. Overall, participants in the personalized group produced between 20 to 46 percent more solutions to transfer problems than the formal group, with effect sizes all above 1. Similar benefits were seen in conversational versions of lessons on how lightning forms and how lungs work.

Note that only some minor changes in language are needed. For example, make use of first- and second-person constructions in which you directly address the learner. In addition, use polite forms of speech rather than impersonal statements. Rather than saying, "Click the ENTER key," use a more socially friendly statement such as "Let's click the ENTER key." Don't go overboard; just a few subtle changes in the narration can help learners feel they are involved in a more personal exchange.

Use On-Screen Agents in Multimedia to Personalize Learning

In Figure 9.7, you saw a small on-screen cartoon character. These characters are called *learning agents* or *pedagogical agents.* Learning agents are on-screen characters who guide the learning process during an e-learning episode. Agents are commonly presented visually as cartoon-like characters, as talking head-video, or as virtual reality avatars. What evidence do we have about the effectiveness of learning agents?

Evidence for Learning Agents. Before investing effort in constructing learning agents, we need to know whether they offer any learning benefits. Based on research to date, the answer is yes. For example, Moreno and Mayer (2004) compared a guided discovery e-learning game called Design-A-Plant described in the previous section. One version included Herman the Bug, a learning agent who poses problems, offers feedback, and generally guides the learner through the game. A comparison version uses the same words and visuals without Herman. Across two separate experiments, the agent group generated 24 to 48 percent more solutions in transfer tests than did the no-agent group. Although we need more studies to make a definitive statement about agents, so far the results look promising.

If agents offer learning value, what do we know about how agents should look, sound, or act to be most effective? Do you need to include a highly realistic avatar like the type found in video games? Or will a simpler visual like the one in Figure 9.7 be as effective? Does it matter how the agent communicates with the learner? Finally, what types of activities should the agent support during learning? Should the agent present content, offer advice, or give feedback?

Features of Agents That Matter

Although we have technology to create very realistic avatars such as those found in video games, research does not support the need for a high degree of realism. In comparing Herman the Bug with a talking-head video of a young man in the Design-A-Plant game, there were no real learning differences (Moreno, Mayer, Spires, & Lester, 2001). Based on evidence to date, a simple figure like the one shown in Figure 9.7 is as useful as a realistic image. However, there is compelling evidence that the agent needs to sound conversational. Clark and Mayer (2008) summarize four studies in which learning was better in the Design-A-Plant game if Herman's words were spoken rather than on-screen text and were conversational rather than formal. These results reflect the modality and

Figure 9.9. A Learning Agent Provides Feedback to the Learner

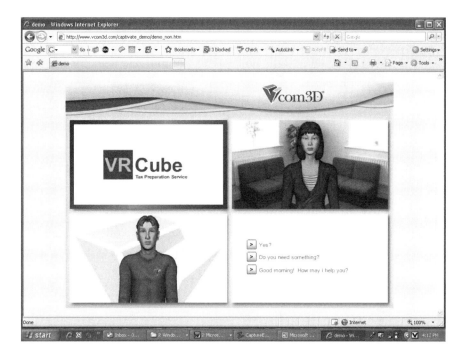

personalization principles described in Chapter 6 and in previous paragraphs. Finally, it is important that the agent serve some useful instructional purpose, rather than appear simply as a decorative element. For example, the agent in the lower left-hand corner of Figure 9.9 gives feedback to the learner's response that includes lesson content as well as provides directions for the next step.

To summarize, when designing asynchronous e-learning, include learning agents that guide the learner's cognitive processes. Your learning agent can be a simple drawing but ideally should speak with conversational audio.

Include Deep-Level Learning Agent Dialogs

In the previous section, I recommended using learning agents to guide cognitive processes during e-learning. We have preliminary evidence that learning can be as effective from observing agent dialogs that involve deep-level questions and answers as from actively responding to questions. Gholson and Craig (2006) and Craig, Sullings, Witherspoon, and Gholson (2006) use an *e-learning environment* called AutoTutor to compare learning from active responding to questions to learning from observing on-screen agents engaged in question-answer dialogs. The research team refers to vicarious learning environments as "those in which learners see or hear content for which they are not the addressees and have no way of physically interacting with the source of the content they are attempting to master" (p. 566). Vicarious learning environments are one form of implicit instructional method. The potential of vicarious learning environments has important practical significance because if learning can be as effective from observing as from overt engagement, considerable time and money might be saved on e-learning design and implementation.

The learning content in their experiments was twelve computer literacy topics such as why random access memory is important, what the CPU does, and the advantages of parallel processing. Learning was measured with multiple choice pre- and post-tests. In the interactive condition, AutoTutor initiated each topic with a brief explanation from an on-screen agent followed by a question for the learner to answer. The learner typed an answer into a dialog box. AutoTutor evaluated learning by comparing the learner's answer to an ideal answer. Once the learner's response incorporated the desired content, AutoTutor moved to another topic. Four vicarious learning conditions were compared to this interactive version.

The most effective vicarious learning version consisted of an interactive dialog in which a virtual tutee asked deep-level questions and the on-screen virtual tutor responded stating the ideal answer such as:

Virtual Tutor: *There are many important issues to be considered when buying a computer. Compatibility is one important issue, but such issues as speed also need to be considered.*

Virtual Tutee: *Why is speed important?*

Virtual Tutor: *The faster the CPU, the faster it can process data, exchange information with RAM, and communicate with peripherals.*

Virtual Tutee: *How can a manufacturer increase the speed of the computer? What can they do to make it faster?*

Figure 9.10 shows the results from the interactive and the vicarious interactive dialog condition from two experiments. The research team reports that learning was as good or better in the agent dialog observation conditions as in the interactive setting.

Can Interactive Environments Be Replaced with Dialogs?

We don't yet have sufficient research to say that vicarious environments are as effective as making overt responses. However, should these guidelines prove effective for diverse learners and content, a great deal of time and money can be saved by converting didactic content into a series of deep-level question–answer responses to be viewed by learners. Rather than constructing questions for learners to answer, adding answer judging routines, and feedback, an equally effective observational learning environment would save development time and costs.

Figure 9.10. Learning from Vicarious Observation Is Better Than Active Engagement

Based on data from Craig, Sullings, Witherspoon, and Gholson, 2006

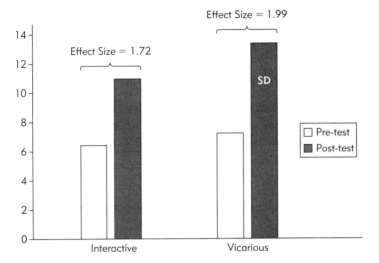

Based on current evidence, I recommend that you replace straight content delivery with a series of agent-based deep-level questions and answers. In synchronous e-learning that will be viewed as a recording in a vicarious learning mode, instructor teams might emulate a tutor-tutee dialog, as shown above. We will need more data to determine the situations in which vicarious learning can replace overt learner engagement.

Provide Examples and Encourage Their Processing

Examples are instances of your lesson concepts, procedures, processes, and principles. Examples to illustrate a concept coupled with non-examples to show the boundaries of what a concept is not, are especially useful to build conceptual mental models. In a lesson on graphics, I show several visual examples. Some samples reflect and others violate research guidelines on effective visuals. The surface features of these examples vary widely and include photographs, illustrations, and animated demonstrations. Through an analysis of these divergent examples and counter-examples, learners build a mental model of what constitutes an effective visual.

Learners love examples. In fact, they prefer them to explanations. When faced with a choice between study of an example or reading of an explanation, most learners choose the example (Anderson, Farrell, & Sauers, 1984; Lefevre & Dixon, 1986). Since examples are both popular and effective, design and use them frequently and effectively.

Maximizing Learning from Examples

Examples are effective ways to build mental models of moderate to high complexity. In Chapter 6, I summarized research showing that rather than asking learners to solve many problems themselves, irrelevant cognitive load can be reduced by providing a number of worked examples. In this way learners can devote mental effort to learning rather than problem solving. However, examples won't be effective unless learners actively process them. If learners ignore the examples, they will not build mental models. In the same way, if learners give examples only cursory processing, their benefits will be limited.

Successful learners generate many more self-explanations of examples than less successful learners (Chi, 2000; Chi, DeLeeuw, Chiu, & LaVancher, 1994). Further, the quality of the self-explanations makes a difference. Better learning results when those explanations articulate the principles behind the examples. Many learners process examples in a shallow way and thus do not maximize their value. However, you can train learners to effectively process examples (Renkl, Stark, Gruber, & Mandl, 1998). Learners trained to carefully study accounting worked examples produced twice as many deep explanations twice as often as untrained learners. Further, those learners who processed the worked examples deeply, did better on far-transfer test items (Stark, Mandl, Gruber, & Renkl, 2002).

One of the recurrent themes of this edition of *Building Expertise* is the power of examples. In Chapter 10, I will illustrate explicit techniques to promote deeper processing of examples by inserting self-explanation questions for learners to answer. In Chapter 12, I will show you how to design examples to build far-transfer mental models. As you will see throughout the book, the frequent and effective use of examples is one of the most powerful tools in your arsenal of teaching techniques.

Provide Effective Analogies

An instructional *analogy* is an explicit, non-literal comparison between two objects or sets of objects that describes their structural, functional, and/or causal similarities (Stepich & Newby, 1988). The purpose of an analogy is to promote understanding by helping learners map critical information from familiar knowledge to knowledge that is new. In other words, the analogy helps the learners understand new information in terms of existing knowledge.

With the aid of a good analogy, learners can construct better mental models than could be constructed without it. For example, an analogy to support the physiological concept of peristalsis is:

> "Peristalsis is like squeezing ketchup out of a single-service packet. You squeeze the packet near one corner and run your fingers along the length of the packet toward an opening at the other corner. When you do this, you push the ketchup through the packet, in one direction, ahead of your fingers until it comes out of the opening."
> (Newby, Ertmer, & Stepich, 1995)

What Makes Analogies Effective?

While some educators are very positive about the value of analogies, empirical comparisons of learning with and without analogies have yielded mixed outcomes. To be effective, an analogy must serve as a cognitive aid for your learners. Some reasons that analogies have not always proven effective include:

- Analogies must successfully draw on knowledge familiar to the learner.

- Analogies from domains similar to the target domain may result in learner misconceptions; it is better to draw on unrelated domains.

- Learning from analogies may require more time than other instructional aids.

In a study that effectively implemented analogies, learners could spend as much time as they wished studying materials that included clear presentations of the analogies which were drawn from far-domains (Newby, Ertmer, & Stepich, 1995). Immediate and delayed learning of physiological concepts such as peristalsis was better when analogies like the ketchup packet were included. Learning was measured by an application (versus a recall) test and therefore evaluated the effect of analogies on building of moderately complex mental models. The authors conclude: "Their effectiveness comes during the initial encoding of information and has little bearing on later recall and application" (p. 16).

Here are three important steps to take to develop effective analogies:

1. Determine the features most important to the new mental model you wish to build based on an analysis of the to-be-learned information. For example, for the concept of peristalsis, the main idea is sustained pressure to move material through a tube-like structure.

2. Identify one or more concrete items from a different domain than the target information with features that overlap the target concept. Be sure the analogy will draw on knowledge familiar to the learners. For example, squeezing toothpaste from a tube was an alternative to the ketchup packet. Both the toothpaste tube and the ketchup packet are from different domains than physiology and would be familiar to the audience.

3. Present the analogy by describing the similarities between the chosen base (the ketchup packet) and the to-be-learned knowledge (peristalsis).

Include Process Content in Your Instruction

Take a look at the equipment panel in Figure 9.11. What if you were asked to make the PF indicator flash on a functional version of this panel? You would have to use a trial-and-error approach until you obtained the desired result. On the other hand, suppose that, before you were asked to make the PF indicator flash, you

---

Figure 9.11. A Control Panel

Adapted from Kieras and Bovair, 1984

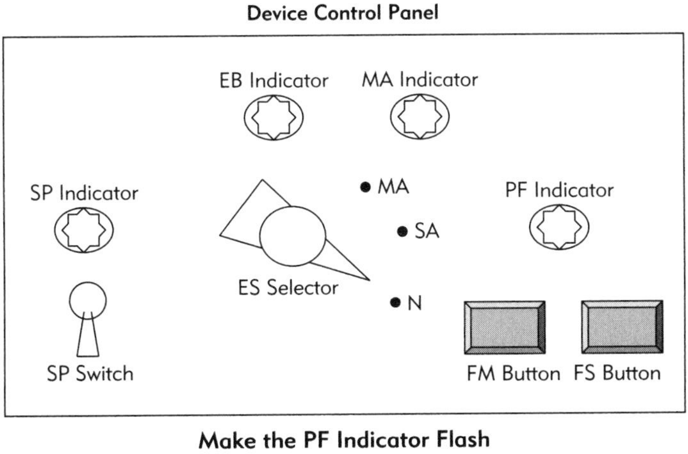

Device Control Panel

Make the PF Indicator Flash

had a process lesson on how the equipment works that used text describing the schematic diagram shown in Figure 9.12. As you read the text and study the schematic, you learn that the panel controls the phaser banks in the Star Ship Enterprise. You further learn how the different panel controls access the ship's power, boost the power, and store the power in one of two accumulators. Would this knowledge improve your ability to make the PF indicator flash? Kieras and Bovair (1984) compared performance of two training conditions. In one condition, the steps were trained. In the second condition, prior to learning steps, the process lesson was given. Individuals who received the process lesson learned procedures faster, spontaneously revised procedures to be more efficient, and were able to troubleshoot malfunctions effectively.

Figure 9.12. An Interpretive Schematic Diagram of the Control Panel
Adapted from Kieras and Bovair, 1984

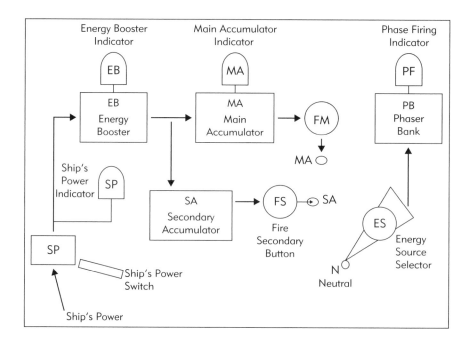

An especially important mental model for individuals involved in design or troubleshooting work is a *cause-and-effect* mental model. Understanding the components and how the components interact with each other will enable the software designer or the troubleshooter to work on the basis of understanding rather than trial and error. One way to build a cause-and-effect model is to teach *process* knowledge. Process knowledge is information about "how it works" and can be trained by way of interpretive diagrams such as schematics, operational simulations, and explanations of parts and functions.

Offer Cognitive Support for Novice Learners

In this chapter, I have reviewed research showing the learning benefits of implicit instructional methods, including explanatory visuals, personalization, agent dialogs, examples, analogies, and process lessons. Many of these methods are effective because they provide cognitive substitutes for mental models lacking in novice learners. However, we have consistent evidence that implicit instructional methods such as graphics or worked examples have no effect or can even depress learning of learners with relevant background knowledge! Learners with background knowledge in the instructional domain have sufficient mental models to process new content on their own. Additional support in the form of worked examples or graphics, for example, either adds nothing or can actually conflict with the experienced learner's pre-existing mental models.

Evidence That Graphics Benefit Novices

Earlier in the chapter, I summarized a number of research studies that support a multimedia principle: Adding explanatory visuals to text will improve learning. However, the multimedia principle applies primarily to learners who are new to the lesson content. In a series of three experiments involving lessons on brakes, pumps, and generators, Mayer and Gallini (1990) reported novices learned better from text and illustrations than from words alone, but experts learned equally well from both conditions. In Figure 9.5 you saw the learning benefits of an audiovisual explanation of legal concepts compared to audio-alone. These benefits, however, applied to legal novices. The law students performed equally well from audio alone as from audiovisual formats.

The Expertise Reversal Effect

There is growing evidence that instructional methods such as visuals are most beneficial for novice learners. These observations led Kalyuga, Ayers, Chandler, and Sweller (2003) to propose the *Expertise Reversal Effect*—the idea that instructional supports that help low-knowledge learners may not help (and may even hurt) high-knowledge learners. As we will see in Chapter 10, there is even some evidence that high-knowledge learners achieve as much in receptive learning environments as in interactive environments. High-knowledge learners already have sufficient mental models to support their own internal cognitive processes and require little or no external support. A practical implication is that the majority of instructional resources should be invested in learning environments intended for novices.

COMING NEXT

Helping Leaners Build Mental Models: Explicit Methods

Explicit instructional methods require learners to respond in visible ways. Do learning environments that include explicit opportunities for encoding result in greater learning than more passive environments? If yes, what types of explicit methods are most effective? I will address these questions in the next chapter.

INSTRUCTIONAL METHODS THAT PROMOTE MENTAL MODELS IN THE ABSENCE OF EXTERNAL ACTIVITY

To recap the evidence about implicit encoding methods, apply the following guidelines.

☐ Include explanatory visuals that help learners understand content relationships relevant to the instructional goal.

☐ Make instructional environments personal by using informal polite conversational style and by including learning agents in e-learning.

☐ Present content in a virtual tutor-tutee dialog in which one agent asks a deep-level question and the second agent responds.

☐ Include frequent examples.

☐ Train learners to self-explain examples.

☐ Include analogies that model the features or functions of new content using illustrations from a different content domain that is familiar to the learners.

☐ Teach process content for learners whose work will benefit from a deeper understanding of systems.

Recommended Readings

Butcher, K.R. (2006). Learning from text with diagrams: Promoting mental model development and inference generation. *Journal of Educational Psychology, 98,* 182–197.

Clark, R.C., & Lyons, C. (2004). *Graphics for learning.* San Francisco, CA: Pfeiffer.

Gholson, B., & Craig, S.D. (2006). Promoting constructive activities that support vicarious learning during computer-based instruction. *Educational Psychology Review, 18,* 119–139.

Clark, R.C., & Mayer, R.E. (2008). *e-Learning and the science of instruction* (2nd ed.). San Francisco, CA: Pfeiffer.

CHAPTER 10 TOPICS

Is Active Learning Better? A Tale of Six Lessons

Case 1: Lecture vs. Problem-Based Discussions

Case 2: Text Reading vs. Computer Simulation

Case 3: Author-Provided vs. Learner-Generated Graphic Organizers

Practice vs. Deliberate Practice

Building Mental Models Principle

What Are Mental Models?

Explicit vs. Implicit Methods for Building Mental Models

Maintenance vs. Elaborative Rehearsal

Maintenance Rehearsal

Elaborative Rehearsal

Incorporate Frequent Elaborative Practice Exercises

Design and Assign Elaborative Practice Exercises

Assign Argumentation

The Law of Diminishing Returns

Consider Cost-Benefit When Planning Practice Exercises

Distribute Practice Assignments

Provide Explanatory Feedback

Evidence for Explanatory Feedback

Intrinsic vs. Instructional Feedback

Use Effective Questioning Techniques in the Classroom

Promote Psychological Engagement with Graphics

10

Helping Learners Build Mental Models: Explicit Methods

What we learn to do, we learn by doing.

ARISTOTLE

HELPING LEARNERS build appropriate mental models is the focus of Chapters 9 and 10. This chapter describes instructional methods that promote behavioral activities that help learners build mental models, which form the basis for expertise. Some guidelines for explicit learning activities include:

- Incorporate frequent elaborative exercises
- Distribute practice throughout your learning event
- Provide explanatory feedback
- Use effective classroom questioning techniques
- Engage learners with graphics
- Promote self-explanations of content
- Incorporate collaborative learning opportunities
- Provide student notes during instructor-led instruction

Is Active Learning Better? A Tale of Six Lessons

Is learning always better when participants are actively engaged? Can learning happen in a passive didactic instructional setting? Let's compare three research studies that addressed this question.

Case 1: Lecture vs. Problem-Based Discussions

Haidet and his colleagues (2004) compared immediate and delayed learning of medical residents from an active and a passive learning event. In the active version, residents were put into small groups and discussed a case problem assigned by the instructor. After a brief discussion, the instructor presented content that resolved the case. This active learning pattern was repeated four times. In the passive version, the same content was presented by the instructor in the form of a traditional didactic lecture. The active and the passive learning events each lasted one hour and each included the same basic technical information. Learning was measured immediately after the session and one month later. In addition, learner satisfaction with the program was also measured.

As you can see in Figure 10.1 both groups realized considerable learning from pre-test to post-test and there were no statistically significant differences in learning between the two groups either immediately or on the delayed assessment. Further, residents in the didactic session were more satisfied with their experience! Most instructional professionals are drilled in the value of "active" aka "experiential" aka "collaborative" learning environments. But in this research we have evidence that overt activity may not always result in better learning or greater satisfaction among learners!

Figure 10.1. There Were No Significant Differences in Learning Between Active and Passive Groups
Based on data from Haidet, Morgan, O'Malley, Moran, and Richards, 2004

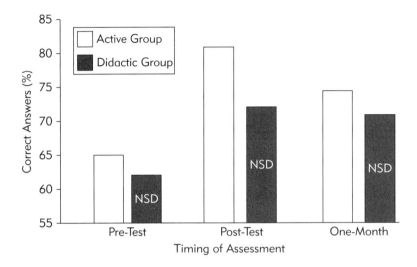

Case 2: Text Reading vs. Computer Simulation

Taylor and Chi (2006) compared learning project management skills by undergraduates from working for two hours in one of two environments: a simulation case-based condition and a text reading condition. Both learning environments presented basically the same information regarding factors that influence project outcomes, such as budget, schedule, customer satisfaction, and team morale. After the two hours, both groups were given two tests. One test asked them to reply to two open-ended questions. For example, they were asked, *What are some ways to tell whether a project is ahead of, behind, or on schedule?* The second test consisted of four case-study scenarios that required test-takers to judge the appropriateness of project management actions taken by a manager in case-based scenarios. The active simulation environment resulted in much more pre- to post-test

Figure 10.2. An Active Learning Environment Resulted in Better
Application Learning Than a Passive Learning Environment
Adapted from Taylor and Chi, 2006

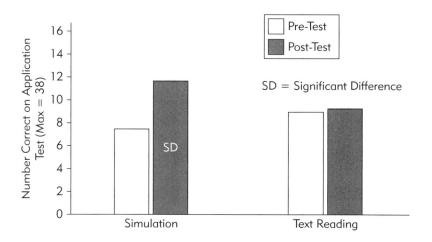

application learning gain on the scenario test items than the text reading environment. On the knowledge test, there were no significant differences in learning between the simulation and text groups. The results are summarized in Figure 10.2 above. The research team concluded that their results "provide strong empirical support for the implementation and utilization of instructional computer simulations, particularly in complex domains that are rich in implicit knowledge" (p. 312).

Case 3: Author-Provided vs. Learner-Generated Graphic Organizers

Stull and Mayer (2007) compared study time and learning from a science text reading in which graphic organizers were provided by the author with study time and learning from the same text in which learners completed organizer templates. A control group read the text with no organizers. As you can see in Figure 10.3, learners who constructed their own organizers took twice as long to complete the lesson and actually scored lower on the test than the control group that had no organizer. Stull and Mayer comment: "Both treatments—learning by viewing and learning by doing— can encourage generative processing, but learning by doing may create so much extraneous processing that insufficient capacity is available to actually engage in generative processing" (p. 817).

In these research studies, we see conflicting results. In the medical resident study, a didactic lecture was just as effective (and more highly rated) than an active discussion-based environment. Similarly in the graphic organizer study, learning was faster and better from viewing author-supplied graphics than from learner-generated graphics. In contrast, in the project management study, the active simulation environment resulted in better case application (although not explicit knowledge) learning than a passive reading assignment.

Figure 10.3. Faster and Better Learning from Text with Author-Supplied Graphic Organizers

Adapted from Stull and Mayer (2007), Experiment 3

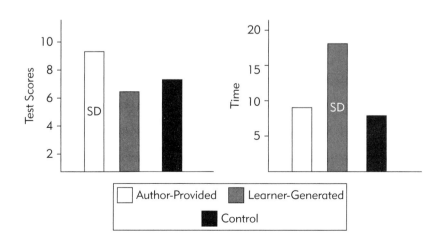

Since active learning environments are generally more expensive than passive learning environments, when should you invest the time and resources to build in practice exercises, group discussions, simulations, or other engagement strategies? When you do include various types of active techniques, how should they be designed for maximum learning? In this chapter we will review some guidelines and research on active learning.

Practice vs. Deliberate Practice

Studies of experts in various domains find top performers in the arts and sports do devote considerably more time to practice than performers who do not reach world-class status. Musicians who had reached an elite status at a music conservatory had devoted more than 10,000 hours to practice by the age of twenty! However, practice alone does not guarantee high levels of proficiency. Ericsson (2006) refers to practice that leads to expertise as *deliberate practice*. He defines deliberate practice as tasks presented to performers that "are initially outside their current realm of reliable performance, yet can be mastered within hours of practice by concentrating on critical aspects and by gradually refining performance through repetitions after feedback" (p. 692). Note that his definition of deliberate practice incorporates the idea of a tailored focused activity aimed at just the right level of challenge to extend expertise. Too much challenge results in extraneous mental load. Too little challenge will not foster the skills needed. As the custodians of expertise in our organizations, we need to consider the design of practice environments that foster deliberate practice—practice that stretches the learner to build new skills just beyond his or her competency level.

In summary, we see that learning by doing may not always lead to greater learning than learning by viewing. Behavioral activity may not translate into effective mental activity. Some types of overt activities such as simulations may build a different type of knowledge compared to a more passive activity such as reading. As with all instructional methods, there are few absolute rules. Instead, we must consider our learners as well as our outcome goals when defining instructional environments. In this chapter, I will review what we know about when, how, and for whom overt activity during training is most beneficial. I will also consider the features of practice assignments that make them successful.

Building Mental Models Principle

In Chapter 9 I introduced the *Mental Models Principle* by emphasizing that the role of the instructor in building expertise is to create an environment that enables learners to construct the best mental models to perform job tasks. The active nature of learning is the basis for the *Mental Models Principle* of instructional design:

Mental Models Principle: Provide learners with an instructional environment that promotes their active construction of new mental models.

What Are Mental Models?

In Chapter 9, I described the concept of mental models. To briefly recap, *mental models* are memory structures (also called *schemas*) stored in long-term memory that are the basis for thinking. Good mental models enable you to: distinguish and generalize concepts, solve problems, make predictions, and interpret situations. I distinguish between two types of mental models:

1. Simple mental models that support cognitive operations such as discrimination and generalization of concepts and situations and implementation of routine procedures

2. Complex mental models that support problem solving— both routine and novel

Simple mental models help you identify new concepts and generalize them to new settings. *Complex mental models,* which incorporate many simple mental models, are the basis for more complex forms of problem solving. Expertise is based on the many complex mental models that the performer has built in long-term memory over years of experience. For example, chess masters are estimated to have approximately 50,000 play patterns stored in their long-term memory (Simon & Gilmartin, 1973).

Explicit vs. Implicit Methods for Building Mental Models

In Chapter 9, we discussed implicit instructional methods that facilitate encoding of new information into existing memories. Implicit methods, such as graphics, promote active learning processes. However, the activity is psychological and thus usually does not involve overt learner responses. For example, when you view a relevant graphic, you form two memory codes—one corresponding to the visual and the second to the verbal expressions of content. The two codes result in two memory traces that increase learning.

In this chapter, I summarize the following *explicit* instructional methods—methods that promote mental activity by way of visible learner activity.

- Develop and assign elaborative practice exercises.
- Distribute practice throughout your events.
- Include explanatory feedback for learner responses.
- Use effective questioning techniques in the classroom.
- Actively engage learners with your content.

- Develop and facilitate effective collaborative learning activities.

- Provide learners with lecture notes or job aids to free limited instructional time for more productive activities.

Maintenance vs. Elaborative Rehearsal

The encoding of new information into existing knowledge in long-term memory occurs through rehearsal processes in working memory. There are two types of rehearsal: maintenance and elaborative.

Maintenance Rehearsal

Maintenance rehearsal is the rote repetition of information in working memory. Repeating a telephone number over and over until you dial it is an example of maintenance rehearsal. An exercise that asks learners to list the five benefits of a new product that have just been presented in a lecture is another example. I call maintenance rehearsal *regurgitation* practice. Maintenance rehearsal is a good way to keep information alive in working memory (as long as the rehearsal continues). However, maintenance rehearsal does not build mental models. Look at the relationship graphed in Figure 10.4 between the number of times a word is repeated and later recall of that word. As you can see, the line is fairly flat, indicating little relationship between the amount of rote rehearsal and learning.

There is an exception to the lack of correlation between rehearsals and learning. Any information or task repeated hundreds of times becomes automated. In Chapters 4 and 5, I mentioned that any skill—cognitive or motor—that is repeated hundreds of times becomes hard-wired into long-term memory. Sheer repetition does work eventually. However, repetitive

Figure 10.4. Maintenance (Repetitive) Rehearsals Do Not Improve Recall
From Craig and Watkins, 1973

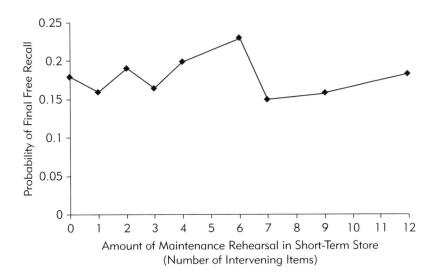

practice exercises during training are labor-intensive and should be reserved for situations in which performing complex tasks relies on automatic performance.

Elaborative Rehearsal

Elaborative rehearsal helps learners build mental models because it promotes the integration of new content with existing knowledge. Elaborative rehearsal thus leads to deeper learning and, with the exception of information that must be automated, is the preferred type of rehearsal during training. An example of elaborative rehearsal is an exercise in which a learner must present the benefits of a new product based on a client's needs. This exercise requires the learner to take new information—the new product benefits—and transform it based on the specific client's requirements. Another example of elaborative rehearsal is the mental processing that occurred during a project management simulation that requires learners to explore a virtual workplace, interpret project outcome measures, and infer causal relationships between project management decisions and subsequent project outcome measures (Taylor & Chi, 2006). Elaborative rehearsals are the basis for deep mental processing in contrast to shallow processes of rote rehearsal.

Incorporate Frequent Elaborative Practice Exercises

As you plan practice exercises to help learners build mental models, consider: the type of practice to design, the amount and frequency of practice, and feedback provided to learner responses.

Design and Assign Elaborative Practice Exercises

It's important that most practice exercises stimulate elaborative rehearsals that incorporate the context of the job. For example, the screens in Figures 10.5 and 10.6 show two exercises from a lesson teaching airline gate agents reasons to deny passenger boarding. The interaction in Figure 10.5 promotes maintenance rehearsal because it requires the learner to merely repeat the content provided on a prior screen. The repetition of information already provided does not require any transformation of information by the learner and results in little or no encoding. In contrast, the interaction in Figure 10.6 requires the learner to apply new information to a work-related scenario. Here's how the practice in Figure 10.6 works. When a learner clicks on a particular passenger, he hears a brief dialog. For example, one passenger responds, *"Yes, I've had a few beers. . . . How many? Well . . . maybe fifteen."* The learner responds by dragging each passenger onto the concourse or onto the airplane. Although this is a nice application of a drag-and-drop feature in e-learning, a question

Figure 10.5. Maintenance Rehearsal Practice

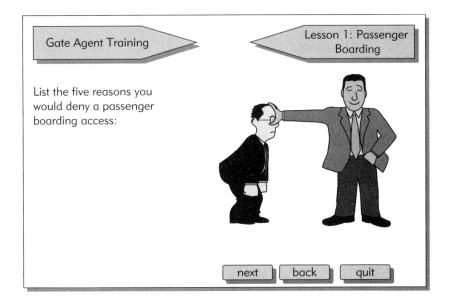

Figure 10.6. Elaborative Rehearsal Practice

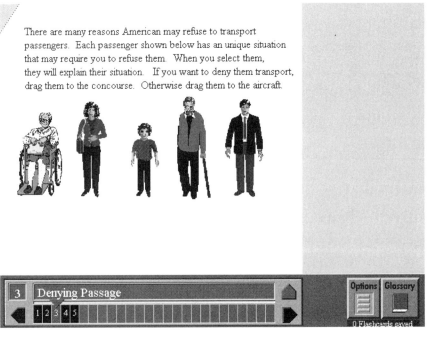

presented in a multiple-choice or dichotomous format would be just as effective. It's not the format of the question that is important; rather it's the mental process that the question stimulates. The interaction in Figure 10.6 requires learners to apply rules to job-realistic situations, whereas the interaction in Figure 10.5 merely requires regurgitation.

Assign Argumentation

Argumentation refers to creating reasoned positions on a topic or controversy. In one experiment, learners were assigned one of four types of essays to write while researching a historical event from a textbook or from Internet sites. The essay types were (1) a summary of the readings, (2) a narrative of what happened, (3) an explanation of what happened, or (4) an argument that discussed two opposing interpretations of the events. Wiley and Voss (1999) measured the quality of the essays produced and far-transfer learning based on a test that required application of the concepts to new historical situations. They found that the argument assignment, especially when learners had to draw information from Internet sites, resulted in more complex essays and in better scores on the final test. The mental work of synthesizing diverse sources into a pro and con discussion fostered the greatest amount of elaboration with subsequent deepest learning.

The Law of Diminishing Returns

While practice may never make perfect, it does improve performance indefinitely, although at diminishing levels. Timed measurements of workers using a machine to roll cigars found that, after four years of practice that involved thousands of trials, proficiency continued to improve (Crossman, 1959). Similarly, a series of twelve practice sessions on manipulating an angled laparoscope reported dramatic improvements in the time to complete the task from the first to the last practice session (Keehner, Lippa, Montello, Tendick, & Hegary, 2006). Figure 10.7 shows the average improvement over practice sessions, along with the distribution of results at each trial among individual participants. First, you can see that the greatest performance improvements occurred on the first five trials. Second, you can see that the performance differences among individual participants were large on the first few practice sessions, but diminished as practice continued. Over time, effective practice exercises even out initial variations among individuals, resulting in consistent performance. Diminishing skill improvements over time is referred to as the *Power Law of Practice,* which has been shown to apply not only to motor skills like the laparoscopic task but also to intellectual skills such as writing (Rosenbaum, Carlson, & Gilmore, 2001).

Figure 10.7. Performance Was Faster and More Consistent with More Practice
Based on data from Keehner, Lippa, Montello, Tendick, and Hegary, 2006

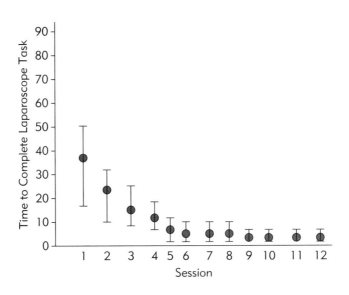

This is why world-class performers such as Tiger Woods continue to practice. One of the most important findings about expertise is that performance proficiency is strongly related to the time and efficiency of *deliberate practice*. The more one practices, the better one becomes, regardless of initial talent and ability. In fact, in the absence of practice, the more talented individuals will lose their edge compared to the less talented individuals who continue a regimen of deliberate practice (Ericsson, 1990). Remember however, that deliberate practice means a concentrated focus on skill areas that specifically need improvement.

When comparing outcomes from e-learning lessons with higher and lower numbers of practice exercises, Schnackenberg, Sullivan, Leader, and Jones (1998) found that both better and poorer learners (as defined by grade point average) improved their test scores when taking lessons with more practice. However, as you can see in Table 10.1, the amount of improvement was not proportional to the amount of extra practice time invested. In fact, poorer learners invested 75 percent more time for a 14 percent gain in scores.

Table 10.1. Learning Improvement Is Not Proportional to Time Invested

	Sixty-Six Practices		Twenty-Two Practices	
Ability Level	Low	High	Low	High
Test Scores	32.25	41.82	28.26	36.30
Time to Complete (Minutes)	146	107	83	85

Adapted from Schnackenberg, Sullivan, Leader, and Jones, 1998

Consider Cost-Benefit When Planning Practice Exercises

As you consider how much practice to include in your training, weigh the cost-tradeoffs of the extra time learners will need to complete practice. For critical tasks such as those with safety consequences, high amounts of practice are justified to bring skills to an automatic level. On the other hand, for tasks that are less critical, fewer practice exercises may achieve outcomes that are acceptable for entry-level job performance.

Furthermore, in some situations, behavioral activity can take more time and result in less learning. As described previously in this chapter, Stull and Mayer (2007) found better learning when they *provided* graphic organizers in an instructional text than when learners created the organizers themselves. Learners who created graphic organizers by filling in templates required twice as much study time and scored significantly lower on a transfer test. In this experiment, behavioral activity actually interfered with psychological activity leading to learning.

Distribute Practice Assignments

One way to get more mileage out of your practice exercises is to distribute them throughout your training sessions rather than lumping them in a single lesson or in one place in a lesson. "The so-called *Spacing Effect*—that practice sessions spaced in time are superior to massed practices in terms of long-term retention—is one of the most reliable phenomena in human experimental psychology. The effect is robust and appears to hold for verbal materials of all types as well as for motor skills" (National Research Council, 1991, p. 30). The advantages of spaced practice have been documented *as long as eight years after the original training!* (Bahrick, 1987).

Rohrer and Taylor (2006) recently compared two groups learning a mathematical procedure. Each group worked ten practice problems. One group completed all of the practice in a single session. The other practiced five problems in week one and the remaining five problems in the following week. As you can see in Figure 10.8, there were no differences in learning on an immediate test, but those in the spaced practice group had much better retention four weeks later. The authors recommend that in math textbooks, rather than assigning a large number of practice problems of the same type at the end of a lesson, the practice should be spread out among several lessons. For example, "Each lesson is followed by the usual number of practice problems, but only a few of these problems relate to the immediately preceding lesson. Additional problems of the same type might also appear once or twice in each of the next dozen assignments and once again after every fifth or tenth assignment thereafter" (p. 1,218).

Because most training programs do not measure long-term retention, the value of spaced practice is rarely salient to training

---

Figure 10.8. Better Long-Term Retention with Spaced-Out Practice
Based on data from Rohrer and Taylor, 2006

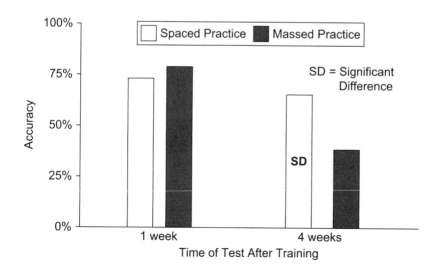

professionals. Naturally, practical constraints will limit the amount of spacing that is feasible in any given situation. Based on this research, I offer a *Spaced Practice Principle*.

Spaced Practice Principle: Distribute practice exercises throughout the instructional event rather than placing them all together in one time and place.

Provide Explanatory Feedback

When learners finish a practice exercise, they need to know whether their responses are correct as well as the reasons their answers are correct or incorrect. Feedback that provides reasons for correct or incorrect responses is called *explanatory feedback*. For example, in an e-lesson on databases, rather than simply saying, "*Sorry, that is incorrect*" explanatory feedback would say: "*Sorry that is incorrect. Remember, records are analogous to rows in a spreadsheet. Try again.*"

Evidence for Explanatory Feedback

Moreno (2004) compared learning from two versions of a computer botany game called Design-A-Plant. In the game, participants construct plants from a choice of roots, leaves, and stems in order to build a plant best suited to various environments. The object of the game is to teach the adaptive benefits of plant features for specific environments such as heavy rainfall, sandy soil, and so forth. Some learners received corrective feedback and others received explanatory feedback such as, "*Yes, in a low sunlight environment, a large leaf has more room to make food by photosynthesis.*" As you can see in Figure 10.9, better learning resulted from explanatory feedback—with a large effect size of 1.16.

Figure 10.9. Better Learning with Explanatory Feedback
Based on data from Experiment 1, Moreno, 2004

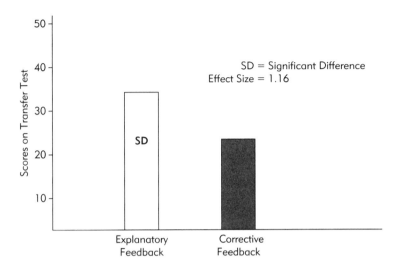

Intrinsic vs. Instructional Feedback

Some tasks provide *intrinsic feedback*. With intrinsic feedback, the results of a given action are immediately apparent to the learner. For example, when you try a golf putt, you immediately see where your ball goes and can infer the quality of your technique. However, *instructional feedback* can add much more. For example, a coach can give you advice regarding your club, your swing, your body positioning, and so on. Thus learning is best promoted by a combination of intrinsic and instructional feedback. Environments that rely on intrinsic feedback alone miss a good opportunity to accelerate learning.

Guided discovery lessons often use intrinsic forms of feedback. After taking an action to solve a problem, the learner "lives out" the consequences, reflects on how the action led to the consequences, and repeats the activity. For example, in a computer simulation teaching appropriate sales closing techniques,

inappropriate responses lead to loss of a sale. The reasons for
the loss can be made salient by showing a customer's thoughts
and follow-up reactions. This type of intrinsic feedback may
be strengthened by offering the learner additional instructional
feedback. For example, an on-screen tutor can explain why the
learner's actions did not lead to intended outcomes and provide
ideas for alternative approaches. Figure 10.10 shows a screen shot
from a sample e-lesson that incorporates intrinsic and instructional feedback. The learner selects one of three potential client
responses from the box in the lower right side of the screen. The
response selected results in appropriate body language and dialog
from the client shown in the upper right side of the screen. The

Figure 10.10. The e-Learning Offers Intrinsic and Instructional Feedback
With permission from Vcommunicator® elements, characters and all related
indicia TM & © 2007 Vcom3D, Inc. All rights reserved.

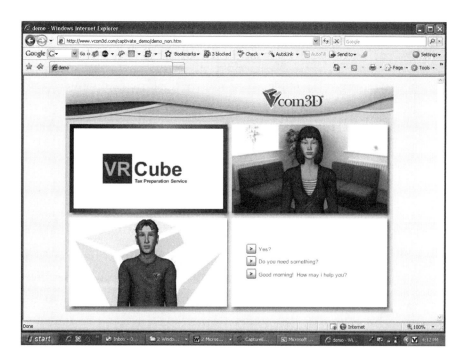

client response is a form of intrinsic feedback. The agent in the lower left corner then provides explanatory feedback and invites the learner to move ahead or try again.

Although providing tailored feedback will add time to your development effort, evidence suggests that it is time well-invested. Therefore, I offer the following *Explanatory Feedback Principle*:

Explanatory Feedback Principle: Provide both implicit and instructional feedback that informs the learner of the correctness of their response and gives an explanation.

Even correct answers to questions such as those shown in Figure 10.10 may have been selected by chance and thus can benefit from explanatory feedback.

Use Effective Questioning Techniques in the Classroom

Classroom instructors tend to overuse close-ended factual-type questions—the kind that promote maintenance rehearsal and don't build mental models (Gall & Artero-Bonare, 1995). Instead, they should ask elaborative questions that promote deeper learning. Some tips to maximize the value of questions asked during training include:

- Ask a single question that uses clear concrete language.

- Ask questions that will stimulate elaborative rather than maintenance rehearsal.

- To develop an elaborative question, elicit or show a sample and ask learners to connect the sample to lesson concepts.

- Wait at least three seconds before calling for an answer. This pause leads to deeper student processing. Research on the influence of wait time on learning suggests that an average three- to five-second wait time enhances achievement (Tobin, 1987).

- Target questions in ways to maximize the response of the whole class

  - Ask a question, pause, call on a specific individual

  - Ask for a show of hands

  - Assign learners to formulate an answer in a small group

- Respond to questions effectively

  - If an answer is correct but hesitant, affirm the correct answer and explain why

  - If an answer is incorrect, give feedback in the form of hints, a different question, or a re-explanation.

As an example, a lesson for sales associates that has presented the features of a new product line might include the following questions:

- *How many of you have heard comments from your clients that reflect a need for one or more of the products we have just described?* (Ask for a show of hands).

- *Could I get a few examples?* (Pause for volunteers).

- *What kinds of questions might you ask your clients to probe for their interest in feature Y? Work with your class colleague for two minutes and write down at least three questions you could use.*

- *Feature Z is especially appealing to our younger clients. Why do you think this is true?* (Pause). *Sam, what do you think?*

Asking effective questions in the classroom is a demanding task. I recommend that the instructor guide include several potentially effective questions that instructors can select. Alternatively, during their pre-class preparation period, instructors can write out several questions to use during the class.

Promote Psychological Engagement with Graphics

In Chapter 9, I showed research underscoring the value of adding relevant visuals and examples to help learners build good mental models. In the case of relational graphics (bar charts, line graphs, and so forth), is it more valuable to provide the graphic in the training materials OR to ask learners to construct their own graphic? Several research studies compared learning from text that included the graphic with the same text that required learners to construct their own graphs. For example, Natter and Berry (2005) gave learners a text regarding side-effects from a fictitious medication. One group saw a bar chart in the text illustrating the probabilities of side-effects, and a second group constructed their own chart. All participants were asked to rate the likelihood of side-effects. Active participants were more correct in their probability and frequency estimates.

Stern, Aprea, and Ebner (2003) gave learners a text explanation of the costs of outsourcing versus self-storage of inventory as a function of the quantity of goods to be stored. One lesson version included a linear graph of the relationship. A second version required the learners to construct their own graphs. Learners who were familiar with graphic representations learned more from the active graphic condition than the passive graph! Cosmides and Tooby (1996) report similar results among learners who actively constructed a visual frequency graph versus those who saw a pre-constructed graph.

In spite of the apparent benefits of active graph construction, it may not be necessary to require learners to actually construct a graph. It could be that those learners who reviewed text with already-constructed graphics simply did not pay attention to those graphics. Perhaps as effective as constructing a graph would be questions that required learners to review a pre-constructed graphic in a meaningful manner. In fact, Stull and Mayer (2007) found better and faster learning from author-provided organizational graphics than from asking learners to construct the graphics themselves. If a behavioral activity included in a lesson adds too much extraneous cognitive load, it may defeat its purpose. We need additional research on the conditions under which learning benefits from active engagement with visuals.

Promote Explicit Self-Explanations of Content

In Chapter 9, I mentioned the benefits of training learners to self-explain new content. A considerable body of evidence shows that learners who give good self-explanations of content learn more than learners who do not self-explain. A good self-explanation is one that goes beyond a mere paraphrasing of the lesson ideas to make inferences that link individual sentences together or connect new ideas to existing knowledge. Here I summarize three studies that illustrate the benefits of self-explanations for various types of demonstrations and examples.

Self-Explanations of Chess Move Examples

De Bruin, Rikers, and Schmidt (2007) compared learning of an end-game chess move among college freshmen with no chess experience. Everyone learned the basic rules of chess, followed by assignment to one of three conditions. Learners in one condition observed examples of a computer end game. Individuals in a second version viewed the same computer end game examples and were asked to predict the outcome of each move. Those in a third version predicted the outcomes AND gave an explanation for their predictions. Those in the self-explanation conditions performed the checkmate maneuver more often. There were no significant differences between the observation and the prediction groups. The authors suggest that the self-explanation condition could be made even more effective had learners received feedback on the accuracy of their self-explanations.

Self-Explanations of Correct Responses in Guided Discovery Learning

Moreno and Mayer (2005) found better far-transfer learning from students who were asked to explain *correct answers* from agent responses in a botany game than from students who explained their own answers (some of which were incorrect). In the game, either an agent or the learner selected the best combination of leaves, stems, and roots to help a plant survive in a given environment. Learners who gave their own answers were asked to give an explanation for their answers. Learners who observed the agent's responses were asked to explain the agent's selections. Learning was better among those who explained the agent's answers, which were correct, rather than those who explained their own answers some of which were wrong. The effect size for explaining correct answers was 1.10, which is high. The authors conclude: "Active reflection alone does not foster deeper learning unless it is based on correct information" (p. 127).

Self-Explanations of Worked-Out Steps in Math Examples

In e-learning, you can actively engage learners in self-explanations by attaching explanation-type questions to the content. For example, Atkinson, Renkl, and Merrill (2003) found that learning from a course on probability was better when learners were

Figure 10.11. Self-Explanation Questions Ensure Review of a Math Example

From Atkinson, Renkl, and Merrill, 2003

Problem: From a ballot box containing three red balls and two white balls, two balls are randomly drawn. The chosen balls are not put back into the ballot box. What is the probability that a red ball is drawn first and a white ball is second?

First
Solution
Step

Total number of balls: 5
Number of red balls: 3
Probability of a red ball first 3/5 = .6

Probability Rules/
Principles:

Please enter the letter of the rule/principle used in this step:

a) Probability of an event
b) Principle of complementarity
c) Multiplication Principle
d) Addition Principle

Next

required to respond to a question about a step shown in a problem example. In Chapter 6, I reviewed research showing that worked examples (demonstrations) are very powerful instructional devices. However, often learners either skip examples completely or give them only shallow processing. In Figure 10.11 the first step of a probability problem is worked out for the learner. The box on the right side asks the learner to identify which of four principles apply to that step. By requiring learners to answer principle-based questions such as these, they will have to carefully review the worked example.

In summary, I recommend the *Self-Explanation Support Principle*.

Self-Explanation Support Principle: Ask learners to give explanations for worked-out steps in demonstrations. Learners can select the principle illustrated by worked-out steps in a multiple-choice format or provide free-form explanations of demonstrated steps.

Incorporate Collaborative Learning Opportunities

Many research studies conducted with all age groups over the past forty years provide consistent evidence that, *under the right conditions,* participants who study together learn more than those who study alone. This holds true for many different subject areas and a wide range of tasks completed by learners who work in small groups or in pairs (Cohen, 1994; Johnson, Johnson, & Smith, 2007; Lou, Abrami, & d'Apollonia, 2001; Qin, Johnson, & Johnson, 1995; Springer, Stanne, & Donovan, 1999).

Johnson, Johnson, and Smith (2007) summarize the results of 168 research studies comparing outcomes of college and adult learners in cooperative, competitive, and individualistic learning environments. "Cooperative learning promoted higher individual achievement than did competitive (effect size = .49) or individualistic (effect size = 0.53). Students who would score at the 53rd percentile when learning individualistically, will score at the 70th percentile when learning cooperatively. These results held for verbal tasks (such as reading, writing, and orally presenting), mathematical tasks, and procedural tasks (such as swimming, golf, and tennis)" (p. 19).

Conditions for Collaborative Learning Success

It's not sufficient to simply assemble learners into a group and ask them to work together. There are five important conditions that ensure the benefits of collaborative learning:

1. Assign structured tasks to the collaborative team.

2. Create smaller groups (two to five members) that will provide more opportunities for each person to engage in the assignment.

3. Create heterogeneous groups.

4. Develop a collaborative assignment that requires everyone's input.

5. Ensure that the outcome (grade or score) is based not solely on the group project but on individual contributions to the group.

The goal of these conditions is *promotive interaction*. In promotive interaction each individual member of a group encourages and facilitates the efforts of the others to complete tasks and achieve group goals. For example, they might help each other, exchange needed resources, provide mutual feedback, challenge other's conclusions, and/or advocate for harder work (Johnson, Johnson, & Smith, 2007).

Structured Controversy

Previously in this chapter, I mentioned the benefits of argumentation, including, for example, Wiley and Voss's (1999) findings that individual learners assigned to write a pro-and-con argument learned more than learners asked to write either a narration or a summary. The deeper processing stimulated by synthesizing opposing aspects of an issue led to more learning than merely writing a summary. You can embed argumentation into a collaborative framework called *structured controversy*.

Johnson and Johnson (1992) developed a structured methodology for group argumentation (summarized in Figure 10.12). You can use this technique in classroom or in synchronous or asynchronous e-learning formats. Here's how it works. First set up heterogeneous teams of four and assign each team an issue or problem that lends itself to a pro-and-con position. Divide each team into two sub-teams of two each—one to take the pro and the other to take the con position. The pairs work together to research, develop, and present a solid argument for their position. After both sides have presented, the team of four integrates

Figure 10.12. The Structured Controversy Method

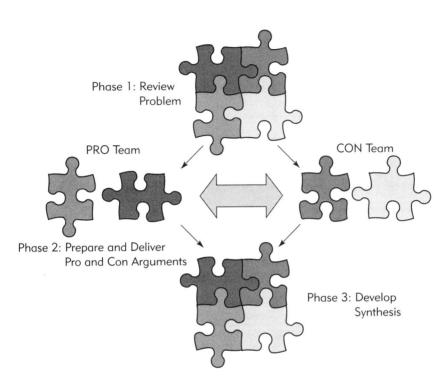

Phase 1: Review Problem

PRO Team

CON Team

Phase 2: Prepare and Deliver Pro and Con Arguments

Phase 3: Develop Synthesis

the two perspectives into a single reasoned position in a culminating report or presentation.

When comparing this structured controversy method with several alternative structures including traditional debates, individual learning, or groups that stressed concurrence, the structured controversy method was more effective with effect sizes ranging from .42 to .77.

The Collaborative Learning Principle

When you have a group in a learning environment, why not leverage the learning opportunities of that group? To do so effectively, I recommend the *Collaborative Learning Principle*.

Collaborative Learning Principle: Provide structured assignments to learning teams of two to four members in which consequences depend on the progress not only of the team but of each member in the team.

Minimize Note-Taking in Instructor-Led Presentations

Some instructors consider note-taking a useful form of active engagement that leads to learning. The effect of note-taking on learning is an important issue because students are commonly expected to take notes during classes. It's also an important economic factor because taking notes during lectures is a time-consuming task and will affect the total class time needed to present relevant job content. Instructional notes can serve two purposes: (1) the act of note-taking may promote attention or encoding during the learning event and (2) notes may serve as a reference source after the class (Kiewra, 1989).

Taking notes in an instructor-led class with unfamiliar content can lead to split attention, which in turn reduces learning. The cognitive effort required to take notes absorbs mental capacity that could be devoted to processing the content in ways that lead to learning. Note-taking does not benefit higher-order learning of adult learners (Kobayashi, 2005). Benton, Kiewra, Whitefill, and Dennison (1993) asked learners to write essays immediately and one week after a lecture (without referring to notes). They found that learners who took notes did not write any better essays than learners who just listened. In additional experiments in the same study, all learners listened to a lecture without taking notes. One week later they wrote essays based on the lecture. Some learners used notes prepared by the instructor as a resource, while others did not have any notes for reference. Learners who used instructor-prepared notes wrote better essays than those who had no reference notes. These experiments suggest that notes serve primarily a reference function after the training event is completed and that this is true whether learners take their own notes or whether notes are provided.

I recommend that detailed notes in a job-aid reference format be provided to learners in instructor-led training events. A job-aid handout is useful because: (1) many learners don't know how to take effective notes and the act of taking extensive notes becomes a source of divided attention and (2) training events in workforce learning often attempt to convey a great deal of content and build numerous skills in a limited time frame. Providing learners with complete notes will allow training to become more learner-centered and relevant because, rather than listening to lectures (and taking notes), instructional activities can be assigned that will require learners to process information in job-related ways.

In contrast to the research on note-taking from instructor-led events, note-taking from texts has been shown to improve learning when learners write notes using their own words and organizational framework rather than just copy information verbatim (Slotte & Lonka, 1999). Because reading is a self-paced activity, taking notes from a text or an asynchronous e-learning lesson *is not as likely* to promote divided attention as taking notes from a lecture or video. Converting text information into your own words requires deeper encoding than merely copying information and subsequently leads to better learning.

Who Benefits from Practice?

In the chapter introduction, I described three research studies with conflicting results. In one case, medical residents learned as much from listening to a lecture as from actively participating in small group problem-solving sessions. In this research, the learners were advanced in their medical background knowledge and in their learning skills. In addition, the instruction was one hour. No doubt, residents who listened to the lecture were able to mentally process the content as effectively as those who participated in discussions. In another experiment, learning of novices was faster and better with author-provided graphic organizers than when learners provided their own organizers. Perhaps novices reading a complex science text found that creating graphic organizers imposed so much mental work that there was no capacity left over for deep processing of the material.

In the third case, application learning (although not knowledge learning) was better from a computer simulation on project management than from reading a text that included similar information. In this experiment, learners were novice to the content. Because learners who were actively engaged in a project-management simulation practiced skills similar to those required by the application test, their learning was better than that of those who read text without practice. Had the text included some worked examples similar to the cases worked in the simulation, perhaps learning would have been equivalent.

The bottom line is that, while we have learned about some of the conditions that promote learning from practice assignments, we still have much to learn about passive and active learning environments. Specifically we need to know more about the types of learners (novice versus expert), engagement types (practice questions, simulations, collaborative exercises, or creating organizers), as well as desired learning outcomes (knowledge acquisition, application, and learner motivation) that can be achieved from passive and active learning environments. Because lessons with behavioral activity generally require more learner time than lessons without behavioral activity, learning more about the conditions under which that time is well invested is an important pragmatic issue for workforce learning.

INSTRUCTIONAL METHODS THAT PROMOTE
MENTAL MODELS THROUGH ACTIVE
ENGAGEMENT STRATEGIES

This chapter has presented a number of ways to promote elaborative rehearsals through questions asked by instructors or assigned as practice exercises to individuals or to groups. Guidelines for implementing explicit rehearsal methods include:

☐ Design questions and exercises to promote elaborative rehearsals.

☐ Distribute practice exercises throughout the learning events.

☐ Include explanatory feedback.

☐ Adjust the amount of practice based on the criticality of the task and the requirement for automaticity.

☐ Engage learners in graphics and worked examples by asking deeper-level questions about them.

☐ Incorporate collaborative learning assignments such as structured argumentation.

☐ Provide the core lesson content in handouts or job aids allocating instructional time to exercises rather than in-class note-taking.

☐ Minimize the amount of extraneous cognitive processing imposed by behavioral activities for your learners and for your desired content.

COMING NEXT

Learning vs. Performance: The Psychology of Transfer

Throughout the past five chapters I have reviewed instructional methods that lead to the encoding of content in ways that build more elaborate mental models in long-term memory. However, it's not sufficient to have mental models stored in long-term memory unless they can be retrieved back into working memory in the workplace. Retrieval is the basis for transfer of learning. In Chapter 11, I summarize the psychological basis for transfer, and in Chapter 12, I focus on instructional methods that promote transfer.

Recommended Readings

Atkinson, R.K., & Renkl, A. (2007). Interactive example-based learning environments: Using interactive elements to encourage effective processing of worked examples. *Educational Psychology Review, 19*, 375–386.

Clark, R.C. (2008). *Developing technical training* (3rd ed.). San Francisco, CA: Pfeiffer.

Clark, R.C., & Mayer, R.E. (2008). *e-Learning and the science of instruction* (2nd ed.). San Francisco, CA: Pfeiffer. See Chapter 11 on Practice.

Haidet, P., Morgan, R.O., O'Malley, K., Moran, B.J., & Richards, B.F. (2004). A controlled trial of active versus passive learning strategies in a large group setting. *Advances in Health Sciences Education, 9*, 15–27.

Johnson, D.W., Johnson, R.T., & Smith, K (2007). The state of cooperative learning in postsecondary and professional settings. *Educational Psychology Review, 19*, 15–20.

Stull, A.T., & Mayer, R.E. (2007). Learning by doing versus learning by viewing: Three experimental comparisons of learner-generated versus author-provided graphic organizers. *Journal of Educational Psychology, 99* (4), 808-820.

Taylor, R.S., & Chi, M.T.H. (2006). Simulation versus text: Acquisition of implicit and explicit information. *Journal of Educational Computing Research, 35*(3), 289–313.

CHAPTER 11 TOPICS

Transfer: The Bridge from Training to Performance

Four Tales of Transfer Failure

    Case 1: Poor Organizational Support

    Case 2: Failure of Creativity Training

    Case 3: Training How But Not Why

    Case 4. Transfer and Context

Causes of Transfer Failure

    A Culture of Transfer

    Transfer of General Skills to Specific Situations

    Learning How It Works

    Learning Is Context Bound

The Transfer Challenge

Specific Versus General Theories of Transfer

    Brain Builders: A General Transfer Theory

    Context Is King: A Specific Transfer Theory

    Transfer of Mental Models

The Transfer Continuum

    Zero Transfer

    Near Transfer

    Moderate Transfer

    Far Transfer

Surface Versus Deep Structure and Transfer

Transfer and Intelligence

11

Learning vs. Performance:
The Psychology of Transfer

Most researchers agree that transfer of learning seldom occurs

HASKELL, 2001

EVEN IF YOU SUCCESSFULLY build new mental models in long-term memory, when new knowledge and skills fail to transfer to the work environment, your efforts have failed. In this chapter, I summarize the psychological basis for transfer of learning to provide background for the transfer training methods described in Chapter 12. The topics include:

- Transfer: The bridge from training to performance

- Four tales of transfer failure

- Causes of transfer failure

- General versus specific theories of transfer

- Near-, moderate-, and far-transfer tasks

- Surface versus deep structure of tasks

Transfer: The Bridge from Training to Performance

Transfer of learning is the ultimate goal of training. Unless new knowledge and skills acquired in the training setting translate into new or improved job skills, the investment in training is wasted. Ideally, learners transfer most knowledge and skills acquired during training into improved job performance. In reality, transfer is very disappointing. "Most of the research on employee training clearly shows that, although millions of dollars are spent on training in the public sector, there is little empirical evidence linking training to improved job behavior or employee attitudes" (Haskell, 2001, p. 5).

Successful learning as evidenced by attending a training event or even passing a test is not the same as successful transfer of learning as evidenced by improved job performance. It's an unwarranted assumption to equate training participation or even learning outcomes with job performance improvement.

In the global economy, competitive advantage relies on innovation. Innovation in turn is the result of *creative* and *critical thinking*. While we often use these terms interchangeably, I like the distinction made by Mayer and Wittrock (2006): "Creative thinking involves *generating ideas* that could be used to solve a problem, whereas critical thinking involves *evaluating ideas* that could be used to solve a problem" (p, 288, emphasis mine). Both forms of thinking are important to innovation and both lead to far transfer. What are the different forms of transfer and how can each form be optimized in training and in organizational environments? Those are the questions addressed in Chapters 11 and 12. Because the topic of transfer is fairly extensive, this chapter will deal with the psychological basis for transfer. It will set the stage for Chapter 12, in which I describe the instructional methods proven to promote transfer.

Four Tales of Transfer Failure

There are various reasons for transfer failure—some organizational and some psychological. As you read the following short vignettes, see whether any of them are analogous to situations you've encountered in your organization.

Case 1: Poor Organizational Support

John takes a blended computer and classroom course on planning and conducting effective meetings. All supervisors are required to complete the course. John finds the class well-organized, and he demonstrates competency with a project in which he prepares an agenda, conducts a meeting, and develops follow-up action plans. John is enthusiastic about what he learns and prepares agendas for meetings he is scheduling for the next week.

However, as work pressures mount, John finds that planning agendas and sending them ahead cuts into his project time. John's manager talks to him about project deadlines—not about meeting agendas. Further, John's manager does not seem to set agendas herself. Within a few weeks after class, John is back to his old habits of "on-the-fly" meetings.

Case 2: Failure of Creativity Training

To improve problem-solving abilities of workers, all employees are required to complete a two-day Effective Thinking Skills program. The training gets high ratings from the participants. It is very interactive and it's fun! Participants work on a number of puzzle problems such as the one shown in Figure 11.1 to illustrate some general approaches to solving problems such as *think outside the box*. The training also includes some visual thinking tools such as flow charts and compare-and-contrast charts to help employees find better ways to represent their problems.

Figure 11.1. A Puzzle Problem from a Creative Thinking Skills Class

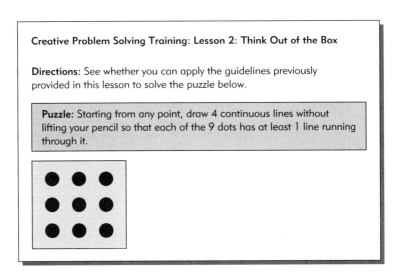

An evaluation six months after class reveals no differences in how employees are approaching problems or in the number of innovative solutions documented in the corporate knowledge base.

Case 3: Training How But Not Why

Marcie and Dean attend two separate classes to learn how to use a new computerized control system that manages plant production. After class Marcie and Dean are able to apply their new skills to routine production activities. However, when the shift team meets to discuss optimization of product output, Marcie has more ideas than Dean on how to adjust the control system values to meet their goals. While both Marcie and Dean achieved equal transfer on procedures they learned in class, Marcie's training prepared her more effectively than Dean's for making adjustments. Both Marcie and Dean experienced some transfer, but Marcie's transfer went further.

Case 4. Transfer and Context

Take a minute to read the tumor problem shown in Exhibit 11.1. This problem was the basis for a number of experiments on transfer (Gick & Holyoak, 1980, 1983). Prior to tackling this problem, participants were given a variety of stories to read. One of them was about a general who attacked a fortress. The many roads radiating out from the fortress were mined in such a way that any large invading force would set off the mines. The general divided his army into small units and deployed them along the various roads to the fortress. Only a small percentage of individuals who read the fortress story transferred the analogous convergence solution to the tumor problem. The experiment illustrates transfer failure. The participants know about the fortress problem. A quiz on the facts of the story yields high recall. Nevertheless, when faced with the tumor problem, readers of the fortress story do not transfer the knowledge. Why was there so little transfer from one situation to another that could benefit from a similar approach?

EXHIBIT 11.1. THE TUMOR PROBLEM

Suppose you are a doctor faced with a patient who has a malignant tumor in his stomach. It is impossible to operate on the patient, but, unless the tumor is destroyed, the patient will die. There is a kind of ray that at a sufficiently high intensity can destroy the tumor. Unfortunately, at this intensity, the healthy tissue that the rays pass through on the way to the tumor will also be destroyed. At lower intensities, the rays are harmless to healthy tissue but will not affect the tumor either. How can the rays be used to destroy the tumor without injuring the healthy tissue?

From Dunker, 1945

Causes of Transfer Failure

These four cases reflect transfer failure. But the causes for each are different. They illustrate failures to:

- Create a culture of transfer and innovation in the work environment
- Transfer general skills to specific job situations
- Adapt a procedural skill when the job situation requires change
- Transfer a skill from one context to a very different context

A Culture of Transfer

Learning can fail to transfer due to lack of what Haskell (2001) calls a "culture of transfer" in the workplace. That was the situation with John's meeting class. An organizational culture of transfer relies heavily on managers and requires established practices such as:

- Ensuring that participants who attend training will be able to apply the skills and knowledge on their jobs relatively soon after training
- Management discussions of learning with training participants
- Assigning job tasks and goals that will require use of new skills
- Providing related feedback and incentives in the workplace for application of new skills
- Providing resources needed to operationalize new skills, including working aids and sufficient time and equipment
- Modeling new skills at all levels of the organization

Quite often, participants in my training sessions say, "*If only my boss were here!*" They know they will go back to a work environment that does not support the application of the new skills they have learned. A major management role is to work with employees to match job-skill requirements with employee competencies, help employees find ways to build competencies, and manage the performance environment to ensure that employees apply new knowledge and skills. Managers should also model all new skills that are applicable to their role.

A visible gap in the culture of transfer was documented in the investigation of police training following the 1991 riots in Los Angeles. New recruits were commonly told to "Forget everything you learned at the Academy" when they received their first field assignments (Independent Commission Report, 1991).

Transfer of learning depends on cultural support in the work environment. This view of transfer places much of the responsibility on the learner's manager and the culture of the organization. Although my focus will be on psychological rather than cultural reasons for transfer failure, training based on the best transfer psychology in the world will not counteract a culture that does not support transfer.

Transfer of General Skills to Specific Situations

The critical thinking skills training is a contemporary version of an old view that training in generic skills can build mental muscle. According to the general skills theory, building analytic muscle on problems like the nine-dot puzzle will pay off on job problems far removed from those in the training. An earlier version of this transfer view was the idea that taking Latin or geometry will improve mental skills. A more contemporary version trained children in LOGO programming in an attempt to build logical thinking skills (Mayer, 1999, 2004).

All of these programs attempt to build general problem-solving skills that will then enable the worker to more effectively tackle job tasks. Unfortunately, we have a lot of evidence that these general skills programs fail to transfer because they train skills out of the context of the job domain. Increasingly, we have to recognize that expertise is tightly wedded to the specifics of the application setting.

Learning How It Works

Dean and Marcie both learned the procedures to use a new software system. However, Marcie's class enabled her to adjust procedures because it not only trained Marcie in the steps to use the system, but it also explained how the system influenced operations in the plant. By understanding not only *what to do* but *how the system interacted* with plant operations, Marcie acquired a deeper knowledge that resulted in greater transfer of learning. In Chapter 9, I reviewed research on worker adaptation of control panel procedures from training that did and did not include a system model (of the Star Ship Enterprise). Workers who received a system model were able to make efficient adaptations when working with the system (Kieras & Bovair, 1984). When job performance benefits from workers who can adapt procedures to changing situations, how-it-works mental models will improve performance.

Learning Is Context Bound

Solvers of the tumor problem who read the fortress problem suffered from what psychologists call *inert knowledge.* Inert knowledge refers to situations in which the needed knowledge is stored in memory—a test of that knowledge would confirm its presence. But in situations in which that knowledge would be useful to solve a different problem, it is not activated—it remains inert. For example, the fortress story embodies a convergence solution. However, when faced with a different context in the tumor problem, readers of the fortress story did not transfer the convergence idea.

In the tumor experiment, the convergence principle used to solve the fortress problem was not sufficiently separated from the specific context of the military setting to be useful in other contexts. Haskell (2001) concludes that "a consistent finding in the transfer literature is that learning tends to be welded to the context in which it is learned" (p. 136).

The Transfer Challenge

We have seen four different versions of transfer failure—all based on documented situations. Transfer of learning is critical to a return on investment in training. Yet it has proven to be a difficult challenge. Haskell (2001) summarizes the situation: "The aim of all education, from elementary, secondary, vocational, and industrial training to higher education, is to apply what we learn in different contexts and to recognize and extend that learning to completely new situations. This is called transfer of learning. . . . Most researchers and educational practitioners agree that meaningful transfer of learning is among the most—if not the most—fundamental issue in all of education. They also agree that transfer of learning seldom occurs" (p. 3).

Specific Versus General Theories of Transfer

How transfer works has been debated among psychologists for over one hundred years. All of the theories represent some variation along a continuum from general to specific accounts of transfer. In the next section, I describe three theories that fall along this continuum. These are (1) formal discipline, (2) identical elements, and (3) mental models.

Brain Builders: A General Transfer Theory

The critical thinking course described previously failed to transfer general problem-solving principles such as "think outside the box" to specific job situations. Mayer and Wittrock (1996) conclude that "Modern attempts to find mind-improving subject matter such as Head Start in preschool or LOGO have not been more successful than historical attempts to use Latin to improve minds. A consistent theme is that a short course of study in one subject-matter area does not have enduring effects on solving radically different problems in other subject matter domains" (p. 52). Technically called the *Formal Discipline* Transfer model, the idea that training on quite general skills will pay off in specific job improvements has proven untenable.

You save your organization a great deal of time and money when you steer them away from very generic skill-building courses that are intended to transfer to many types of job tasks. Critical thinking courses that use general puzzle-type problems to build "general" analytic skills that will apply across many job roles are one example. Another is the use of outdoor experiential training to build leadership and teamwork skills. Because the outcomes of these courses are so general, they are rarely measured beyond learner satisfaction ratings. And learning ratings are often high because these types of courses are usually quite engaging. Therefore, these types of learning events perpetuate themselves in spite of little return on investment.

Context Is King: A Specific Transfer Theory

As an alternative to the brain-building general approach, Thorndike and Woodworth in 1901 suggested *identical elements* as a specific transfer mechanism. According to the identical elements view, transfer is enhanced to the extent that two tasks share common elements. For example, when I first starting using

Microsoft Windows, I found the transition very easy. I was puzzled by classes filled with new Windows users who were struggling with the mouse. Then I realized that I had come to Windows from a Macintosh environment that used a mouse and similar interface. The number of common elements between the two operating environments was high, giving me a positive transfer. In contrast, people learning Windows who had worked in a DOS environment had many new skills to learn because there were few common elements. For training purposes, the identical elements view suggests that the activities and interfaces in instruction should match those of the job as closely as possible.

The identical elements perspective is the basis for high fidelity simulation training in which the training environment looks and feels and sounds like the work environment. It suggests that transfer of training will be limited to those job tasks that are very similar to those learned during the training. Failure to solve the tumor problem reflects a lack of common elements between the learning setting (the fortress problem) and the performance setting (the tumor problem).

The identical elements view suggests that all training should teach tasks in the same context as that in which they will be encountered on the job. If the identical elements theory is valid, we will have to give up on instruction that will transfer much beyond exactly what is trained. In other words, there will be no transfer to significantly new or different problems on the job.

Transfer of Mental Models

Is there an approach that can take advantage of both a general and a specific view of transfer? A third, more recent perspective suggests that transfer takes place not only on the basis of shared elements among tasks but also as a result of understanding (Mayer & Wittrock, 2006). If general principles can be taught and sufficiently robust mental models formed, these can be applied to job problems beyond those practiced during training. The mental models theory is more specific than the brain building approach because it does focus on building of relatively specific mental models—not on general analytic power. At the same time, it's more general than the identical elements view because an understanding of principles can apply to tasks beyond the ones encountered during training.

Recall the transfer failure from the fortress story to the tumor problem. The research team found that if they built a mental model of convergence they could break the context barrier. They helped learners build a convergence mental model by providing not only the fortress story but also a story about putting out a fire on an oil rig. Since a single hose was not large enough to deliver sufficient foam, a number of smaller hoses arranged in a circle around the rig dispensed enough foam to put out the fire. After reading the fortress and fire stories, learners completed an activity such as drawing a picture or stating the common principle between the stories. Later, when faced with the tumor problem, a much higher proportion of these participants were able to solve it, compared to individuals who had read only the fortress story. As a result of actively processing the two stories, participants built a mental model that could override the constraints of context.

I recommend that you make use of the identical elements and the mental models approaches to transfer, depending on whether your training goals focus more on near-, moderate-, or far-transfer tasks. I define a transfer continuum in the next section.

The Transfer Continuum

In Table 11.1, I summarize a transfer continuum with four main levels, ranging from no transfer to far transfer involving creative and innovative thinking. I introduce these transfer levels here

Table 11.1. Four Levels of Transfer

	Transfer Level			
	Zero	Near	Moderate	Far
Description	No transfer from instructional environment to job	Transfer of step-by-step skills as learned in training to the job; ability to solve well-defined routine problems practiced during training	Transfer of skills to new situations or problems not encountered in training. Ability to solve non-routine problems not encountered during training.	Invention of new solutions not addressed in training. Ability to solve ill-defined problems not encountered during training.
Example	Learners complete class that demonstrates spreadsheets but are unsuccessful when trying to use them three months later to prepare budget reports.	Learners complete spreadsheet class and work with job aids to produce routine budget reports on the job as practiced in training.	Learners complete spreadsheet class and create new formulas and spreadsheets to apply to inventory tasks not discussed in class.	Learners design spreadsheets and report formats for use by revenue managers throughout the organization.
Resulting from	New skills not learned during training/New skills not applicable to the job/New skills learned but not supported in work environment	Rote learning of routine tasks/Practice of procedures/Step-by-step working aids	Learning the how and why of tasks/Building mental models that support understanding/Practice with multiple contexts/Strategic working aids	Deep knowledge/Collaborative work/Thinking outside domain-specific solutions/ High productivity/Cultures that encourage innovative thinking
Based on	Lack of knowledge/Lack of working aids/Lack of job standards, feedback, incentives etc.	Emphasis on factual and procedural knowledge	Emphasis on conceptual, process, and strategic knowledge/Crystallized intelligence	Emphasis on conceptual, process, strategic and metacognitive knowledge/Crystallized and fluid intelligence

and will describe how to promote them in your training and performance environments in Chapter 12.

Zero Transfer

If there is no original learning, naturally there will be no transfer. For example, a class that provides a great deal of information in a receptive format may result in minimal learning. Alternatively, new skills may have been learned but fail to translate into changed work behaviors because the job environment does not support use of new skills. John's meetings class summarized in the beginning of this chapter is a good example. Although John learned new skills, the work environment did not support application of those skills.

Near Transfer

Near transfer results from successful application of the identical elements theory of transfer. Learners practice specific procedural tasks during training—tasks that are very similar to those they will perform on the job. Furthermore, when they return to their jobs they have job aids and organizational support to apply new skills. This approach works well if your performance goal is consistent application of procedures. However, don't expect that your learners will be able to apply their new skills to job situations that differ much from the ones provided in training. For example, you read previously in this chapter about Dean's training in process control software. He was able to use the software effectively, but he was not able to suggest ways to adapt the procedures to accomplish different goals.

Moderate Transfer

Moderate transfer such as that exhibited by Marcie requires a deeper knowledge level—one that will enable workers to go beyond what they learned in training to apply new skills to different contexts than those presented in training. Moderate transfer depends on the mental models theory of transfer in which learners build deep understanding of the processes and principles in their job domains and have the opportunity to try out the new skills on various types of problems during training. Workers who successfully achieve moderate transfer reflect what Bransford and his colleagues (2006) call "routine expertise."

Far Transfer

The most far out types of transfer involve innovative thinking to produce new products and solve non-routine problems not encountered in training. We are really talking about innovation and creativity! Bransford and his colleagues (2006) call these types of workers *adaptive experts.* This type of transfer relies primarily on a depth of knowledge gained not only from formal training but also from years of domain-specific experience. For example, Weisberg (2006) reviews the learning of highly creative icons such as Mozart, Thomas Edison, and The Beatles. He finds that, in most cases, creative advance arose from domain-specific expertise. For example, Mozart and The Beatles studied the musical works of others and had extensive formal or informal coaching and practice. In Chapter 12, I will describe specific strategies that will lead to near-, moderate-, and far-transfer learning.

Surface Versus Deep Structure and Transfer

Surface features refer to the salient context of the task—what images, sounds, or sensations are associated with the task. Near-transfer tasks tend to have consistent surface features. For example, each time you use a particular e-mail system, the interface will look the same. For this reason, the identical elements principle can be effectively exploited in training of near-transfer tasks.

Because surface features are so salient, humans tend to encode new knowledge, tasks, and problems based on their surface features. However, in some situations, the principles beneath the surface features are more important. Moderate- to far-transfer tasks tend to have different surface features but share a similar deep structure. For example, solving the tumor problem is a moderate-transfer challenge. The fortress problem and oil rig fire analogs do not share any surface features with the tumor problem. But they do have a common deep structure—convergence. Because transfer is so context bound, we face our biggest training challenges with moderate- to far-transfer tasks.

Deep structures are the basis for most moderate levels of transfer by experts. An expert views a situation and represents it in terms of its deep structure. However, a wealth of deep structures can also be a barrier to innovative thinking, as domain experts will automatically rely on their mental models to represent and solve novel problems. How can we go beyond deep structures to encourage creative and critical thinking? I will look at that question in Chapter 12.

Transfer and Intelligence

The debate on the contribution of training and intelligence to expertise and performance continues today. Some suggest that expertise is 90 percent perspiration and only 10 percent inspiration. "Thirty years of research suggests that intelligence and talent provide initial advantages, but that high levels of expertise are due primarily to sustained, systematic effort on the part of the learner. Ability alone is not sufficient for high levels of expertise. Ability and sustained practice are ideal" (Schraw, 2006, p. 255).

Others believe that inherited abilities—talents—are a major prerequisite to the highest levels of expertise. A distinction between two types of intelligence—crystallized and fluid—may unlock part of the nature-nurture debate. The concept of multiple intelligences is not a new one. Crystallized and fluid intelligence was first suggested by Cattell in 1943. Basically, *crystallized intelligence* relies on domain specific knowledge—especially the type of knowledge learned in school, such as mathematics and reading. In contrast, *fluid intelligence* is the basis for adaptive expertise. "Crystallized abilities are essential in the development of well-organized knowledge structures that lead to expertise, while fluidization requires that learners revise existing problem-solving strategies, assemble new ones, search for new analogies or new perspectives" (Neitfeld, Finney, Schraw, & McCrudden, 2007, p. 511).

THE PSYCHOLOGY OF TRANSFER

In this chapter. I have reviewed some of the cultural and psychological prerequisites for learning transfer. Many years of research on transfer suggest that:

☐ Organizations need to adopt cultures of transfer to support the application of new knowledge and skills to the job.

☐ General theories of transfer have not paid off in job-specific improvement because of the strong influence of the context of learning on transfer.

☐ The identical elements theory of transfer applies to training of near but not moderate or far-transfer skills.

☐ Moderate transfer tasks require the building of a mental model that helps the performer adapt skills acquired during training to diverse job situations.

☐ Far transfer is the basis for original thought and will likely not emerge from any single training event but rather from a combination of training, a culture of innovation, collaborative work projects, extensive diverse work experience in a domain, and fluid intelligence.

COMING NEXT

Teaching for Transfer

How can you design instructional environments that will maximize transfer? We will tackle that question in the next chapter by looking at instructional methods for near, moderate, and far transfer. Although my focus will be on training methods that will maximize transfer, I will also touch on the transfer culture of the organization as a critical component for success.

Recommended Readings

Haskell, R.E. (2001). *Transfer of learning: Cognition, instruction, and reasoning.* New York: Academic Press.

Mayer, R. E. (2008). *Learning and instruction* (2nd ed.). Upper Saddle River, NJ: Pearson Merrill Prentice Hall.

Mayer, R.E., & Wittrock, M.C. (2006) *Problem solving.* In P. Alexander& P. Winne (Eds.), *Handbook of educational psychology.* Mahwah, NJ: Lawrence Erlbaum Associates.

Renkl, A., Mandl, H., & Gruber, H. (1996). Inert knowledge: Analyses and remedies. *Educational Psychologist, 3*(2), 115–121.

CHAPTER 12 TOPICS

Transfer: It's All About Context

Teaching for Near-Transfer Performance

      Mimic Job Context for Procedural Training

      Use Operational Simulations

Learning Aids for Near-Transfer Learning

      Training Wheels

      Hints

      Part Task Drill and Practice

      Use Audio Narration or Integrated Text for Demonstrations

Teaching for Moderate Transfer

      Move from Specific to General Steps

      Teach How It Works

Teaching for Far-Transfer Performance

      Use Varied Context Examples and Practice Exercises

      Engage Learners in Comparisons of Examples

      Incorporate the Why's and How's

      Use Inductive Techniques

Learning Aids for Guided-Discovery Simulations

      Start with Simple Simulation Goals

      Include Explanatory Feedback

      Optimize Simulation Pacing

      Keep Simulation Interfaces Simple

12

Teaching for Transfer

Intelligent behavior is deeply context bound.

R. RITCHART AND D.N. PERKINS, 2005

IN THIS CHAPTER, I describe instructional methods that promote retrieval of new knowledge and skills from long-term memory after the learning event. I organize the guidelines based on the degree of transfer they support as follows:

- Instructional methods to support near transfer
- Learning aids for near-transfer learning
- Instructional methods to support moderate transfer
- Instructional methods to support far transfer
- Learning aids for far-transfer learning from simulations

Transfer: It's All About Context

Transfer refers to the extent to which a learner can apply new mental models learned in one setting to a different setting. In training, we are concerned about how effectively new skills learned in a formal instructional environmental are later applied to job tasks. Without transfer of learning, all of the powerful instructional strategies I have reviewed throughout this book are for naught. There is little value to mental models in long-term memory that cannot be retrieved back into working memory when needed on the job.

In some situations, job tasks are performed more or less the same way each time. We call these *near-transfer tasks*. In near-transfer learning, we can specify the context of the job, which will remain fairly constant. For example, much software training involves step-by-step procedures using a consistent set of commands. However, in other situations, the context in which new skills will be applied will vary from situation to situation. Customer service and supervisory training are two common examples. We call these *far-transfer tasks*. In this chapter, I focus on instructional methods that deal primarily with context; that is, methods providing the appropriate context in the instructional setting to ensure transfer to the job. I will summarize instructional methods for near-transfer tasks, for tasks that require moderate transfer of learning as well as for far-transfer tasks.

Teaching for Near-Transfer Performance

Near-transfer tasks are performed more or less the same way and in the same environment each time. Some examples of near-transfer tasks are many routine end-user computer tasks and procedures, such as completing standard forms as well as producing and assembling a range of products from hamburgers to computers. Near-transfer tasks often involve decisions that are relatively clear cut with defined actions such as, *If the customer's account balance exceeds $5,000, approve the check. Otherwise, refer to the supervisor.*

Near-transfer tasks typically require little judgment, and job success depends on consistent application of steps in an accurate and efficient manner. With many repetitions, near-transfer skills become automated in long-term memory so that working memory capacity is freed for other tasks. For example, as a result of frequent use, motor skills such as driving and cognitive skills such as reading are automated, freeing you to allocate working memory capacity to additional tasks.

Mimic Job Context for Procedural Training

The identical elements view of transfer described in Chapter 11 can be readily applied to instruction of near-transfer tasks. I refer to training programs based on identical elements as applying the *Mirror the Job Principle*.

Mirror the Job Principle: The learning environment should emulate the performance environment.

When including a mirror of the job in the training environment, the retrieval cues of the job environment are incorporated into memory at the time of learning. For example, when learning a new software application, demonstrations and practice on the real screens or on close simulations will incorporate enough identical elements to enable transfer to the job.

Use Operational Simulations

In this chapter, I will discuss two types of simulations: conceptual and operational. All simulations are models of real-world systems. *Conceptual simulations* such as a genetics simulation are models of how cause-and-effect systems or invisible phenomena work and will be discussed later in this chapter. *Operational simulations* are models of computer or mechanical systems that respond in realistic ways. Operational simulations have been used for training of software applications, medical procedures, and safety-related skills such as aircraft piloting and industrial control operations.

Figure 12.1. This Software Simulation Exercise Created with Captivate Emulates the Job Procedure

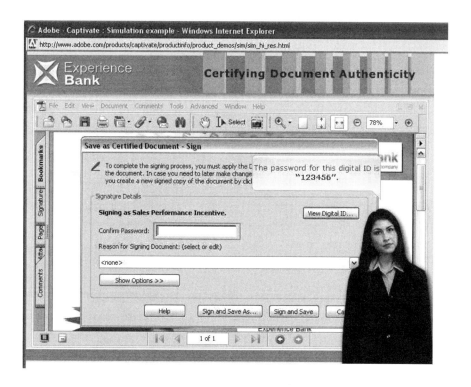

For example, Figure 12.1 shows part of an e-learning software simulation that can provide demonstrations as well as a practice environment. Modern software programs such as Captivate make the creation of software operational simulations fast and simple; little or no programming expertise is needed.

Operational simulations are especially useful when realistic practice is unsafe or unavailable. For example, Issenberg (2005) recommends high-fidelity simulations in medical education because (1) managed health care has resulted in shorter patient stays with consequent fewer clinical teaching opportunities than in the past, (2) patient safety is enhanced when procedures can be learned and practiced on simulators, (3) new medical procedures such as sigmoidoscopy, laparoscopy, and robotics involve motor and perceptual skills that can be effectively practiced via simulators, and (4) deliberate practice involving repetitive performances leads to improved skills.

Learning Aids for Near-Transfer Learning

If the procedural tasks are complex and learners are novice, applying the Mirror the Job Principle can lead to overload of working memory. You will need to manage load during early practice exercises by providing support structures that should be gradually removed as training progresses. Learning aids, also called scaffolds, are designed to provide external supports that manage cognitive load during initial learning. As learning progresses, the learner's new mental models serve as learning aids and external support is no longer needed. I discussed many of these support methods in Chapter 6 on managing cognitive load. Therefore, I will only briefly review the following four key methods here:

- Training wheels

- Hints

- Part task drill and practice

- Use of audio or integrated text

Training Wheels

Training wheels, an apt metaphor suggested by John Carroll (1992), involves providing external support for task performance until the learner is self-sufficient. One approach to training wheels in simulations is to constrain the operational fidelity of the system by disabling some of the functionality. Most online systems have numerous tool bars, menus, and other response facilities. By enabling only those needed to perform a given task in a simulation, learners cannot stray too far during early practice attempts. The training wheels interface looks like the actual interface but much of the functionality is disabled. Since only a limited number of functions are operational, the students can't get into too much trouble if they invoke the wrong commands. As learning progresses, the functionality of the simulated system is gradually expanded.

Modern authoring software simulation programs such as Captivate apply a training wheels approach in creating "hot spots" on the screen interface that respond to the user action. Other areas on the screen simply do not react when the learner engages them. For example, in Figure 12.1, the simulation responds to a user entry into the "confirm password" field. Clicking on other areas of the screen generates no response.

Hints

Another example of scaffolding is to provide various levels of hints during the early practice exercises. For example, on the software practice screen shown in Figure 12.1, the on-screen learning agent can offer hints and a red box is placed around the password entry box to guide the learner to the correct part of the screen.

Part Task Drill and Practice

In jobs that involve many complex procedures, you may need to identify subtasks and ask learners to practice the subtasks until they achieve a sufficient skill level to add another layer to their skill repertoire. Repetitive practice leads to automaticity, which in turn frees working memory capacity for additional tasks. For tasks that are complex and include many interdependent procedures, assign part task practice in the context of the entire task. For example, if learning to fly an airplane, the student can practice one maneuver such as landing while the instructor handles other related tasks that must be performed simultaneously, such as the radio communications. In other situations, you may assign practice on a single skill in isolation from the full performance. For example, in tennis you might practice serving independent of full game play.

Part of your decision about how to segment learning of procedures will depend on the extent to which a single skill can be easily integrated in the final performance. For independent subtasks such as serving in tennis, isolated drill and practice is an appropriate approach. For subtasks that are interdependent with other subtasks, assign drill and practice in context of the entire task.

Use Audio Narration or Integrated Text for Demonstrations

The Modality Effect has been demonstrated for a wide variety of procedures. When your procedural lesson will include a visual as part of the demonstration—and most procedures do involve some type of visual—you can minimize irrelevant cognitive load by explaining the steps with audio narration. Alternatively, if audio is not available, such as in print media, present the steps with text integrated into the visual as callouts.

When it is time to practice, however, other than very simple steps, the directions should be presented in text, thus allowing the learners to review and refer back to each step at their own pace as they complete the exercise. That's why in Figure 12.1 the learning agent displays the directions in text on the screen.

Teaching for Moderate Transfer

In some instructional situations, the job requires learners not only to perform near-transfer tasks but also to adjust the steps to accommodate different situations. For example, an operator learns the basic steps to perform tasks on production equipment.

However, on occasion, changes in the environment require the operator to adjust the steps somewhat. I think of these situations as requiring moderate transfer. To help learners achieve moderate transfer, you need to go beyond teaching specific steps and teach for understanding. Two methods to promote moderate transfer are (1) to present generalized steps and (2) to teach how a system works.

Move from Specific to General Steps

Suppose you are teaching how to perform edits in word processing software. You may want to start with a very detailed step description such as:

"*Move the cursor to the space before the first word in the edit. Left click the mouse and drag the cursor over the words to be edited. Type in this sentence: The brown cow. . . .*" This level of detail is most appropriate for novice learners. However, with greater experience, you can use a more general statement such as: "*When you want to replace text, use the mouse to highlight the text to be replaced and type in the revised text*" (Mayer, 2002*)*. This version teaches more general actions than the first and has greater potential to generalize to more diverse situations. To gain greater transfer of learning, gradually incorporate more general steps or higher-level steps that encompass several smaller steps. For example, in an early lesson you might provide four specific steps to access a document. In a later practice you would start with a higher-level step such as *Access the ZYB document.*

Teach How It Works

In Chapter 9, I described an experiment in which Kieras and Bovair (1984) compared performance of participants who learned procedure steps with another group that learned not only the steps but also how the system worked. The goal of the training was to learn procedures such as *make the PF indicator light up* on a control panel you can review in Figure 9.11. One group was trained by a rote method in which participants were given the steps needed to achieve the goal. The second group was trained by teaching a model of how the system worked prior to learning the steps to perform the procedure. A schematic diagram (shown in Figure 9.12) was used to help learners build a mental model of how the system worked.

Note in Table 12.1 that learners in the system model group were able to find 40 percent more shortcuts, which resulted in a more efficient performance. Note also that procedure training and execution time was lower for the system model group than for the rote group. This study points to the performance benefits of building a deeper understanding of a system.

When should you spend extra time and money teaching a system model? That depends on the degree of transfer you want. If your goal is consistent performance of a procedure, stick

Table 12.1. Learning a System Model Improved Retention and Led to More Shortcuts

Outcome	Rote Training	Model Training	Improvement
Training Time- System Model		1141	—
Training Time- Procedure	270	194	28%
Retention	67%	80%	19%
Shortcuts	8%	40%	400%
Execution Time	20.1	16.8	17%

From Kieras and Bovair, 1984

with just teaching the steps by applying the identical elements principle. For example, if someone needs to use a telephone, the person's performance will not benefit from knowledge of how the telephone works. However, if performance would benefit from adjustment of procedures or troubleshooting of problems, then a deeper understanding of the system justifies the extra investment in training. For example, the telephone repair person needs how-it-works knowledge.

Teaching for Far-Transfer Performance

Unlike near-transfer tasks, there is no single approach to perform far-transfer tasks. Far-transfer tasks involve some degree of problem solving, and successful performance relies on worker judgment to apply guidelines to situations that will be different each time. To apply new knowledge and skills to diverse situations, learners must build mental models that are different from the procedural skills needed for near-transfer performance. For procedural skills, the identical elements transfer view will work well. However, for far-transfer skills, there are no identical elements because the context of performance changes each time. Instead, far-transfer tasks require a combination of knowledge of principles as well as the ability to recognize when a particular problem could benefit from a specific principle. Training of far-transfer skills is a more demanding challenge than training of procedural tasks. You will have to train for understanding. Some proven methods include:

- Use varied context examples and practice.
- Engage learners in comparisons of varied context worked examples.
- Incorporate the whys and hows into worked examples.
- Use inductive instructional techniques.

Use Varied Context Examples and Practice Exercises

Recall from Chapter 11 that learners who studied several problems that reflected a convergence principle were able to solve the tumor problem. All the problems shared a common deep structure (convergence), but varied on the story lines or surface features. Providing examples with different surface features that learners have to process will build a robust mental model in long-term memory that should transfer to other problems. The important elements for successful learning are the use of several examples of different context *and* active learner processing to identify the common principles in the examples.

Paas and van Merrienboer (1996) compared learning from high-variable examples to learning from low-variable examples in two conditions: students solving the problems themselves and students studying the problems as worked examples. Table 12.2 shows the results. As found in previous experiments, worked

Table 12.2. Better Learning from High Variable Worked Examples

Outcomes	Conventional		Worked Examples	
	Low Variable	*High Variable*	*Low Variable*	*High Variable*
Training Time	1230s	1406s	561s	625s
Perceived Mental Effort (1–7)	4.2	4.5	3.2	3.3
% Correct on Test	28.9	27.8	47.8	62.2

From Paas and van Merrienboer, 1996

examples resulted in better learning than asking learners to solve the problems themselves. However, the best results (shown in the lower-right-hand cell of the table) came from the use of worked examples that were *highly variable.* Using high-variable problems that the learners *had to solve themselves* depressed learning because the high variability imposed too much cognitive load. Therefore, for far-transfer learning, it's a good idea to include a number of examples that vary on the surface features but are consistent regarding the principles they reflect. For novice learners, make these varied examples *worked examples,* rather than practice assignments to manage cognitive load during building of mental models.

The value of varied context examples has been demonstrated in a number of experimental studies. Quilici and Mayer (1996) created examples to illustrate three statistical tests of t-test, correlation, and chi-square. Each of these statistical tests requires a different mathematical procedure and is most appropriately applied to different types of data. For each test type, they created three examples. One group of examples used the same surface features. For instance, the three t-test problems used data regarding experience and typing speed; the three correlation examples used data regarding temperature and precipitation; and the three chi square examples included data related to fatigue and performance. A comparison group of examples varied the cover stories. For example, the t-test was illustrated by one example that used experience and typing speed, a second example about temperature and precipitation, and a third example about fatigue and performance. This set of varied examples emphasized the deep structure of the different statistical tests.

After reviewing the examples, participants sorted a new set of problems into groups (Experiment 2) or selected which set of calculations they should use to implement the appropriate statistical

Figure 12.2. Varied Context Worked Examples Led to Better Learning
From Experiment 3, Quilici and Mayer, 1996

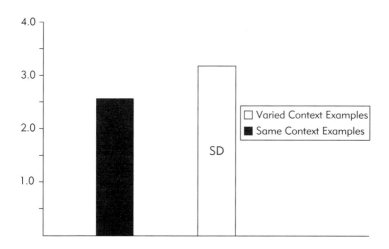

test (Experiment 3). As you can see in Figure 12.2, the varied context example sets led to significantly greater learning.

Engage Learners in Comparisons of Examples

A risk associated with worked examples is that learners may by pass them completely or may give them only cursory processing. Only when learners deeply process worked examples will they produce learning benefits. One way to promote active processing of diverse context examples is to engage learners in a comparison of two or more examples in which the surface features change but the principles remain constant.

We have good evidence for the value of active comparisons from research reported by Gentner, Loewenstein, and Thompson (2003) on learning of negotiation skills. Their training goal was the application of a negotiated agreement based on a "safeguard" solution rather than a less effective "tradeoff" solution.

They presented one worked example of negotiation that involved a conflict between a Chinese and American company over the best way to ship parts. They illustrated both the tradeoff (less effective) and the safeguard (more effective) negotiation strategies in the shipping scenario. In the next part of the lesson, they provided a different worked example involving a conflict between two travelers over where to stay on a vacation trip. On the same page as the traveler negotiation example, the learner viewed a diagrammed summary of the safeguard shipping solution placed next to a blank diagram the learners must complete using the traveler's scenario. To complete the blank diagram, the learners must study the traveler example closely and compare it with the solution summary from the shipping example. This interaction encourages learners to abstract the deep structure (the safeguard principle) from the cover stories of the two examples.

The research team compared three lesson versions, summarized in Figure 12.3. In one version (separate examples) participants saw the shipping and traveling examples each on a separate page. After reading the examples, participants were asked questions about each case such as "*What is going on in this negotiation?*" Answering the questions ensured that these learners did attend to the two examples. In a second lesson version (comparison), participants saw both examples displayed on the same page and were directed to think about the similarities between the two situations. This version supported implicit processing as described in Chapter 9. A third group (active comparison) followed the format summarized in the previous paragraph. Learners were presented the first example on one page. The solution to this example was carried to a second page that contained the second example. On the second page, the learners have to actively respond to questions about the second case. A fourth group received no training.

Figure 12.3. Three Versions of Negotiation Lessons with Different
Support for Active Comparisons of Varied Context
Negotiation Examples

Adapted from Gentner, Loewenstein, and Thompson, 2003

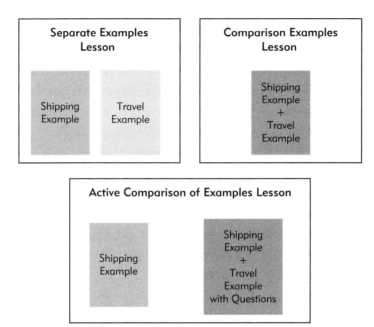

Figure 12.4. Best Learning from Active Comparisons of Examples

Adapted from Gentner, Loewenstein, and Thompson, 2003

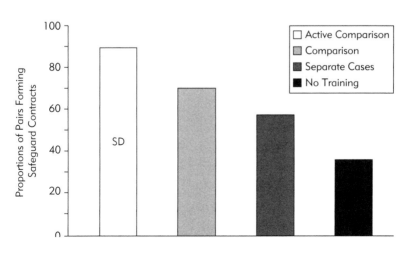

Following training, all participants were tested with a role-play face-to-face negotiation that could be solved with either the safe-guard or the tradeoff solutions. As you can see in Figure 12.4, the lesson that required an active comparison of the two examples resulted in the best learning.

This research is especially useful to workforce learning practitioners because it is a rare example of applying the varied context examples strategy to soft skills. Most research uses more defined skills such as mathematics problems. In addition, this research leaves us with a useful model for how to best present and engage learners in training proven to promote far-transfer learning.

Incorporate the Why's and How's

Most of the worked examples I have described throughout the book focus on the procedural steps and the outcomes of the procedure. Math worked examples typically show each solution step and the mathematical result from that step. Van Gog, Paas, and van Merrienboer (2004) recommend adding content to your worked examples that will help learners build deeper mental models. Specifically, they recommend adding expert rules of thumb (heuristics) as well as basic theory that serves as the rationale for the heuristics. Figure 12.5 shows an example they use to illustrate how to apply their idea to an electronic troubleshooting worked example. The typical worked example is shown in the white boxed steps containing steps 1 through 6. To the steps they have added expert rules of thumb for troubleshooting in the gray box located on the right side of the example. Under some of these rules of thumb the why's behind the rule are displayed in italicized text. In this manner, a basic worked example is beefed up to incorporate expert heuristics (rules of thumb) and the why's behind those heuristics. Alternative techniques might make use of a learning agent to provide the heuristics or the why content.

To ensure learner engagement, Van Gog, Paas, and van Merrienboer (2004) recommend that worked examples such as

Figure 12.5. Include Why and How Explanations for Steps in Worked Examples

Adapted from Van Gog, Paas, and van Merrienboer, 2004

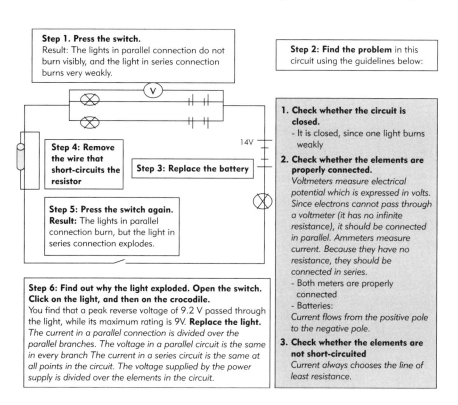

these use the fading technique I described in Chapter 6, whereby the learner has to complete an increasing number of steps with each example. The value of adding heuristics and whys to worked examples has not yet been tested and we will have to wait for further research to define when and how to apply this technique to far-transfer lessons.

Use Inductive Techniques

Traditional instruction uses a *directive* architecture. Directive lessons state the content, provide examples to illustrate the content, and end with practice that requires the learner to apply

Figure 12.6. Reverse the Activity Ratio in Inductive Learning
From Clark and Kwinn, 2007

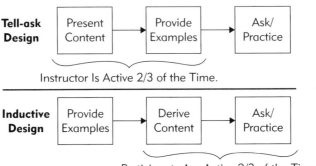

the content. Directive designs follow the two-thirds/one-third rule; namely that the instruction does two-thirds of the work (present content and examples) and the learner is engaged for one-third of the time during the practice assignment.

In contrast *inductive* approaches require learners to derive the content from an instructional experience. Learners derive concept features or guidelines from specific instances. As shown in Figure 12.6, inductive methods reverse the activity ratio. In inductive learning, the learner is actively engaged two-thirds of the time (deriving content and applying content in practice) and the instructor one-third (providing examples).

Inductive learning can be used on a small scale as part of receptive or directive instructional architectures. Alternatively, guided discovery simulation environments rely heavily on inductive learning. In the next sections I summarize each of these approaches.

Mini Inductive Approach.   One way to make traditional directive lessons more engaging is to incorporate brief inductive exercises. For example, in a class on formulas in Excel, the instructor posts two examples of Excel formulas and asks learners to identify the formatting rules for formulas. In this lesson the instructor provides the examples (one-third) and the learners induce the rules (one-third) and are then required to apply the rules by constructing a valid formula (one-third). In our course on design of e-learning, we use an inductive approach to screen design. We begin the lesson by assigning groups of learners a number of screen examples—some more effective than others. Teams are directed to sort the examples into "good" and "bad" piles and then derive the features of the more effective screens. The features are scribed on a wall chart and reviewed and expanded upon by the instructor. Later, teams apply the guidelines by designing sample screens.

Having used both directive and inductive methods to teach the same content, I find that inductive learning leads to a richer and more personal mental model than the directive approach. The reason is that the learners actively engage in building a personal version of the content as a result of their own experience and collaboration with colleagues. The downside to the inductive method is that it usually consumes more training time than the directive approach. The other downside is that if not carefully designed, an inductive experience can impose too much cognitive load. I use an inductive approach in my lessons when the mental model to be taught is of sufficient importance to warrant the time and effort invested and also when I can readily embed sufficient instructional support to manage cognitive load.

Mayer (2002) summarizes an *Inductive Methods* guideline: "Inductive methods of instruction are useful when the goal of instruction is the ability to learn how to form rules (rather than the learning of a specific rule) or how to transfer to new situations" (p. 78). In other words, inductive approaches are best used in far-transfer training.

Induction from Conceptual Simulations. Previously in this chapter, I discussed the use of operational simulations to teach

procedures. The other type of simulation is a *conceptual simulation.*
A conceptual simulation models a scientific or mechanical system
that involves the application of multiple rules. Some practitioners
refer to these as spreadsheet simulations, because they are often
programmed with a number of mathematical statements that
underlie the simulated phenomena. An example of a conceptual
simulation is the genetics simulation illustrated in Figure 12.7.
In this simulation, changes learners make to the genes result in
changes to the dragon features. In conceptual simulations, learners
can use an inductive approach to derive principles or strategies
from their engagement with the simulation.

Of the four architectures I described in Chapter 2, the guided
discovery approach makes the greatest use of inductive learning.

Figure 12.7. A Genetics Conceptual Simulation

From Biological Project

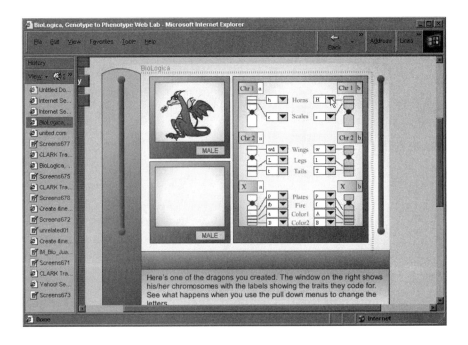

Guided discovery lessons typically provide the learner with a job-realistic case problem and ask them to use various resources to work the case. For example, in the genetics simulation, the learner can manipulate the dragon's genes and see the effects on the dragon. The learner can be given some specific tasks, such as to create a dragon without horns or wings. In performing these tasks, the learner will have to discover the laws of dominant and recessive genes.

Learning Aids for Guided-Discovery Simulations

It's important that simulations be used in a *guided discovery rather than a pure discovery* mode. Research shows that pure discovery instruction fails to achieve good learning outcomes (Mayer, 2004). Open ended simulations can easily impose too much extraneous cognitive processing for optimal learning. Learners need structure to utilize conceptual simulations in ways that will lead to building of accurate mental models in a relatively efficient manner. We are just starting to learn useful techniques that will foster learning in conceptual simulations (Clark & Mayer, 2008). In this section, I will give an overview of a few of these, including:

- Start with simple simulation goals.
- Include explanatory feedback.
- Optimize simulation pacing.
- Keep simulation interfaces simple.

Start with Simple Simulation Goals

Begin a simulation with a relatively low challenge task or goal and move gradually to more complex assignments. For example, in the genetics simulation shown in Figure 12.7 the challenge can be adjusted by changing the number of genes or by adjusting the complexity of the genetic relationships required to "build" a dragon of specific features.

Lee, Plass, and Homer (2006) found better learning from two separate physics simulations—one on Boyle's Law (showing relationship between pressure and volume of a gas) and the other on Charles' Law (showing relationship between temperature and volume of a gas) than on a simulation that combined both laws into a single interface that allowed manipulation of pressure and temperature together.

Include Explanatory Feedback

Moreno (2004) and Moreno and Mayer (2005) compared two versions of a botany simulation game called Design-A-Plant. The simulation goal is to design a plant that succeeds in a specific environment and thus learn how plant features are adaptive to various environmental conditions. In one version of Design-A-Plant, a learning agent provided explanatory feedback to learner responses. For example, the agent might respond to a learner selection with a statement such as: "*No, in soil and moisture conditions such as these, a deeper root system will enable your plant to survive. Select a different root system.*" A comparison version offered only "correct-incorrect" feedback. The researchers found that explanatory feedback resulted in better learning and was also rated as more helpful by the learners. Motivation ratings were the same in both versions. Therefore, adding explanatory feedback increased the learning value of the simulation and did not detract from enjoyment of it.

Optimize Simulation Pacing

Some simulations require learners to respond quickly in order to succeed at their task assignments. Games such as arcade games that are based on fast responses are called "twitch" games. For conceptual learning that relies on reflection, I recommend that you avoid timing features that will defeat learning. In contrast, if your goal is to build automaticity, you may want to design a timing feature into the simulation. For example, train engineers learned to respond to track signals in a simulation that measured both the accuracy and timing of learner responses to signals.

Keep Simulation Interfaces Simple

Contemporary computer and video games rely on highly realistic images and sounds in the interface. However, highly realistic interfaces are more expensive to create and may impose irrelevant mental load. Van Merrienboer and Kester (2005) suggest that "For novice learners, a high-fidelity task environment often contains irrelevant details that may deteriorate learning" (p. 79). Lee, Plass, and Homer (2006) compared learning from a concrete (iconic) representation of Boyle's law shown in Figure 12.8 (top) that used a weight to illustrate pressure along with a slider bar located above the weight to a more abstract (symbolic) representation (bottom) that used only a slider bar positioned in the lower right-hand corner of the screen. They found that learners with little or no science background learned more from the concrete representations. The research team concludes that their findings "provide preliminary evidence that the use of iconic versus symbolic representation of important information in a visual display may reduce extraneous load" (p. 912).

COMING NEXT

Problem-Centered Instruction

In this chapter, we saw that embedding the context of the workplace in the instructional interface is an important ingredient for effective job transfer. A popular strategy in many educational

**Figure 12.8. A Concrete Simulation Interface (Above) Led to Better
Learning of Novice Learners Than Abstract Interface (Below)**
Adapted from Lee, Plass, and Homer, 2006

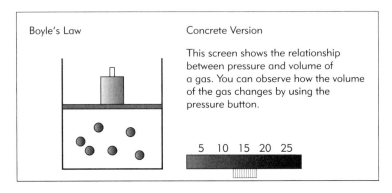

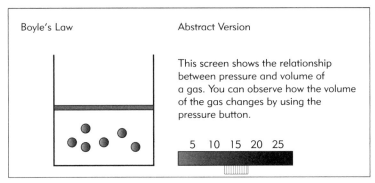

settings is called *problem-centered learning*. In problem-centered learning, a work-relevant problem or task is used to kick off the course, module, or lesson. Starting an instructional experience with a relevant problem creates a moment of need for the content in the lessons. It also risks overloading learners and requires careful implementation for success. In Chapter 13, I summarize techniques and research regarding the use of problem-centered learning.

METHODS TO PROMOTE TRANSFER OF LEARNING

In this chapter I have summarized instructional methods that promote transfer of near and far-transfer tasks. To recap, some important guidelines include:

☐ Apply the Mirror the Job Principle to near-transfer tasks in which demonstrations and practice reflect the environment of the job.

☐ Manage cognitive load by: using a training wheels approach, assigning part-task practice to build automaticity, and using audio and text in ways that minimize extraneous cognitive load.

☐ Include general steps and "how it works" lessons to achieve moderate transfer of procedural skills.

☐ Build flexible mental models to support far-transfer by including highly variable worked examples that engage learners as well as inductive learning environments, including simulation-based lessons.

☐ Avoid cognitive overload in conceptual simulations by constraining initial assignments and interfaces, offering explanatory feedback, and optimizing pacing.

Recommended Reading

Clark, R.C., & Mayer, R.E. (2008). *e-Learning and the science of instruction* (2nd ed.). San Francisco, CA: Pfeiffer. See Chapters 10 and 15.

Gentner, D., Loewenstein, J., & Thompson, L. (2003). Learning and transfer: A general role for analogical encoding. *Journal of Educational Psychology, 95*(2), 393–408.

Mayer, R.E. (2004). Should there be a three-strikes rule against pure discovery learning: The case for guided methods of instruction. *American Psychologist, 59*(1), 14–19.

Chapter 17
Practical Applications in
Building Expertise

BUILDING EXPERTISE IN ACTION

Chapter 13 Problem-Centered Instruction	**Chapter 14** Metacognition and Self-Regulation	**Chapter 15** Motivation and Expertise	**Chapter 16** Motivating Your Learners

PROMOTING ADAPTIVE EXPERTISE AND MOTIVATION

Chapter 11
The Psychology of
Transfer

Chapter 12
Teaching for
Transfer

SUPPORTING TRANSFER OF LEARNING

Chapter 9
Implicit Methods

Chapter 10
Explicit Methods

BUILDING NEW MENTAL MODELS

Chapter 7
Managing Attention

Chapter 8
Leveraging
Prior Knowledge

MANAGING EARLY EVENTS OF INSTRUCTION

Chapter 5
How Working Memory
Works

Chapter 6
Managing Cognitive
Load

OPTIMIZING WORKING MEMORY RESOURCES

Basic Learning Events Proven to Build Expertise

Chapter 1 Expertise in the Global Economy	**Chapter 2** Four Ingredients of Instruction	**Chapter 3** No Yellow Brick Road	**Chapter 4** The Psychology of Building Expertise

FOUNDATIONS OF BUILDING EXPERTISE

PART THREE

Promoting Adaptive Expertise and Motivation

ECONOMIC COMPETITIVENESS increasingly relies on adaptive expertise—expertise that grows from flexible and creative thinking skills. The highest forms of expertise are based on a multi-year sustained effort of deliberate practice. To maintain the discipline to reach high levels of expertise, the performer must have the motivation to initiate and persist in focused regiments of practice. In Section III, I review research and guidelines related to the building of thinking skills and on support of motivation leading to persistence in achieving performance goals.

In Chapter 13, I summarize ways to grow expertise in training that is organized around job-specific problems. Problem-centered instruction has been widely applied in medical education, where it has been extensively evaluated. Adaptive expertise relies on the development of not only job-specific cognitive skills but also thinking skills, called metacognitive skills. In Chapter 14, I review the research on how instructional environments can build metacognitive skills. Recent research on motivation has produced evidence-based models of self-regulatory behaviors that we can draw on to create productive motivational environments. In Chapters 15 and 16, I summarize what we currently know about promoting motivation during learning.

CHAPTER 13 TOPICS

The Revival of Problem-Centered Learning
What Is Problem-Centered Design?

The Benefits of Problem-Centered Design
Problems Promote Transfer
Learners Like Problem-Based Learning
Problems Promote Engagement
Problems Lead to "Teachable Moments"
Problems Provide Vehicles for Integrated Learning
Problems Focus on Thinking and Learning Processes

Three Problem-Centered Design Models

Model 1: Problem-Based Learning (PBL)
What Have Medical Educators Learned About PBL?
What Features Lead to PBL Success?

Model 2: 4C/ID
A Course on Preparing a Legal Plea Designed with 4C/ID
Managing Cognitive Load in 4C/ID

Model 3: Sherlock and Cognitive Apprenticeship

Applying Problem-Centered Design
Low-Complexity Designs
High-Complexity Designs
When to Use Complex Problem-Centered Designs

Issues in Problem-Centered Instruction
Problem Quality
Problem-Solving Support
Reflection on Solutions
Use of Collaboration
Use of Media to Present Problems

Reservations About Problem-Centered Instruction

13

Problem-Centered Instruction

We learn geology the morning after the earthquake.

RALPH WALDO EMERSON

U SING PROBLEMS to initiate and anchor learning is an increasingly popular instructional strategy with roots going back to the early 20th Century. Problem-centered learning under various labels has been applied to diverse learning outcomes and settings, including near- and far-transfer tasks, educational and training goals, and classroom and multimedia delivery. The use of a work-realistic problem as a training centerpiece stimulates learner motivation by creating a "moment of need."

In this chapter, I review three instructional models that use problems to drive learning:

- Problem-Based Learning (PBL)

- The Four-Component ID Model

- A Cognitive Apprenticeship

Based on these models, I recommend some general guidelines to apply to any form of problem-centered learning.

The Revival of Problem-Centered Learning

Using problems to drive training is not new. In the early 1900s, John Dewey (1916) advocated instructional approaches that rooted learning in realistic problems or projects. In the years since the first edition of *Building Expertise,* I have seen increasing numbers of reports about lessons and courses that use problems to start and/or anchor learning events. As is common in our field, instructional approaches that rely heavily on problems have been called by various names. In this edition, I will review three instructional models that rely on problems or cases and that are supported by research evidence: (1) Problem-Based Learning (PBL) prevalent in medical education, (2) van Merrienboer's Four Component ID Model, and (3) A cognitive apprenticeship in the form of Sherlock, an intelligent automated tutor designed to build troubleshooting skills.

Problems in the form of work-related case studies or scenarios are in widespread use as the context for learning. Problems have been used to kick off near- and far-transfer learning in educational and training settings and in synchronous and asynchronous delivery modes. Problems are centerpieces in training designed for solo learning as well as in collaborative learning settings. Given the ubiquitous use of problems as instructional drivers in diverse settings and for diverse content, it is likely that you can adapt some aspects of these designs to your instructional goals. In spite of its popularity, problem-centered learning has its critics and has been the focus of a lively debate in the educational research community (See Kirschner, Sweller, & Clark (2006) and Volume 42, issue 3, of the *Educational Psychologist*).

What Is Problem-Centered Design?

I define *problem-centered design* as an instructional strategy in which tasks or problems relevant to the instructional objective are the context for learning. In problem-centered design, problem scenarios are:

1. Presented in the introductory phases of learning; they are the kickoff events for courses, modules, or lessons,

2. Based on authentic tasks specific to the domain of learning; they are job-specific and they incorporate content related to the job or educational objective.

3. The focal point for teaching knowledge and skills needed to resolve the problem.

Problem-centered designs range from relatively simple approaches in which problems or cases presented in print media serve as a source of learning issues to very complex guided discovery simulation-based multimedia lessons. The more complex designs derive problems and problem solutions from cognitive task analysis and often use simulation, incorporate coaching, and provide ways for learners to review "maps" of their problem-solving steps to compare with expert problem-solving maps.

The Benefits of Problem-Centered Design

Problem-centered designs offer a combination of psychological and motivational advantages, including support for learning transfer, learner popularity, engagement, teachable moments, integrated learning, and an opportunity to focus on problem-solving processes as well as outcomes.

Problems Promote Transfer

Do people learn better from courses that present knowledge and skills in an abstract manner or from courses that focus on specific examples and cases? For example, mathematics classes often teach computations, but not how or when the computations might be used in real-world contexts. This can lead to inert knowledge, as discussed in Chapter 11. Training classes may offer relevant skills and knowledge. However, only when new content is situated in job-realistic tasks are the resulting skills encoded in a real-world context. Proponents of using problems as vehicles to contextualize learning suggest that transfer of learning will be better from instruction that presents content in a relevant context. Problems can bridge the gap between general and specific knowledge since the general knowledge is learned in the context of specific applications.

Learners Like Problem-Based Learning

When learning from problems that are clearly applicable to real-world goals, the relevance of the training is highly salient. In contrast, lessons with content—even relevant content—presented outside of a real-world context often do not engage learners. Failing to see how the knowledge could be applied, learners don't see its value. Vernon and Blake (1993) report that medical students involved in problem-based learning classes like them better than traditional science education classes.

However, not all learners may embrace a problem-centered approach. Depending on their discipline and background experience, some may find it imposes too much cognitive load and therefore prefer a more traditional program that offers greater structure and direction.

Problems Promote Engagement

We know that learners must build their own knowledge and skill base in long-term memory. This is the meaning of constructivist learning. Therefore, active engagement with new content is an essential prerequisite to learning. By basing a lesson around a problem, the engagement process is initiated early in learning. If lessons are based on solving problems, engagement will permeate the entire experience. Starting with a problem makes learning a much more inductive experience, especially when the learner has multiple options to build the knowledge base needed to solve the problem. Alternatively, learning new knowledge and skills while solving a problem may impose too much cognitive load—especially for learners who are novices (Kirschner, Sweller, & Clark. 2006).

Problems Lead to "Teachable Moments"

In the context of trying to solve a problem, the learner realizes she needs related knowledge and skills. Challenged with solving a relevant problem, learners experience a readiness for learning—an openness of the mind to embrace new content and to immediately apply it. Teachable moments point to "just-in-time" instruction—providing relevant information and skills when the mind is most ready to receive them. Many problem-centered lessons begin with problems, followed by instructional resources ranging from traditional lectures to resources for self-study that provide relevant content needed to solve the problem.

Problems Provide Vehicles for Integrated Learning

In the real world, experts draw on integrated multi-component knowledge bases to solve problems. For example, in electronic troubleshooting, an extensive cognitive analysis showed that experts used three knowledge components: (1) a model of how the system works—its components, subcomponents, and the circuitry related to each; (2) procedural knowledge of how to conduct and interpret diagnostic tests; and (3) strategic knowledge of where to test first, based on a blend of pragmatic and theoretical considerations. A typical troubleshooting class might teach test procedures and/or it might teach system knowledge. But without a troubleshooting scenario as a context for learning, the content may fail to integrate around real-world work requirements.

Problems Focus on Thinking and Learning Processes

In jobs that involve problem solving—which include most knowledge worker jobs—learning the mental approaches to solving problems in a given domain is just as important as learning the content. For example, in the electronic troubleshooting training mentioned above, experts use heuristics to guide their action paths. The rationale of many experts solving diverse problems on specific equipment was used as a source to derive general troubleshooting guidelines. These guidelines were then modeled and practiced in the training program. More details are presented in the description of the troubleshooting training later in this chapter.

Three Problem-Centered Design Models

The three instructional models I describe in this section use problems as kickoff and anchoring devices. I will start with models that are less complex and move to more complex implementations. Table 13.1 summarizes their major features. Following a summary of these models, I will discuss the commonalities among them as the basis for a problem-centered approach to instruction.

Model 1: Problem-Based Learning (PBL)

Hmelo-Silver (2004) defines *problem-based learning* (PBL) as "focused experiential learning organized around the investigation, explanation, and resolution of meaningful problems" (p. 236). PBL is considered to be the most significant innovation in medical education in the past fifty years (Norman, 2004). PBL started at McMaster University in Canada in the 1970s and has since been adopted on a world-wide scale. PBL reflects a dramatic shift from "traditional" academic models that relied primarily on

Table 13.1. A Summary of Problem-Centered Design Models

Model	Description	Example	Comments
Problem-Based Learning	Small learning teams initiate a lesson by discussing a job-realistic case scenario. The team defines learning issues and reviews resources to resolve.	See Exhibits 13.1 and 13.2.	Widely used in medical education. The most extensively evaluated of all problem-centered instructional models.
Four Component ID Model by van Merrienboer	Individuals learn while resolving far-transfer tasks. The four components of the model are far-transfer tasks, supportive information, near-transfer tasks, and drill-and-practice of procedures as needed	Law students learn how to prepare a legal plea.	Researchers of this model have focused on techniques to manage cognitive load while learners solve problems.
Cognitive Apprenticeship	Learning occurs while performing tasks under the guidance of a mentor (live or automated).	Sherlock multimedia program trained technicians to troubleshoot electronic equipment	Twenty-five hours on Sherlock resulted in competency of ten-year technician.

large group science-based lectures to small tutorial groups that structure their learning around clinical cases. Although PBL started in medical education, some universities have adopted PBL into diverse curriculum areas, including health sciences, law, economics, and psychology (Schmidt & Moust, 2000). In fact, interest in PBL has grown sufficiently to warrant its own journal that debuted in 2006: *The Interdisciplinary Journal of Problem-Based Learning.*

Problem-based learning is characterized by the following four features:

1. A student-centered approach that relies on the learner to identify and review knowledge needed to resolve a case

2. Use of an authentic problem introduced to the tutorial group prior to any preparation or study

3. Synchronous small group collaborative work supported by a faculty facilitator, combined with self-directed study to investigate learning issues that arise from problem discussion

4. Use of the problem and tutorial discussion of the problem as vehicles to identify the required knowledge (facts and concepts) as well as problem-solving skills to resolve it

A typical PBL session begins with a team review of a case problem such as the story of the miserable stomach shown in Exhibit 13.1. The learning team discusses the case to clarify its meaning and to develop hypotheses to explain it. Known facts are identified as well as knowledge gaps. These are recorded on a white board such as the one shown in Exhibit 13.2 based on discussion of a medical case. Team members then work individually to research the learning issues. At a follow-on session, the team reconvenes to discuss what they learned, refine their initial hypotheses, and identify action steps or problem solutions.

EXHIBIT 13.1.   A PROBLEM FROM A MEDICAL LESSON

The Miserable Life of a Stomach

The protagonist of our story is the stomach of a truck driver who used to work shifts and who smokes a lot. The stomach developed a gastric ulcer and so the smoking stopped. Stomach tablets are now a regular part of the intake.

While on the highway in southern Germany, our stomach had to digest a heavy German lunch. Half an hour later, a severe abdominal pain developed. The stomach had to expel the meal. Two tablets of acetyl salicylic acid were inserted to relieve the pain (the truck driver had forgotten his stomach tablets!). A second extrusion some hours later contained a bit of blood. In a hospital in Munich an endoscope was inserted. The stomach needed to be operated on in the near future.

Explain.

From Schmidt and Moust, 2000

EXHIBIT 13.2. AN EXAMPLE OF A PBL WHITEBOARD

Case Data	Hypotheses	Learning Issues	Action Plan
Fever	Infection	Infectious Strains	Order Lab tests - Blood - Culture
Sore Throat		Disease Cycle	- Xray
Cough-Blood		Treatment Alternatives	Research Drugs

What Have Medical Educators Learned About PBL?

Medical education is critical and expensive. Therefore, a number of research studies have compared learning and motivation among individuals in a "traditional" curriculum with that of learners in a PBL format. The first wave of research asked the question: *Does PBL work?* Enough research has been conducted to support a meta-analysis of results (Dochy, Segers, Van den Bossche, & Gijbels, 2003) as well as several recent reviews, for example, Hmelo-Silver (2004) and Mamede, Schmidt, and Norman (2006). Here are the lessons learned:

1. PBL does not yield better learning of science knowledge and facts. In fact, PBL may be somewhat disadvantageous compared to the traditional curriculum. Dochy and his colleagues (2003) based a meta-analysis on forty-three comparisons that were empirical, carried out in real-life classrooms, and compared PBL with traditional learning of facts and concepts. They found a negative effect of PBL on the student knowledge base, with an average effect size of –0.223. The authors conclude that the negative effect of PBL on knowledge is "small and not practically significant."

2. PBL leads to better clinical problem-solving skills. The Dochy meta-analysis also evaluated PBL versus traditional curricula on application tests–tests that assess how learners can apply their knowledge to medical cases. They found a moderate practical positive effect of PBL on application skills with an effect size of +0.460. Hmelo-Silver (2004) concludes that PBL students perform slightly better than traditional medical students on tasks related to clinical problem solving.

3. Medical students like PBL better than traditional curriculum. The popularity of PBL has been a consistent finding from the earliest research on PBL in medical education. PBL students are more satisfied and confident in their learning than students in traditional programs. Dolmans and Schmidt (2006) gave learners a problem dealing with osmosis (the objective of the lesson) or a problem unrelated to the instructional goal. After the group discussion, all participants were asked whether they were interested in receiving information about the topic of osmosis. Next, all participants read a text on osmosis and were asked again if they would like to read more about it. Groups who discussed the problem on osmosis displayed higher interest in receiving more information immediately after the discussion as well as after reading the text. The researchers conclude that group discussions focused on a relevant problem motivate participant interest in the topics contained in the problems.

However, the enthusiasm for PBL may not apply to all learning audiences. Hmelo-Silver cautions: "It would be naïve to believe that the medical school model of PBL could be imported into other settings without considering how to adapt it to the local context, goals, and developmental level of learners" (p. 260).

4. There is not yet clear or sufficient evidence that PBL builds learners who are more self-directed or are better collaborators. In addition to learning goals, PBL environments with their emphasis on self-study and research as well as collaborative learning could potentially develop professionals with greater self-directed learning skills as well as better collaborative working skills. However, we do not have conclusive evidence on these questions.

What Features Lead to PBL Success?

The initial body of research focused on the question: *Does PBL Work?* Most recently studies have shifted to a different and perhaps more productive question: *What features of PBL lead to success?* Although this research question is relatively new, we do have some findings and conclusions:

1. The problems should be complex, ill-structured, open-ended, and balanced. Problems that are too simple and or have clear "right or wrong" closed responses do not support the collaborative exchanges and individual research in ways that optimize learning. Learning comes from problems that can promote conjecture and argumentation. Problems should be multidisciplinary and realistic and connect to the learner's experiences. Further, across a curriculum, the sequence of problems must be carefully considered in order to give coverage to all the critical competencies needed. If most of the problems focused on broken limbs, for example, we might have really competent doctors when it comes to a broken leg, but not much else!

2. Facilitators should be experts in learning in order to guide participants through modeling of thinking and problem-solving strategies. Hmelo-Silver (2004) suggests that the ability of the facilitator to help participants externalize their thinking, focus attention, and elicit causal explanations is more important than technical content knowledge.

3. Group processes must be effective. Group process effectiveness depends on the skills of the facilitator. Dolmans and Schmidt (2006) show that small- to medium-sized groups are more effective than large groups for outcomes related to remembering of information, self-directedness, and student ratings. Students and faculty agree that quiet students, lateness or absenteeism, and dominant students are the biggest inhibitors of learning. Students report that dominant students, a disorganized tutorial with haphazard discussions, and superficial study of the problem impede PBL success.

Frustration with ineffective and/or inefficient group processes has led some medical schools to move from PBL to *case-based learning* (Srinivasan, Wilkes, Stevenson, Nguyen, & Slavin, 2007). One of the main differences in case-based learning is that group facilitators are more directive during discussions than they are in PBL. For example, facilitators may redirect and explore incorrect statements, provide corrective information, and discuss alternative approaches. A second difference is pre-work assignments. In case-based learning, reading assignments require preparation *before* the group session. In contrast, in PBL, learners are given recommended sources to review *after* problem discussion and are free to select the sources they prefer. In short, the case-based learning approach adds more structure both to the self-study and to the group discussions. Srinivasan and his colleagues (2007) surveyed students and faculty experienced with both PBL and case-based learning and found overwhelming preference for the case-based learning structure. However, there are no conclusions yet on the learning effectiveness of PBL versus case-based learning.

4. Participant experience and available study resources may play a role. Mamede, Schmidt, and Norman (2006) note the positive effects of student clinical expertise on PBL discussions. Clinical experience allows learners to connect their experiences with the problems in ways that enhance learning. They recommend that PBL, which has dominated the first two years of medical school, be extended to higher levels. For example, Kumta, Psang, Hung, and Chenge (2003) found that adding PBL in the form of multimedia cases to a fourth-year three-week rotation in orthopedics resulted in better clinical skills than those students who completed the rotation without PBL. The research team notes that the students felt the "simulations complemented and deepened their understanding of patient care, as they could relate this information to real cases present in the wards. In fact, the scenarios reinforced the need to obtain the necessary clinical history and to complete a comprehensive physical assessment of patients in order to make clinical decisions" (p. 272).

The source and number of resources are other factors that influence the effectiveness of PBL. Resources are categorized as primarily those sources that are assigned by the faculty—and supplementary. Offering diverse sources of information leads to richer group discussions. Participants received higher grades when courses offered more primary learning resources. A question yet to be resolved is whether the resource recommendations should decrease as learners gain expertise and are able to identify good resources for themselves.

As you can see, research has revealed quite a lot about the effectiveness of PBL approaches in medical education. However, keep in mind that these results are based on a specialized population of medical students who have already completed many years of schooling, have demonstrated good academic skills, and who are focused regarding their career aspirations. To what extent these lessons learned apply to learners who are younger or older, less skilled or less focused remains to be seen.

Model 2: 4C/ID

Van Merrienboer (1997) and van Merrienboer and Kester (2005) offer the Four Component Instructional Design (4C/ID) problem-centered model for training of complex cognitive tasks such as advanced programming, air traffic control, and preparation of legal pleas. The four components are (1) far-transfer tasks (called *non-recurrent tasks*), which are the main focus of each lesson; (2) supportive information, which provides guidance on completing far-transfer tasks; (3) near-transfer tasks (*procedural tasks*), which are presented in the lesson at the point at which they are needed to complete a far-transfer task; and (4) drill and practice of procedures as appropriate to automate near-transfer skills.

In the problem-based learning approach used in most medical schools, problems serve primarily as triggers for defining learning issues and researching those issues. In the 4C/ID model, the problem is more than a trigger—it is the core of the lesson. Learners are expected to actively "work" the problem, learning needed knowledge and skills as they go. Recent research on the 4C/ID has focused on ways to manage cognitive load while working on complex realistic tasks (van Merrienboer, Kester, & Paas, 2006; van Merrienboer & Sweller, 2005). To manage cognitive load, the initial lessons focus on the simplest authentic tasks completed on the job and are followed by lessons with more complex tasks. In addition, the initial lessons may incorporate various forms of instructional support. Supporting information includes explanations of concepts (What is this?), processes (How does this work?), and guidelines (How should I approach this task?). Procedural skills are presented just when needed to complete a far-transfer task. Because most complex jobs include both near- and far-transfer tasks, an appealing aspect of the 4C/ID approach is the incorporation of both.

The non-recurrent (far-transfer) tasks are the basis for the core problems that drive the training. Learners complete a series of far-transfer problems using the supporting knowledge provided. The problems presented are diverse to help build more transferable mental models, as discussed in Chapter 12. When the tasks reach a point at which a procedure (near-transfer task) is needed, the steps are taught, along with any associated concepts or facts. In some cases, expert performance requires automaticity of procedures. In these situations, drill-and-practice sessions are included as part of the near-transfer task training segment.

A Course on Preparing a Legal Plea Designed with 4C/ID

Nadolski and others (2001) describe a blended learning course designed to teach law students how to prepare a legal plea using the 4C/ID model. The preparation of the plea is taught via multimedia simulation, and the presentation of the plea is practiced in a classroom role-play exercise. In the online simulation, the learner assumes the role of a trainee in a law firm assigned to prepare pleas for several cases. Online resources include case files, support from a senior employee who serves as a coach, expert advisors, and sample pleas. A process worksheet guides learners through problem-solving stages derived from analysis of expert performance. Some of the tasks included in the lesson are 1) getting familiar with the case file, analyzing the context of the plea, defining a plea strategy, planning steps to translate the strategy into a court plea, delivering the plea in court.

The development team used cognitive task analysis to identify tasks and supporting knowledge from different types of experts, including highly experienced lawyers, new practitioners, and trainers. Interviews from these three groups were used to (1) define task and subtask size, (2) define related knowledge, and (3) derive scenarios. The training starts with an example of practitioners performing the final task—conducting the plea. Next learners receive a process worksheet that summarizes the major subtasks involved in researching and presenting a plea. These introductory elements are followed by the first problem, along with specifications of the resources needed for the problem. Cases used diverse scenarios such as a civil law case followed by a criminal case.

Managing Cognitive Load in 4C/ID

Managing cognitive load imposed on learners tasked with solving a problem at the same time they are learning is one of the major challenges of 4C/ID. van Merrienboer, Kester, and Paas (2006) recommend imposing productive cognitive load by using techniques that promote learning and at the same time reducing unproductive load with techniques that minimize irrelevant load. We know that transfer is enhanced by including problems with high variability. For example, highly variable problems such as a civil law case and a criminal law case impose useful cognitive load.

To offset this load, you may use several instructional strategies that vary the nature and sequencing of supporting information. In particular, consider the complexity of your problem sequences, and the placement and use of process worksheets and procedure aids. van Merrienboer and Sweller (2005) recommend that you:

1. Use whole-task sequencing from simpler to more complex problems. A common instructional technique to reduce complexity is to break the content of a lesson into two or more parts. For example, if teaching a procedural task, you might first teach the parts and functions of the equipment or interface, followed by teaching the steps. This chunking of content is called a *part-task sequencing procedure.* In contrast, van Merrienboer recommends starting the early phases of learning with the simplest task that is representative of an authentic complete job task. He suggests that it's important for the learners to form an early quick impression of the whole task that can be further elaborated as the course evolves. For example, in the plea preparation class, learners begin by viewing a video of an in-court plea.

2. Support whole-task solutions with process worksheets and procedural steps. Even a simple whole task may be too complex for new learners as it may impose too much cognitive load. Therefore, guidance can be offered with process worksheets and procedural steps. A *process worksheet* is a working aid that summarizes the guidelines for tackling a far-transfer problem. The list below shows part of a process worksheet from a case-based lesson on analyzing a client loan for funding. Research with process worksheets has found that presenting them while the learner is solving a problem may add too much cognitive load. Instead, consider presenting the process worksheets *before the problem* and the procedural guides in the context of the problem at the time of need rather than presenting both forms of support during the problem-solving phases.

Part of a Process Worksheet from Analyzing a Loan

1. What is the amount of the requested loan?

2. What are the client's credit scores?

3. What is the current cash flow?

4. What collateral does the client have?

5. Which credit criteria are most important in this situation?

6. What are the financial consequences if the client defaults on the loan?

3. Use worked examples to model approaches to solving complex problems. Worked examples in the form of demonstrations are an effective approach to guiding novices through the early stages of working through a problem. In previous chapters I have reviewed guidelines for constructing and engaging learners effectively in worked examples.

4. Use collaborative teams to enhance problem-solving efforts. Hummel, Paas, and Koper (2006) compared the effects of process worksheets and small group discussions on learning how to prepare a plea in court. They found that both the worksheets and collaborative problem solving individually improved learning outcomes. However, they note that the benefits of collaboration increased in the absence of the worksheets and decreased when more worksheets were available. They suggest that learners who worked individually with the process worksheets had less to gain from collaborative discussions. Therefore, collaboration is a feasible option to substitute for process worksheets when training complex tasks. However, adding collaboration to lessons that have process worksheets may not add much value.

Model 3: Sherlock and Cognitive Apprenticeship

For over twelve years, a research team developed and evaluated a multimedia tutorial called Sherlock, designed to teach troubleshooting of specific electronic test equipment. Training on Sherlock accelerated the expertise of technicians not only on the equipment trained but also on different equipment. Post-tests showed that technicians who worked with the Sherlock tutor for an average of twenty-five hours over a fifteen-day period, *were able to outperform master technicians with ten years of experience* (Gott & Lesgold, 2000)! Sherlock is an example of a *cognitive apprenticeship* approach to learning. As with a real apprenticeship, learning occurs in the context of actual work. But as a result of instructional control over the type and sequence of problems, the training mitigates the inefficiencies of real-world apprenticeships.

The goal of the Sherlock project was to develop better training models for information-age workers in technical domains. The research team emphasized the need to gain a through understanding of performance as a prerequisite to course design. Extensive cognitive analysis based on interviews of technicians with a range of expertise served as the foundation for their design.

From this analysis, the team found three main knowledge and skill components linked to troubleshooting: (1) an understanding of the device, (2) specific procedures involved in performing tests and interpreting the results, and (3) troubleshooting heuristics. They summarize these as *system knowledge* (how it works), *procedural knowledge* (how to do it), and *strategic knowledge* (decisions on what to do when). The troubleshooting problems in the training are used to teach all three of these forms of knowledge in an integrated manner. This approach differs from traditional training, which typically teaches one or two of these knowledge components outside of a specific context.

Applying Problem-Centered Design

Of the types of problem-centered instruction that I've summarized, some are clearly more complex to design and implement than others. Complexity depends on the instructional role the problem is designed to serve, the techniques used to derive the course content, the delivery media used, and whether simulation is involved. The 4C/ID and Sherlock examples represent complex problem-centered design. The problem-based learning models represent low-complexity problem-centered design.

Low-Complexity Designs

Low-complexity problem-centered designs, while not as ambitious as the more elaborate cognitive apprenticeship models, do offer practical cost-effective ways to contextualize learning and boost motivation. The scope of the design is relatively limited. In most situations, the problem is not intended to be solved but rather to offer kickoff opportunities for participants to define learning issues.

For example, a classroom session could begin with small group discussions of a problem related to the objectives of the lesson. Groups could list what knowledge and skills are needed to solve the problem. One problem could be used for all groups, or several different problems could be assigned to different groups in order to provide more diverse examples. The class might be conducted in a relatively traditional manner ending with a revisit of the initial problem. The problems could additionally serve as the basis for after-class research with postings of findings on a class web page. Problem cases could be short and apply to one or two sessions or they could be more comprehensive, lasting for the duration of a course.

The goals of these lower complexity designs are to:

- Activate prior knowledge or to build prior knowledge in situations in which the content is new to the learners

- Provide a context for learning so that new knowledge and skills are acquired in an integrated fashion

- Promote transfer of learning by building multiple examples of skill application in job-like contexts

- Increase motivation by making the relevance of the new knowledge and skills immediately apparent

High-Complexity Designs

The more complex designs use problems to drive comprehensive learning of far-transfer tasks. These designs stress learning of problem-solving *processes* as much as learning of related knowledge and skills. I think of problems in the *less complex designs* as acting like ignition switches and knowledge blueprints – a way to kick start the learning and guide knowledge construction. In contrast, the problems in the high complex designs *are the engines*—they are the primary vehicles for learning cognitive skills. The more complex designs stress:

- ***Cognitive task analysis*** used to derive work-specific mental models and problem-solving approaches, scenarios, and procedural knowledge. Feldon (2007) notes that the performance of highly skilled experts relies on automatic knowledge that is difficult to articulate. For example, when an experts physician's explanation of his diagnostic techniques was noted by a researcher to differ from the techniques he actually used, he responded: "You *see, I don't know how I do diagnosis, and yet I need things to teach students. I create what I think of as plausible means for doing tasks and hope students will be able to convert them into effective ones"* (p. 102). Many discrepancies between experts' articulated procedures and their actual approaches suggest that cognitive task analysis techniques be used to derive more a accurate set of knowledge and skills. This is a labor-intensive effort. Both the legal plea class and Sherlock used intensive knowledge elicitation techniques as the basis for the design. From a cost-benefit perspective, the transfer of general troubleshooting skills learned in Sherlock to new equipment suggests payoffs that go beyond the context of the actual lessons. I recommend the book by Crandall, Klein and Hoffman (2006) as a starting point for those interested in cognitive task analysis techniques.

- ***Simulation to accelerate expertise.*** The more complex designs focus on building mental models by accelerating the normal processes by which expertise grows. In traditional apprenticeships, learning happens in the context of performing real work tasks under the supervision of a journeyman or expert performer. Since real-world tasks present themselves randomly, there is no logical learning sequence or pace. An instructional apprenticeship selects the best type and sequence of tasks to maximize learning. Simulation allows learners to try out actions and experience the consequences of their actions much faster and more efficiently than real-world practice does. A sophisticated design supports the kind of deliberate practice that Ericsson (2006) recommends as the basis for expertise. Deliberate practice is supported by assessing the gaps in each learner's performance and assigning practice with feedback to target those gaps.

- ***Focus on the problem-solving processes.*** Learning the process is as important as learning the content needed to solve problems. Learners are required to reflect on how they solved problems. In technology-delivered training, maps of the learners' problem-solving paths can be viewed and compared with maps based on expert solutions. Figure 13.1 shows a student map from a multimedia course on commercial loan analysis. Learners can explain how they would approach the problem differently next time as part of a debrief exercise. These techniques help externalize

Figure 13.1. A Learner's Problem Steps

With Permission from Moody's Analytics

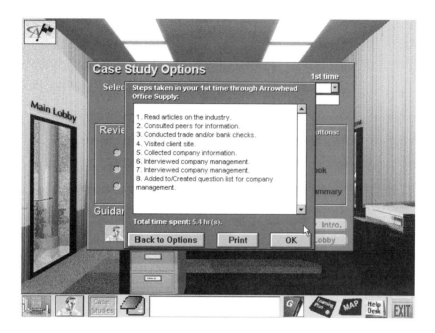

problem-solving processes, making them explicit skills to be acquired.

When to Use Complex Problem-Centered Designs

Because of the labor intensity of these complex models, they are most practical for training when the job context and guidelines are stable and resources are available for an extensive instructional design and development effort. For example, the knowledge and guidelines for plea bargaining are not likely to change significantly in the near future. The more complex models are also applicable to critical jobs where the acceleration of expertise will compensate for the time and cost involved in the analysis.

La Joie and her colleagues (1998) have adapted the techniques used in Sherlock to training for critical care nurses. A third application is situations in which a problem-solving heuristic could be reused with updated specific content. For example, an effective sales process could form the basis for instruction that is updated with new product knowledge. In contrast, for jobs for which knowledge and skills are more volatile and a strong case cannot be made for cost-benefit of acceleration of expertise, consider a less complex design.

Issues in Problem-Centered Instruction

Whether you choose to implement a high- or low-complexity design, there are several issues you will need to address, including assuring high-quality relevant problems, building in instructional support, and including opportunities for reflection.

Problem Quality

Schmidt and Moust (2000) conclude that it is not easy to define what makes up a good problem and that there will be no substitute for prototyping and refining problems during development. An effective problem needs to be:

- Related to the instructional goal. In the case of training, this means the problem must be related to the job performance. Therefore, the problems are best derived from performance analysis of practitioners.

- Job-specific. Problems that work well for training troubleshooting won't apply to training medical personnel. And very general problems will have limited transfer.

- At the "right" level of complexity. If problems are too complex, learners are overwhelmed. If problems are too simple or close-ended, learners won't engage for maximum learning. An optimal sequence of problems from easier to more complex is required.

• Designed to integrate the major knowledge components of the work. These include the procedural components, the knowledge components, and the strategic components.

Problem-Solving Support

Support during problem solution should be liberal in the beginning and fade over time. Early support might include models of good performance or products, worksheets that provide problem-solving flow charts, and explicit hints about how to tackle a problem. Problem support is removed gradually as the course proceeds. Typically, beginning problems are easier, with fewer variables and require less related knowledge and skills.

Reflection on Solutions

When your goal is learning problem-solving heuristics, include opportunities for reflection. These can be traces of learner problem-solving approaches, opportunities for learners to plan their actions, or opportunities to review solution consequences and revise approaches. For example, the screen in Figure 13.1 shows the steps a learner took to research a credit application. These steps can be compared with the steps an expert would take.

Use of Collaboration

For far-transfer learning outcomes that involve problems with multiple approaches and diverse solutions, structured collaborative learning opportunities will generally yield better learning than solo work. Collaborative work can involve group identification of learning issues or group production of a product related to the problem.

Use of Media to Present Problems

Some of the problem-centered design models I have summarized made use of print media, while others used audio and video multimedia features. Does the delivery media make a difference to learning?

Kamin, O'Sullivan, Deterding, and Younger (2003) compared the depth of discussion in groups who received a medical case on video with groups who received the same case in print. They report that the video case stimulated deeper discussions. Although the evidence is preliminary, it may be that the additional fidelity offered by multimedia provides more information or offers a more engaging experience, leading to deeper processing. For example, in presenting a medical case, seeing and hearing patient data provides additional cues. We need more research to define learning situations that profit from richer media presentations of problems.

Reservations About Problem-Centered Instruction

Kirschener, Sweller, and Clark (2006) suggest that problem-based learning is a form of instruction that uses minimal guidance leading to inefficient and ineffective learning. Specifically, they say: "Based on our current knowledge of human cognitive architecture, minimally guided instruction is likely to be ineffective. The past half-century of empirical research on this issue has provided overwhelming and unambiguous evidence that minimal guidance during instruction is significantly less effective and efficient than guidance specifically designed to support the cognitive processing necessary for learning" (p. 76). Essentially, the authors argue that asking learners to simultaneously solve a problem and learn new knowledge and skills overloads memory resources.

Responses to their challenge claim that problem-based learning does not equate to unguided instruction because it is highly scaffolded (Hmelo-Silver, Duncan, & Chinn, 2007; Schmidt, Loyens, van Gog, & Paas, 2007). You may want to read these arguments as an interesting current debate in the learning psychology community.

LESSONS LEARNED FROM PROBLEM-CENTERED INSTRUCTIONAL DESIGNS

In this chapter I have reviewed the features, benefits, and lessons learned about training that is designed around real-world problems. To recap, the main lessons-learned to date are:

☐ Problem-centered designs are useful to promote transfer of learning, motivate learners, promote engagement, lead to "teachable moments," provide a context for an integrated learning experience, and focus on thinking skills.

☐ Extensive evaluation of problem-based learning designs in medical education finds that learners may experience a slight disadvantage on science knowledge and facts tests but have better clinical problem-solving skills; learners rate PBL more favorably than traditional programs.

☐ Recent research on features of PBL that lead to success include the use of complex open-ended problems, effective group facilitation, and availability of study resources.

☐ The 4C/ID model of problem-centered learning focuses on ways to manage cognitive load as learners tackle complex tasks. Some learning supports include starting with simple problems, providing templates to guide performance, and using worked examples to model correct approaches.

☐ A problem-centered multimedia environment called Sherlock that focused on electronic troubleshooting demonstrated that a well-designed sequence of problems can accelerate expertise.

☐ Tradeoffs in design and use of high- and low-complexity problem-centered designs were summarized to help you select a cost-effective approach for your environment.

COMING NEXT

Metacognition, Self-Regulation, and Adaptive Expertise

Some learners are better at learning than others based on their metacognitive skills. Learners with good metacognitive skills are able to set goals, select effective learning tactics, monitor understanding, and make adjustments as needed. In other words, they are self-regulated learners. Learners with high metacognitive skills benefit from different instructional methods than those lacking these skills. As a trainer or instructional designer, the metacognitive skill level of your target audience will be one factor to consider as you plan your instruction.

Metacognitive skills also play a major role in adaptive expertise. To encourage development of adaptive expertise, you will want to support building not only cognitive skills but also metacognitive skills in far-transfer learning environments. You will learn how to do so in the next chapter.

Recommended Readings

Crandall, B., Klein, G., & Hoffman, R.R. (2006). *Working minds.* Cambridge, MA: MIT Press.

Feldon, D.F. (2007). The implications of research on expertise for curriculum and pedagogy. *Educational Psychology Review, 19,* 91–110.

Gott, S.P., & Lesgold, A.M. (2000). Competence in the workplace: How cognitive performance models and situated instruction can accelerate skill acquisition. In R. Glaser (Ed.), *Advances in instructional psychology: Educational design and cognitive science.* Mahwah, NJ: Lawrence Erlbaum Associates.

Hmelo-Silver, C.E., Duncan, R.G., & Chinn, C.A. (2007). Scaffolding and achievement in problem-based and inquiry learning: A response to Kirschner, Sweller, and Clark (2006). *Educational Psychologist, 42*(2), 99–107.

Hmelo-Silver, C.E. (2004). Problem-based learning: What and how do students learn? *Educational Psychology Review, 16*(3), 235–266.

Hung, W., Jonassen. D.H., & Liu, R. (2008). Problem-based learning. In J.M. Spector, M.D. Merrill, J. van Merrienboer, & M.P. Driscoll, Handbook of research on educational communications and technology (3rd ed.). New York: Taylor & Francis Group.

Jonassen, D.H. (2003). *Learning to solve problems: An instructional design guide.* San Francisco, CA: Pfeiffer.

Kirschner, P.A., Sweller, J., & Clark, R.E. (2006). Why minimal guidance during instruction does not work: An analysis of the failure of constructivist, discovery, problem-based, experiential, and inquiry-based teaching. *Educational Psychologist, 41*(2), 75–86.

Mamede, S., Schmidt, H.G., & Norman, G.R. (2006). Innovations in problem-based learning: What can we learn from recent studies? *Advances in Health Sciences Education, 11*, 403–422.

Schmidt, H.G., Loyens, S.M.M., van Gog, T., & Paas, F (2007). Problem-based learning is compatible with human cognitive architecture: Commentary on Krischner, Sweller, and Clark (2006). *Educational Psychologist, 42*(2), 91–97.

Sweller, J., Kirschner, P.A., & Clark, R.E. (2007). Why minimally guided teaching techniques do not work: A reply to commentaries. *Educational Psychologist, 42*(2), 115–121.

van Merrienboer, J.J.G., & Croock, M.B.M. (2002). Performance-based ISD: 10 steps to complex learning. *Performance Improvement. 41*(7) 33–38.

van Merrienboer, J.J.G., & Kester, L. (2005). The four-component instructional design model: multimedia principles in environments for complex learning. In R.E. Mayer (Ed.), *The Cambridge handbook of multimedia learning.* New York: Cambridge University Press.

van Merrienboer, J.J.G., & Sweller, J. (2005). Cognitive load theory and complex learning: Recent developments and future directions. *Educational Psychology Review, 17,* 147–177.

CHAPTER 14 TOPICS

Cognition, Metacognition, and Adaptive Expertise
What Is Metacognition?

Routine Expertise vs. Adaptive Expertise

Metacognition and Self-Regulation
What Is Self-Regulation?

Are Learners Self-Regulated?
Do Learners Know What They Know?

Do Students Select Instructional Methods That Promote Learning?

Do Practicing Professionals Accurately Assess Their Competence?

Can Learners Monitor Understanding as They Study?

The Bottom Line: Don't Rely on Learner Judgment!

Supporting Self-Regulation During Learning
Assess Self-Regulated Learning Skills of Your Audience

Build in Support Structures to Guide Selection and Completion of Learning Events

Design Instruction to Accommodate Metacognitive Learning Skills

Domain-Specific Metacognitive Skills

Building Domain-Specific Metacognitive Skills
Include Worked Examples of Metacognitive Skills

Build Learner Awareness of Problem-Solving Strategies

Use Guided-Discovery Architectures to Build Metacognitive Skills

Promote Deliberate Practice by Teaching Self-Regulation Skills

14

Metacognition, Self-Regulation, and Adaptive Expertise

They know enough who know how to learn.

HENRY ADAMS

METACOGNITIVE SKILLS help learners and workers set goals, select strategies, monitor results, and adjust based on outcomes. In other words, these skills serve as the mind's operating system. In this chapter I focus on metacognition applied to (1) self-regulated learning skills and (2) solving job-specific far-transfer problems. Experts who are able to go beyond what they know and invent new and creative solutions are called adaptive experts. Metacognitive skills are an important element of adaptive expertise.

Cognition, Metacognition, and Adaptive Expertise

Consider the following math problem: *An army bus holds thirty-six soldiers. If 1,128 soldiers are being bused to their training site, how many buses are needed?* On a multiple-choice test, 70 percent of the respondents did the math correctly. However, 29 percent selected the answer: *31 remainder 12.* Eighteen percent said *31 buses needed,* while 23 percent gave the correct answer of *32* (Schoenfeld, 1987). In this situation, most of the test-takers had the cognitive skills; they knew how to do the required division. However, for the majority, the metacognitive skills that support monitoring and reflection were lacking. Consequently, they chose either too few buses or fractions of buses. They failed to ask themselves: "Does *31 remainder 12 buses* make sense in the context of the question?"

What Is Metacognition?

Metacognition is the skill that sets goals, plans an approach to accomplish a goal, monitors progress toward the goal, and makes adjustments as needed along the way. Think of metacognition as the operating system of the brain. People with good metacognitive skills focus not only on the outcome of the lesson or the job task, but also on the steps and decisions they make to achieve that outcome. When working in a team, the person with high metacognitive skills might say: "*Wait! Let's stop and see whether we are making progress. Will we have time to integrate our efforts effectively?*" When in an Excel class, he or she might say: "*I'm not really understanding how to set up pivot tables. I need to ask the tutor and then retry the practice problems in section four.*" In other words, individuals with high metacognitive skills are mindful of their work. When they don't see progress toward a goal, they shift gears and try another approach.

Routine Expertise vs. Adaptive Expertise

"Houston, we've got a problem." This message from the Apollo 13 spacecraft on April 13, 1970, initiated one of the better-documented creative approaches to problem solving. Early in the mission, a loud bang aboard the Apollo spacecraft signaled the loss of two of the three fuel cells responsible for providing power, oxygen, and water for the trip. Without power, oxygen, or water, the astronauts did have a problem! One potentially lethal hazard was the loss of mechanisms to remove carbon dioxide, which would soon reach life-threatening levels. Luckily, the lunar module contained lithium hydroxide canisters that trapped carbon dioxide. Unfortunately, they could not access them because the canisters in the lunar module were square, while the holes connecting the main craft to the lunar module unit were round. Unless they could find a way to access the square canisters, the carbon dioxide content of the cabin air would soon rise to poisonous levels. The fix came in the form of an ingenious repurposing of materials available on the spacecraft, including suit hoses, cardboard, and plastic stowage bags, which allowed the astronauts to access the square canisters via a filter device. Happily, the cobbled-together solution worked! Thinking outside the box led to survival of the crew!

Throughout this book, I have primarily focused on building of schemas in long-term memory that support what Bransford and his colleagues (2006) call *routine expertise.* Routine expertise refers to the solving of problems based on schemas residing in long-term memory. We saw that chess masters have built up literally thousands of chess play patterns as a result of extensive and deliberate practice. However, extensive schemas that work well to solve familiar problems often aren't helpful when faced with a unique situation like the Apollo 13 problem. The Apollo 13 crew owe their lives to creative problem solving, also known as *adaptive expertise.* Adaptive expertise is called into play when experts must go beyond their schemas developed in long-term memory to structure their experience in new ways.

Adaptive expertise is not just of psychological interest. It may speak to the economic survival of your organization in a time of a growing global talent pool. Uhalde and Strohl (2006) suggest two main actions to remain competitive in a global economy: (1) improve educational attainment and quality and (2) nurture innovative thinking. They recommend thinking and reasoning competencies as one of three core skills needed for success in the new economy.

Can adaptive expertise—the basis for innovative thinking— be trained? The answer is yes, and part of that training involves learning activities that offer opportunities for building metacognitive skills.

Metacognition and Self-Regulation

Effective learners apply metacognitive skills by (1) setting relevant and realistic goals, (2) determining how best to achieve a goal, (3) monitoring progress toward the goal, and (4) making adjustments as needed. Greene and Azevedo (2007) consider students to be self-regulated "to the degree that they are metacognitively, motivationally, and behaviorally active participants in their learning. Self-regulated learning is a constructive process wherein learners set goals on the basis of both their past experiences and their current environments" (pp. 334–335). Self-regulatory skills are most important in instructional environments that depend on self-directed learning and as the basis for innovative thinking that will keep your organization competitive in the new global economy.

When I started my doctoral program, I was told that only about 40 percent of all participants who finish their course work complete their dissertations. I believe the attrition reflects the self-regulatory demands required to achieve learning goals outside the structure of the classroom. During the classroom portion of the graduate program, regular classes are scheduled and managed by the instructor. Relatively few decisions are left to the learner. Once coursework is completed, however, it's up to the learner to work with an advisor to develop a dissertation plan, conduct the study, analyze the data, write it up, and have it approved.

Self-study e-learning is documented to have higher attrition rates compared to face-to-face or virtual classrooms. The need for self-regulatory skills in the face of competing demands for time and attention in the workplace is an important factor determining initiation and persistence to complete a learning goal on one's own.

What Is Self-Regulation?

Self-regulation involves a synergistic cycle summarized in Figure 14.1. The activities include: (1) setting specific goals and completion timelines, (2) managing time to allocate regular periods to study, (3) defining the best tactics to achieve a specific learning goal 4) Investing effort to achieve goals, (5) monitoring understanding during the learning process, and (6) adjusting goals

Figure 14.1. The Self-Regulation Cycle of Learning

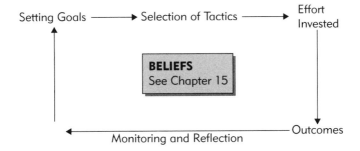

and study tactics based on self-monitoring and external feedback. In achieving a learning goal, the self-regulated learner uses a number of learning tactics—techniques that will support the learning processes described in this book. Some of the more important tactics are those that focus attention, rehearse content in ways that will promote encoding into long term memory, and monitor progress to diagnose and remedy pockets of misunderstanding.

Are Learners Self-Regulated?

Do learners know what they know? Can they make good choices about learning tactics? Can learners assess their knowledge status during a learning event? There is considerable evidence that many learners of all ages and professions *lack self-regulatory skills.*

Do Learners Know What They Know?

One of the core skills of self-regulation is the ability to assess your current knowledge status. For example, when preparing for a test, the self-regulated learner is able to determine what he or she doesn't know and needs to work on. Accurate self-assessment is called *calibration.* Although most of us may feel we have a general sense of what we do and do not know, our specific calibration accuracy tends to be poor (Stone, 2000). Glenberg, Sanocki, Epstein, and Morris (1987) asked learners to predict their scores on a test and then compared those predictions with actual results. They found calibration correlations close to zero. They concluded: "Contrary to intuition, poor calibration of comprehension is the rule, rather than the exception" (p. 119). When comparing knowledge estimates among year 1, year 2, and year 3 medical students, Eva, Cunnington, Reiter, Keane, and Norman (2004) found no evidence that self-assessments improved with increasing seniority. They concluded: "Self-assessment of performance remains a poor predictor of actual performance" (p. 222). Glenberg (1992) refers to the subjective assessment of knowledge as "illusions of knowing."

Do Students Select Instructional Methods That Promote Learning?

Schnackenberg, Sullivan, Leader, and Jones (1998) surveyed participants before taking a course regarding their preferences for amount of practice—high or low. Participants were then assigned to two e-learning courses—one with many practice exercises and a second identical course with one-third the amount of practice. Half the learners were matched to their preference and half mismatched. Regardless of their preference, those assigned to the version with more practice achieved significantly higher scores on the post-test than those in the shorter version. The authors conclude: "The results are more consistent with past evidence that students' preferences and judgments often may not be good indicators of the way they learn best" (p. 14).

Do Practicing Professionals Accurately Assess Their Competence?

Violato and Luckyer (2006) compared performance ratings of peers with self-ratings of specialist physicians from internal medicine, pediatrics, and psychiatry domains. They found that physicians whose colleagues placed them in the lowest and highest quartiles rated themselves 30 to 40 percent higher and lower, respectively, than their peers. In other words, those perceived as performing in the lower quartile over-estimated their performance, while those rated in the higher quartile under-estimated their competency. The authors conclude: "Practicing physicians are inaccurate in assessing their own performance" (p. 235).

Can Learners Monitor Understanding as They Study?

Hacker, Bol, Horgan, and Rakow (2000) evaluated the monitoring skills of college students during a semester course. Participants were asked to predict their test performance before they took a test and after they took the test (but before they knew the actual scores). Students also recorded their study time for each test. The goal of the research was to see how accurately learners could monitor their learning and whether, based on results from a prior test, they would adjust their study time for the next test. Better-performing students accurately predicted their test scores, while poorer students did not. In fact, the poorest learners were grossly overconfident in their pre-test predictions. All students, however, were fairly accurate on their test performance *after* taking the test—before seeing their scores.

You would expect that after scoring low on a test, learners would increase their study time for the next test. However, there was not a strong association between prior test scores and study time for the next test. Instead, learners based their study time on their predictions of performance (which in the case of poorer learners were inaccurate), rather than on actual results of prior tests. The authors noted: "Rather than basing judgments on actual performance, students continued to give greater weight to their expectations for performance" (p. 168). In the case of poor-performing students, low test scores did not translate into increased study time. This may be because poor performers inaccurately believe they will do well on a test. However, when they don't do well, rather than take responsibility, they assign their poor scores to external causes such as a tricky test or poor instructor. In this study we see that low levels of metacognitive monitoring skills lead to poor learning outcomes.

The Bottom Line: Don't Rely on Learner Judgment!

Taken together, there is considerable evidence that many individuals do not make good judgments about their competency, what they do and do not know, and what instructional methods are most appropriate to help them achieve learning goals. This general lack of metacognitive skills suggests that instructional professionals either compensate by embedding metacognitive support into the instructional materials *or* by providing metacognitive skill training to build these skills.

In the next section, I discuss how to support metacognitive skills that underpin learning. Then I turn to ways to support metacognitive skills during domain- or job-specific problem solving.

Supporting Self-Regulation During Learning

What can instructional professionals do to promote self-directed learning skills? Some options include: (1) use self-regulated learning skills inventories to assess learners' metacognitive strengths and weaknesses; (2) provide support structures and metacognitive training when using learning environments, such as self-directed training that heavily rely on self-regulated learning skills; and (3) design training, especially online training, to accommodate the metacognitive skills of your learners.

Assess Self-Regulated Learning Skills of Your Audience

A number of tests can help learners assess their skills and attitudes related to success in self-directed learning environments. For example, the Strategic Assessment of Readiness for Training (START) developed at the University of Texas at Austin is designed to provide a diagnostic assessment of adults' strategic learning strengths and weaknesses in a work setting. It includes the following scales: anxiety, attitude, motivation, concentration, ability to identify important information, knowledge acquisition techniques, learning, and time management. Likewise, the Learning and Study Skills Inventory (LASSI) for learning online assesses skills and aptitudes linked to success in a distance-learning educational program. You can learn more about START and LASSI at www.hhpublishing.com. The Learner Autonomy Profile (see www.hrdenterprises.com) is another resource that provides data on learner desire, resourcefulness, initiative, and persistence.

You could use the assessment results as needs assessment data to help you profile your learning audience and design self-directed learning environments accordingly. You could also make these instruments available to help learners do self-inventories with follow-up resources to boost areas of weaknesses.

Build in Support Structures to Guide Selection and Completion of Learning Events

As you plan training that relies heavily on self-direction and persistence, provide support structures that encourage learners to initiate and successfully complete training. For example, one large organization found that, by sending e-learning registration notices to the manager as well as to the learner, the percentage of learners who initiated their learning increased. Managers decrease attrition by setting outcome goals for the learners, collaborating with learners to set aside regular work time to devote to the instruction, and monitoring the results of the training.

Another approach is to create blended learning that combines traditional classroom sessions and online learning. Traditional classroom events tend to be well attended and can serve as anchors for self-study episodes in your blend. For example, completion of an online course might be required as a prerequisite to a follow-on classroom session. Or a classroom session might initiate a series of online learning events that must be completed to get credit for the class. In these blends, the classroom not only incorporates instructional methods not easily accomplished online, but it also serves as a gatekeeper to promote completion of self-study work.

Third, you can provide direct training in use of self-regulatory learning techniques. Azevedo and Cromley (2004) demonstrated successful learning from hypermedia materials dealing with the circulatory system among learners who received training on self-regulation techniques compared to learners who received no training. The researchers compared the growth in circulatory mental models among two groups of learners who had forty-five minutes to study a hypermedia lesson on the circulatory system. Prior to working with the hypermedia, one group received a thirty-minute face-to-face training on self-regulatory skills. The training included an explanation of the different stages involved in self-regulation as well as seventeen techniques associated with high self-regulatory skills. For each technique, a description and an example were provided such as those illustrated in Table 14.1.

The researchers used a pre-post test essay describing the circulatory process as well as student drawings of the circulatory system to measure changes in mental models. In addition, participants were asked to talk aloud during their study of the hypermedia. The talk-aloud scripts were used to identify which learners made use of the various self-regulatory strategies.

They found that learners who received self-regulatory training had greater growth of their initial mental models and made greater use of self-regulatory techniques. They concluded: "Training

Table 14.1. Samples of Self-Regulation Training Content

Monitoring Behaviors	Description	Example
Judgment of learning	Learner becomes aware that she doesn't know or understand everything he or she reads.	"I don't know this stuff, it's difficult for me."
Content Evaluation	Monitoring content relative to goals.	"I'm reading through the information, but it's not specific enough for what I'm looking for."

Adapted from Azevedo and Cromley, 2004

students to self-regulate their learning on the basis of a thirty-minute training period on the use of specific empirically based self-regulatory learning variables . . . led to significant increases in their understanding of the circulatory system" (pp. 529–530).

Design Instruction to Accommodate Metacognitive Learning Skills

Three major design decisions shaped by your audience's level of metacognitive skills are: the degree of learner control to include in your training, the inclusion of instructional methods that promote deeper learning, and the selection of an appropriate instructional architecture.

Learner Control Relies on Good Metacognitive Skills. Learner control refers to the extent to which learners are allowed to make instructional decisions during training. For example, most traditional classroom environments are relatively low in learner control. The instructor typically orchestrates the learning, which includes the same content and exercises provided at the same pace for all participants. In contrast, some e-learning programs are designed to allow high levels of learner control. Learners can decide which lessons to take in which order and whether or not to review examples or complete practice exercises. Figure 14.2 is from an online course that allows high learner control over content and instructional methods. From this screen, the learner has options to select other topics from the left-hand navigation menu links, and tabs leading to additional information.

Learners with good metacognitive skills generally do quite well in environments of high learner control. They set appropriate goals and manage their time accordingly, apply or select effective study tactics, and monitor their understanding. In contrast, learners with weaker metacognitive skills will often not make good choices in environments of high learner control.

Figure 14.2. Learner Control Provided Through Menus, Links, and Tabs

With permission from Element K

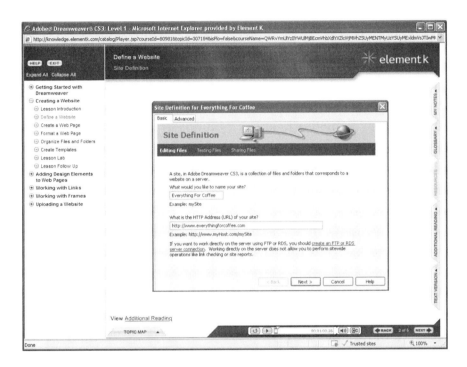

One consistent finding is that learners prefer learner control to instructional control (See Clark & Mayer, 2008, for a review). Therefore, to get positive learner ratings of your courses, provide high levels of control. At the same time, learners low in meta-cognitive skills will struggle in these environments. Two ways to allow control but at the same time improve learning are (1) allow moderate levels of learner control but give suggestions regarding the lessons and lesson sequences and (2) make important instructional elements such as examples and practice exercises the default navigational route. For example, rather than asking learners to overtly select a practice, set up the navigation so that pressing the continue button leads to practice. Schnackenberg and Sullivan (2000) showed that most learners take the default route and, when these lead to important instructional elements, learning is better.

Embed Instructional Methods That Promote Deeper Learning and Monitoring. Many learners do not use effective study skills or tactics. The instructional professional can override poor learning strategies and monitoring failures by adding self-explanation questions to course examples and by administering frequent practice exercises with feedback not only regarding content accuracy but also regarding the learner's overall level of understanding.

I reviewed self-explanation questions in Chapter 10. Recall that, when showing a worked out example of how to solve a problem, you include a question that requires the learner to carefully study the example and to process it deeply. Answering self-explanation questions mitigates the tendency to skip examples or give them only cursory processing during self-study. Requiring learners to self-explain can turn a potentially passive instructional device (a worked example) into an active learning opportunity.

We also saw that many learners fail to accurately assess their knowledge and they fail to monitor their own understanding. You can help learners monitor by including skill practice that provides feedback—not only on the content itself but also on how the learner is doing. For example, after completing a skill assessment that includes sixteen items requiring identification of content types and level of performance in my ISD class, I grade the assessment and give each participant feedback on items they missed along with review and additional practice that focuses on those specific items. My test is a *diagnostic* assessment—one used to help learners and the instructor to identify the knowledge and skill gaps of the participants. Too many training events omit assessments in any form. This omission creates an "illusion of competence" among participants and by the instructor.

Select an Architecture That Matches Your Learners' Metacognitive Skills. For learners who are low in metacognitive skills, I recommend using a directive architecture that does much of the metacognitive work for the learner. First, a directive architecture is typically low on learner control. A directive design orchestrates many instructional methods, including segmenting and sequencing of content and the inclusion of many learning aids discussed throughout this book, such as learning objectives, cues to direct attention to important knowledge points, signals such as text headers to help learners organize new information, and practice exercises to stimulate the rehearsal that builds mental models. Directive architectures support monitoring of learning by including diagnostic assessments that inform the learner of their level of understanding, as mentioned in the previous paragraphs.

Unfortunately, directive architectures are unlikely to help learners build good self-regulatory skills themselves. If your goal is more to build self-regulated learning skills than teaching the actual domain knowledge, you may want to use a guided discovery architecture with an emphasis on goal setting, planning, monitoring, and reflection.

In contrast, if your learners are high in metacognitive skills and have some relevant domain knowledge as well, the degree of support provided in directive architectures may actually be counter-productive. These learners have their own learning strategies, and the imposition of different strategies can cause interference. Instead, these learners would do well in a guided discovery or exploratory environment characterized by high learner control and rich and varied learning resources.

Domain-Specific Metacognitive Skills

Adaptive expertise relies on a combination of metacognitive problem-solving skills and content knowledge. Think of metacognitive skills as a hand. A hand is a powerful and flexible tool— but only when it has something to grasp. And the way a hand grasps a baby will be different from how a hand grasps a hammer. Therefore, problem-solving or metacognitive skills must be tailored to the types of problems faced in a given domain. The most appropriate metacognitive skills in a troubleshooting job will be different from those most applicable to engineering or writing. Therefore, metacognitive skills are best trained in concert with job-specific knowledge and skills (Perkins & Saloman, 1989).

For example, in the electronic troubleshooting tutor Sherlock (described in Chapter 13), cognitive task analysis of multiple experts diagnosing real equipment failures provided the basis for a set of heuristics or best practices for troubleshooting. Learning these metacognitive heuristics is most effective when they are integrated with other important domain knowledge such as a system model and test procedures (Gott & Lesgold, 2000).

Alan Schoenfeld, a mathematics professor, has focused on ways to build metacognitive skills in his students. He began by comparing the problem-solving approaches of expert and novice mathematicians. He asked them to talk aloud while solving problems. He then coded the resulting scripts and graphed their problem-solving patterns, as shown in Figure 14.3 (Schoenfeld, 1987).

Figure 14.3. A Comparison of Metacognitive Thinking Patterns of Expert and Novice Problem Solvers

From Schoenfeld, 1987

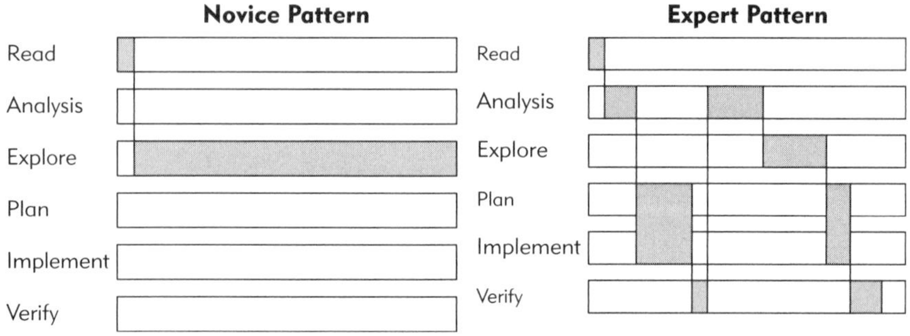

As you compare the expert and novice patterns, note that the novices latch onto a solution and keep working it until the time runs out. In contrast, the expert tries many different approaches but is fast to verify the effectiveness of each approach and to discard those that lead to blind alleys.

Building Domain-Specific Metacognitive Skills

How can you build expert-like job-specific metacognitive skills? Several encouraging results have been reported by instructors who tackled this challenge. The main techniques are (1) modeling of metacognitive skills through demonstrations and (2) assignments that grow learner awareness of their own metacognitive approaches. These methods have proven successful in classroom and online instruction.

Include Worked Examples of Metacognitive Skills

Metacognitive activities of expert performers *are not* usually explicit because they are invisible mental processes automatically applied by experts. Learners are not usually exposed to the goal-setting, planning, and monitoring techniques used by the expert practitioner. Instead, when experts serve as instructors or SMEs, they "magically" display the correct solutions and demonstrate the cognitive (but not the metacognitive) approaches to solve problems. Classroom and online instruction can make these metacognitive activities explicit to learners with worked examples that focus on problem-solving processes.

Schoenfeld (1987) describes a semester-long class in which he focused on the building of metacognitive skills in mathematics graduate students. He used video examples and instructor demonstrations to make these skills explicit. He would show a video of expert and novice mathematicians solving a sample problem.

In these videos the participants talk aloud as they work on the problems. By directing the students to attend to problem-solving process as well as to the results, he makes the relationship between problem-solving processes and outcomes explicit. Schoenfeld also models metacognitive skills during class demonstrations. He does this by "voicing over" his demonstration with metacognitive editorials such as *Is this approach working? What alternatives might I consider?* On occasion, he will deliberately move down a wrong solution path and then stop, evaluate out loud, and change direction. In this way he makes the metacognitive thinking processes of the expert practitioner visible.

e-Learning lessons can use similar techniques. For example, in training designed to teach LISP programming, a video shows an expert solving problems and then reflecting on and revising his solution (Lin, Hmelo, Kinzer, & Secules, 1999). The solution focuses on the cognitive aspects of the problem. However, the retrospective evaluations and revisions focus on the metacognitive processes. Consistent with the research on self-explanation questions for worked examples, Bielaczyc, Pirolli, and Brown (1995) reported that requiring learners to respond actively to the video models resulted in better outcomes than asking learners to merely watch the video. Requiring an active response to a video model ensures that the learner processes it meaningfully. Some ways to promote active engagement with examples include asking learners to (1) graph or record the strategies used by the expert, to compare expert with novice strategies and (2) describe how they will apply expert approaches to their own assignments.

Build Learner Awareness of Problem-Solving Strategies

Merely observing examples of metacognitive skills is not enough. Learners also need to apply metacognitive skills themselves and receive feedback on their attempts. This type of practice and feedback can only be achieved in the context of solving job-authentic problems.

Following the video examples and instructor demonstrations described above, Schoenfeld assigns math problems to small groups. As learners work on the problems collaboratively, he moves from group to group asking questions that will lead to metacognitive monitoring, such as: *What are you doing now? Why are you using that approach? What other alternatives have you considered?* Soon students realize they will be consistently asked these questions, so they need to be prepared to answer them. In this way, they learn to incorporate metacognitive planning and monitoring as part of their routine problem-solving process.

One of the unique contributions of technology to metacognitive training is the ability to give the learner a visual map of her problem-solving steps or thinking processes to compare with an expert map. The computer program can track the learner's path or reasoning through a problem-solving simulation. Making the track visible provides a unique opportunity for self-awareness. For example, in Bioworld, learners are asked to provide a diagnosis for a case study of a medical patient. Learners support their diagnosis with a list of data (symptoms, medical tests) prioritized in order of evidential weight. As shown in Figure 14.4, they can compare their priorities to that of an expert.

Use Guided-Discovery Architectures to Build Metacognitive Skills

Learning metacognitive skills will be best achieved in a guided discovery architecture in which learners have the opportunity to try out actions, make mistakes, and learn from those mistakes. In Chapter 13, I described the Sherlock tutor designed to build

Figure 14.4. Bioworld Compares Novice and Expert Reasoning Processes
With permission of Susanne Lajoie

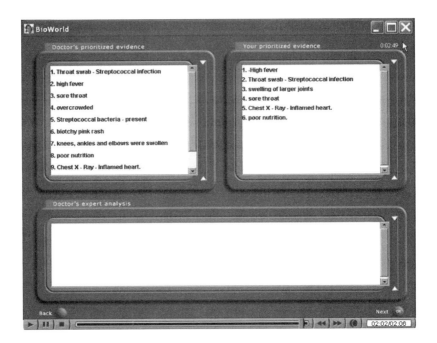

troubleshooting skills. An integral part of the tutor is a reflection component in which learners can review their troubleshooting steps, compare them with those of an expert, and receive commentary from the tutorial (Gott & Lesgold, 2000).

Promote Deliberate Practice by Teaching Self-Regulation Skills

In Chapter 1, I noted that expertise requires not just sustained practice over time but practice that focuses on specific techniques that lead to outcome success. This type of practice is called *deliberate practice* (Ericsson, 2006). When facing a job-specific problem, the activities of goal setting, investing effort, and assessing outcomes to make adjustments are the basis of a self-regulation cycle that leads to deliberate practice. Research supports the benefits of directly training self-regulatory skills as part of a domain-specific learning event.

Zimmerman (2006) evaluated an experimental three-phase self-regulation training program aimed at improving free-throw performance of college basketball students. The phases included (1) goal setting, (2) performance monitoring, and (3) self-reflection to make needed adjustments after missed throws. Four groups of learners were compared. One group received phase 1 only, a second group received phases 1 and 2, a third group received all three phases, and a fourth control group engaged in practice only without self-regulatory training. Phase 1 asked participants to set technique goals such as grip, elbow position, knee bend, and follow-through. Phase 2 assigned participants a self-recording form to monitor the steps of the strategy they were focusing on while shooting. During phase 2 participants could monitor whether they missed a shot and the reason they missed the shot. Phase 3 focused on training participants how to link poor shots with one or more of the shooting techniques in order to refine techniques on the next throw.

The researchers measured outcomes in two ways. First, they evaluated shooting accuracy using a 5-point scoring system. Second, they monitored whether individual participants adapted their techniques after missing a shot. The group averages on both measures improved based on the number of phases included in their training. Those who received multiple-phase self-regulation training showed greater accuracy when shooting and also improved more poor shots with a follow-up attempt. The phase 2 and phase 3 groups took significantly fewer practice shots than the phase 1 and non-training groups, most likely because the quality of their practice was improved through monitoring of results and focus on technique adaptation after a missed shot. The self-regulation training led to deliberate practice in which participants focused on specific techniques needed to improve performance gaps.

METHODS TO BUILD LEARNING AND DOMAIN-SPECIFIC METACOGNITIVE SKILLS

In this chapter, I have reviewed ways to support metacognitive skills that apply to monitoring and managing learning processes and to build metacognitive skills that will improve job-specific problem solving. To recap, the main guidelines are to help learners to learn by:

☐ Assessing the self-regulatory learning skills of your audience

☐ Building surrounding learning events that support initiation and completion of optional training

☐ Providing training in self-regulatory skills

☐ Embedding learning tactics into your training with techniques such as self-explanation questions

☐ Aligning your instructional architecture to the metacognitive strengths and goals of your learners

Help learners build job-specific metacognitive skills by:

☐ Including worked examples of metacognitive skills applied to job-specific problems

☐ Building learners' awareness of their problem-solving strategies

☐ Using guided-discovery architectures

☐ Teaching self-regulatory skills to promote deliberate practice

---

COMING NEXT

Motivation and Expertise

In this chapter, I introduced the importance of a self-regulated approach to learning and job-specific problem solving. All of the main self-regulation events such as goal setting, investment of effort, and reflection on outcomes are fueled by beliefs.

Learners' beliefs about themselves, their goals, the content, and the consequences of learning drive self-regulations. It is these beliefs that lead to selection of a learning event or goal, setting of specific learning goals, and interpretation of outcomes. In other words, motivation to initiate and persist in training rests on beliefs. In Chapter 15, I will summarize five types of beliefs that underlie self-regulation, along with strategies that instructional professionals can use to encourage productive beliefs.

Recommended Readings

Clark, R.C., & Mayer, R.E. (2008). e-Learning to build thinking skills. In *e-Learning and the science of instruction*. San Francisco, CA: Pfeiffer.

Clark, R.C., & Mayer, R.E. (2008). Who's in control? Guidelines for e-learning navigation. In *e-Learning and the science of instruction*. San Francisco, CA: Pfeiffer.

Ley, K., & Young, D.B. (2001). Instructional principles for self-regulation. *Educational Technology Research and Development, 49*(2), 93–2001.

Lin, A., Hmelo, C., Kinzer, C.K., & Secules, T.J. (1999). Designing technology to support reflection. *Educational Technology Research and Development, 47*, 43–62.

Mayer, R.E., & Wittrock, M.C. (2006). Problem solving. In P. Alexander & P. Winne (Eds.),. *Handbook of educational psychology* (2nd ed.). Mahwah, NJ: Lawrence Erlbaum Associates.

Schoenfeld, A.H. (1987). What's all the fuss about metacognition? In A. Schoenfeld (Ed.), *Cognitive science and mathematics education*. Mahwah, NJ: Lawrence Erlbaum Associates.

CHAPTER 15 TOPICS

Motivation for Learning

Motivation, Self-Regulation, and Beliefs

What Is Motivation?

External vs. Internal Views of Motivation

Beyond Carrots and Sticks

Beliefs and Learning Choices

Is the Outcome Important?

Am I Capable and in Control?

Is It Interesting?

Emotional and Cognitive Situational Interest

Motivational Theories and Choices

Beliefs About Learning Outcomes and Persistence

Attribution Theory

Goal Setting and Motivation

1. Challenging Specific Goals Lead to Better Performance and Persistence
2. Goals That Focus on Task Techniques Lead to Expertise
3. Mastery Goal Orientations Lead to Deeper Learning Strategies
4. Intrinsic Goals Lead to Greater Voluntary Commitment

15

Motivation and Expertise

The thing always happens that you really believe in;
and the belief in a thing makes it happen.

FRANK LLOYD WRIGHT

AS AN **EXPERIENCED INSTRUCTOR** and learner, you know first-hand that motivation fuels learning. This chapter summarizes recent perspectives on motivation that focus on beliefs and goals. Productive beliefs fuel a cycle of self-regulation activities that promote expertise. Beliefs guide the selection of learning events, the focus of effort on task-relevant techniques, and the persistence needed to achieve goals. My focus in this chapter is the psychology of motivation as a prerequisite for Chapter 16 that summarizes techniques you can use to foster motivation in your learning environments.

Motivation for Learning

My son-in-law teaches CPR to adults. His learners come from two quite different populations. Nursing home staffs, including nurses' aides, are required by law to take periodic CPR training and demonstrate competency. Many of these participants lack motivation. They do not ask questions. They don't volunteer for demonstrations. Sometimes they are overtly inattentive. Because the training is compliance mandated, perhaps they feel they already have the skills and the training is redundant. Other classes are made up of corporate staff. These participants typically exhibit greater interest, ask relevant questions, and participate proactively. Perhaps many of these participants attend training voluntarily and see relevance in these skills to aid their co-workers or families in the event of an emergency.

Any experienced instructor knows that motivation or the lack thereof has a major impact on learning. In fact, motivation has been reported to predict close to 50 percent of the variance in achievement (Means, Jonassen, & Dwyer, 1997). What accounts for differences in motivation among individual learners? What are the factors that prompt an individual to persist through lengthy periods of focused practice that are requisite for expertise? Is there a science of motivation? These are some of the questions I consider in this chapter.

Motivation, Self-Regulation, and Beliefs

As summarized in Figure 15.1, cognitive models of motivation emphasize self-regulation based on personal beliefs. You can see that the beliefs box occupies center stage in this model. The learners' beliefs influence the main events in the self-regulation cycle, including selection of a task or learning event, setting of goals, effort invested in achieving a goal, and the interpretation of outcomes from that effort. We saw in Chapter 1 that practice alone is an insufficient condition to build expertise. Instead, it is *deliberate practice* that leads to the highest levels of expertise. Deliberate practice focuses effort on goal-relevant techniques designed to close performance gaps. In the previous chapter, I reviewed the self-regulated performance cycle from a

Figure 15.1. A Self-Regulatory Cycle Fueled by Beliefs

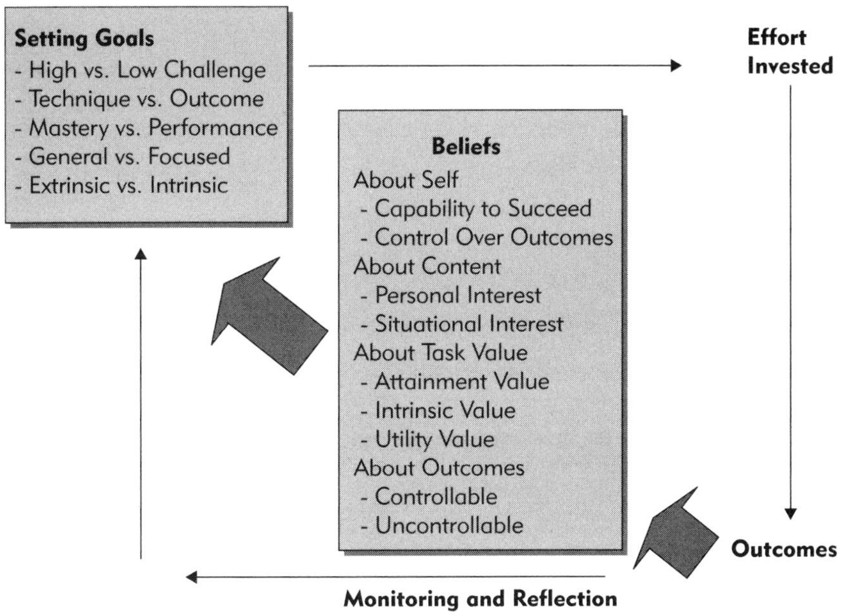

metacognitive perspective. In this chapter, we will look at self-regulation through the lens of beliefs that are the basis for motivation. Table 15.1 summarizes the motivation theories that are the basis for the self-regulatory model of motivation.

What Is Motivation?

The term "motivation" stems from a Latin root word meaning "to move." I define motivation as the mix of beliefs that causes one to initiate a learning activity, to adopt goals related to the activity, to invest effort to achieve the goals and to reflect on outcomes in ways that lead to improved and sustained effort. Beliefs are the fuel that trigger and sustain these activities. In fact, coaches and expert performers consider desire to succeed as the most important factor for success in any given domain (Zimmerman, 2006).

Table 15.1. Five Cognitive Theories of Motivation

Theory	Description
Expectancy-Value	Beliefs about likelihood of success and the value the learner perceives in the learning outcomes
Self-Confidence	Beliefs about self. Learners' beliefs in their ability to achieve learning goals
Goals:	
– Mastery	A focus on improving one's performance over time
– Performance	A focus on doing better than others
Interest	Interest arising from
– Personal	– The learner
– Situational	– The instructional materials and environment
• Emotional	– Evocative content
• Cognitive	– Coherent content
Attribution	Beliefs about outcomes. Learners assign their outcomes to causes that are: internal or external, controllable or uncontrollable, and stable or unstable

External vs. Internal Views of Motivation

Based on Thorndike's (1932) *Law of Effect,* a carrots-and-sticks approach to learning holds that a correct answer followed by a reward is reinforced. For example, after a student correctly answers a math problem, the teacher responds: *Your answer is correct. Good job!* The reward strengthens the association between the question and its answer and increases the probability of a similar correct response next time. This *behavioral view of motivation* emphasizes the role of the external environment (namely the consequences of correct or incorrect responses) on subsequent behavior. It assumes that all individuals will react in similar ways to positive or negative learning outcomes.

Beyond Carrots and Sticks

In contrast to carrots and sticks, cognitive views of motivation put the individual's beliefs into the center of the equation. I have organized motivational beliefs into four main categories:

1. Beliefs about your self—especially your ability to succeed and to control factors that will lead to success

2. Beliefs about the content—primarily your interest in that content

3. Beliefs about the importance or value of a task or outcome

4. Beliefs about the reasons for a learning success or failure

These core beliefs will guide the selection of learning events, support the types of goals relevant to a specific learning opportunity, foster the type and persistence of effort, and serve as filters for the interpretation of performance outcomes.

Beliefs and Learning Choices

Should I pursue an MBA? Should I try out for the basketball team? To learn spreadsheets, should I choose Course A or Course B? Beliefs that affect selection will be most important when individuals have a choice to adopt a learning goal or to select specific learning events to achieve that goal. Selection of an instructional goal or event is influenced by beliefs related to task value, self-confidence, and content interest. Let's look at these three core beliefs.

Is the Outcome Important?

Mark and Jeanne decide to pursue an MBA program. Mark is already a supervisor and feels that what he learns can help him work better with his team. Mark generally did well in school and looks forward to the challenge of academic tasks that are relevant to his work. Jeanne, in contrast, always hated school. But she sees that all of the vice presidents have their MBAs and that if she is going to get ahead, she needs to get that certificate. Both Mark and Jeanne believe getting their MBA is important, but their values—the type of importance they assign to it—are different. Three common types of value are attainment value, intrinsic value, and utility value.

Attainment value refers to personal importance of doing well on the task. For example, an individual who sees him- or herself in a future organizational leadership role may see an attainment value in investing in and doing well in classes leading to an MBA. Earning an MBA confirms his or her leadership self-image.

Intrinsic value refers to the enjoyment an individual derives from undertaking and succeeding in a learning goal. For example, individuals taking elective classes have usually made their selections based on their own interest in the topic. Learners with high intrinsic interest may take a class or pursue a degree primarily out of personal interest and enjoyment in the challenge.

Utility value is based on the importance of achieving learning outcomes in terms of some future gain. For example, Jeanne will pursue an MBA—not because she values the achievement for her self-image (no attainment value), and not because she finds the activity enjoyable (no intrinsic value). Jeanne sees a utility value in receiving her MBA because it is a prerequisite to a management promotion at her company.

Am I Capable and in Control?

Most of us will not select a learning event or goal if we do not believe we will succeed. No one likes to set himself up for failure. Belief in success stems from self-confidence and from feeling that one has control over the events that will lead to success. Self-confidence, also called *self-efficacy,* is domain-specific. I am self-confident when planning and delivering a presentation, but not when playing on a baseball team. Planning and delivering a presentation is a task for which I have a history of experience, some success, and that fits with my verbal strengths. Playing baseball is just the opposite! A meta-analysis of 109 research studies reported that academic self-efficacy was the strongest predictor of cumulative grade point average (Robbins, Lauver, Le, Davis, Langley, & Carlstrom, 2004).

In addition to self-confidence, you must also believe that you can influence the outcomes. For example, if you feel that a class grade will be determined by an unfair grading scheme or by luck, you are less likely to invest effort in studying or completing assignments linked to the grade.

Is It Interesting?

How much easier it is to choose a class when you are interested in the content! There are two types of interest: *personal* and *situational.* For example, Paul is interested in sports—especially basketball. He will read lengthy articles on basketball techniques, even when they are quite technical and dull. His motivation stems from personal interest. Sam is not interested in sports but watches a documentary on professional team sports because the documentary is engaging. In this case, Sam is motivated by situational interest—interest triggered by a well-crafted presentation. Figure 15.2 shows a taxonomy of types of interest, including personal and situational interest.

Personal interest is domain-specific, relatively stable, and tied to the individual. Personal interests usually drive our selection of leisure-time activities, such as viewing or participating in sports, listening to music, or pursuing a hobby. Personal interests may also lead to selection of classes, such as quilting, flying an airplane, or tennis. In contrast, situational interest is a feature of the

Figure 15.2. The Evolution of Interest

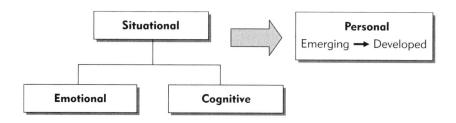

environment, and it is relatively transient. Eccles and Wigfield (2002) characterize situational interest as "an emotional state aroused by specific features of an activity or a task" (p. 114). As you will see in Chapter 16, instructional environments promote situational interest when they incorporate comprehensible text, personal relevance, novelty, concreteness, and learner activity. Situational interest plays a big role in getting attention, whereas personal interest is more relevant to longer-term goals and invested effort.

Hidi and Renninger (2006) propose a four-phase model of interest development. Initially, situational interest is triggered by the learning environment. Situational interest may be maintained over a period of time. A sustained situational interest gradually leads to emerging personal interest, which may then evolve into well-developed personal interest.

Emotional and Cognitive Situational Interest

Instructional professionals can incorporate situational interest as they develop and deliver training materials. They look for ways to make the learning more engaging. For example, the motivational appeal of digital games suggests that we might be able to use some game features in learning environments. Dickey (2005) identifies first-person perspective, narratives, and interactive design as three game elements that can be incorporated into learning environments in order to increase situational interest. The use of stories and games as instructional methods in training are popular recommendations in practitioner journals and conference presentations (Thiagarajan, 2006; Wacker & Silverman, 2003).

However, research on lessons highly charged with emotional situational interest sounds a cautionary note. In Chapter 8, I reviewed research from Mayer, (2005) showing that adding short interesting visuals and stories about the effects of lightning to a lesson on how lightning forms depressed learning, compared to a lesson that omitted the stories and visuals. Along similar lines, learning from games in which game progress depended on activities that were not congruent with the instructional objectives defeated the learning goals of the game (Clark & Mayer, 2008). For example, early versions of The Oregon Trail game included facilities for shooting animals and for moving covered wagons across varied terrain. Children co-opted those features by turning the game into an arcade and racing adventure. Their attention was diverted to more salient goals of greater intrinsic interest such as shooting and racing. Based on consistent negative results from the use of seductive elements, I recommend that you avoid the temptation to rely heavily on emotional interest as a motivational technique.

Instead, promote cognitive interest. In several research studies, the learning and interest ratings from different versions of instructional materials were compared to determine what text features lead to increased interest and subsequent learning (Sadoski, Goetz, & Rodriguez, 2000; Schraw & Lehman, 2001). In Chapter 16, we'll look at features of training materials associated with increased interest and better learning.

Motivational Theories and Choices

In Table 15.1, I summarized five current theories of motivation. The theories related to selection of learning goals or specific training options are Expectancy-Value Theory (Eccles & Wigfield, 2002) and Interest Theory (Hidi & Renninger, 2006). Expectancy refers to the extent to which an individual feels he or she can succeed at a task, whereas value focuses on reasons for engaging and investing effort in a task. Schunk and Zimmerman (2006) conclude that research on expectancy-value theories have supported many of the predicted inter-relationships. Values in particular seem most related to selection of learning opportunities. "Values have been shown to be positively related to achievement, although when both expectancies and values are used as predictors, expectancies are typically stronger. In contrast, values—especially attainment, intrinsic, and utility value beliefs, are excellent predictors of intentions to take courses and enrollment in them. Values seem more important for learning choices, whereas expectancies bear a stronger relation to achievement" (p. 354).

Beliefs About Learning Outcomes and Persistence

In the previous section, we reviewed the role of beliefs in deciding to pursue a specific learning goal or event. Now we turn to how beliefs about outcomes will influence decisions to persist—especially in the face of failure. Even the greatest experts will have failures along the way. Tiger Woods sometimes makes poor shots, loses a tournament, or both. High performers attend to the causes of failures and make attributions to controllable causes. To gain the most value from outcomes, learners need to keep a record of their results and to formulate productive reasons for those results that generate a cycle of refined goals, refocused effort, and improved outcomes. Beliefs about outcomes are called *attributions*.

Attribution Theory

When we succeed or fail at a learning task, we generally give ourselves a reason for that outcome. Psychologists call these reasons *attributions*. Attributions refer to our beliefs about the results we achieve. For example, Marcie and Rajeev both fail a test. Marcie decides that unfair grading was the reason she failed, whereas Rajeev decides he did not study hard enough. How will these reasons for failure influence their actions?

Attribution theory grew from research by Weiner (2000) and focuses on the motivational consequences of beliefs about the reasons for performance outcomes—especially outcome failures. The most common attributions are ability, effort, task difficulty, and luck. Thus, learners may tell themselves they failed to reach a goal because they lack the ability, they did not invest the amount or type of effort needed, the task was too hard, or they were unlucky. Attributions to causes that are controllable are the most productive. In other words, the learners believe that improved or increased effort will make a difference the next time they attempt to achieve their goal. It is more likely that Rajeev will increase his study effort for the next test, whereas Marcie will not, because she attributed her failure to an uncontrollable cause. While many factors influence attributions, instructors can create learning environments that foster controllable attributions. We will review some techniques in the next chapter.

Goal Setting and Motivation

As you can see in Figure 15.1, goals assume a central role in the self-regulatory cycle. Some goals are more productive than others in promoting the type of effort that leads to expertise. In Table 15.2, I summarize five dimensions of goals: (1) Challenge: High vs. Low, (2) Focus: Specific vs. Vague, (3) Target: Technique

Table 15.2. Five Dimensions of Goals

Dimension	Value	Description	Example
Challenge	High	A goal that is attainable but will demand considerable effort. High challenge is relative to the performers experience.	Marcie has been typing about thirty words a minute. She sets a goal to reach fifty words a minute with two weeks of practice.
	Low	A goal that is easily attainable and most likely will not elicit high levels of effort.	Marcie has been typing about thirty words a minute. She sets a goal to reach thirty-five words a minute with two weeks of practice.
Focus	Specific	A goal that specifies exact metrics.	Marcie has been typing about thirty words a minute. She sets a goal to reach fifty words a minute with two weeks of practice.
	Vague	A goal that specifies general approaches or outcomes.	Jane has been typing about thirty words a minute and wishes to type faster. She sets a goal to work harder during her practice sessions.

Target	Technique	A goal that focuses on techniques that lead to better performance.	Sam's typing errors reflect keystrokes from his left hand. He sets a goal to increase left-hand exercise proficiency by 20 percent.
	Outcome	A goal that focuses on the final results of the task.	Sam sets a goal of forty words per minute.
Achievement Orientation	Mastery	Goals that focus on individual progress over time.	Marcie has been typing about thirty words a minute. She sets a goal to reach fifty words a minute with two weeks of practice.
	Performance	Goals that focus on outperforming others.	Marcie wants to be the fastest typist in her class.
Drivers	Intrinsic	Goals that increase personal health, such as affiliation with others, health, enjoyment, and self-development.	John studies typing in association with his computing club.
	Extrinsic	Goals adopted to reap future rewards.	Sam studies typing because he wants to earn extra money typing papers for others.

vs. Outcome, (4) Achievement Orientation: Mastery vs. Performance, and (5) Drivers: Intrinsic vs. Extrinsic.

Goals are important because they direct learners' attention toward activities that lead to building of expertise. Counterproductive goals divert attention from the kinds of activities that lead to learning. In the following section, I summarize four proven guidelines for goals that improve performance and learning.

1. Challenging Specific Goals Lead to Better Performance and Persistence

Locke and Latham's (2002) extensive research on goal setting reveals a direct and positive relationship between goal difficulty and subsequent performance with effect sizes ranging from .52 to .82. General goals such as: "*I need to try harder*" or "*Do your best*" do not lead to as good achievement as specific goals such as "*I need to improve by 20 percent*" or "*Type fifty words a minute.*" Goal achievement will be moderated by beliefs about the self. For example, when goal levels are held constant, higher levels of performance come from individuals with high self-confidence who believe that with effort they can attain the goals. In addition, specific goals will be most effective when accompanied by feedback so the performer knows how he or she is doing relative to goal levels.

The right level of challenge has long been identified as an important feature of games that motivates persistence and enjoyment (Malone & Lepper, 1987). I enjoy crossword puzzles—at least puzzles that offer me the right level of challenge. Crosswords that are too easy are boring. On the other hand, the *New York Times* crossword on Sundays is too demanding for my skill level—I don't even give it a try. Optimal engagement comes from learning environments designed to be moderately challenging to the target learners.

2. Goals That Focus on Task Techniques Lead to Expertise

A *technique goal* focuses on specific strategies the learner needs to improve performance. In contrast, an *outcome goal* focuses on the result. For example, in basketball, an outcome goal is to sink eight baskets in ten free throws, whereas a technique goal is "keep my elbow in" or "follow through." A comparison of self-regulation methods of expert and non-expert basketball players found that 60 percent of the experts expressed needs to focus on specific techniques, whereas only 20 percent of the non-experts mentioned specific strategies. Non-experts tended to focus on general strategies such as to "concentrate" or to "try harder" (Zimmerman, 2006).

Great athletes focus on techniques. For example, swimming champion Natalie Coughlin comments: "There's so much technique involved in swimming. . . . You're constantly manipulating the water. The slightest change of pitch in your hand makes the biggest difference" (Grudowski, p. 73). Performance improvement is best mediated by technique goals aligned to specific behaviors the learner needs to achieve the desired outcome. One of the features of deliberate practice is concentration on specific aspects of performance that need improvement—in other words on techniques.

3. Mastery Goal Orientations Lead to Deeper Learning Strategies

Some individuals set goals that are primarily ego driven—they want to look good. For example, they want to shine among their classmates by achieving better grades. These goals are called *performance goals*. In contrast, other learners are more focused on personal improvement over time. Progress goals are called *mastery goals*. Research shows that mastery goals lead to selection of more challenging tasks and investment of effort in activities that will promote individual progress. Selection of a mastery goal activates additional goals that focus on techniques. In contrast, performance goals lead to social comparisons. When an individual does not do as well as his or her peers, his or her self-confidence is eroded as well as his or her subsequent motivation for learning.

Schunk and Zimmerman (2006) conclude that research evidence supports many of the predictions of goal theory. "Students with a mastery goal orientation demonstrate better cognitive monitoring and use of learning strategies. Mastery goals also relate positively to use of better cognitive processes during learning and to many motivational variables such as high self efficacy" (p. 235).

4. Intrinsic Goals Lead to Greater Voluntary Commitment

Table 15.2 includes two different drivers for goals: intrinsic or extrinsic. Imagine that you are asked to study a text about recycling. You are asked to study the text to achieve either an intrinsic goal (to help the community in a recycling campaign), an extrinsic goal (to earn additional income), or both intrinsic and extrinsic goals. An *intrinsic goal* is related to core psychological or physical health needs such as competence, affiliation with others, health, and autonomy (Greene & Azevedo, 2007). An *extrinsic goal* emphasizes external rewards such as monetary gain, image, grades, or other incentives. Note that extrinsic goals are closely aligned to utility values, for example, I work on the task not because it is satisfying or enjoyable but because it will reap future rewards. How will intrinsic or extrinsic goals affect your study process, learning experience, learning outcomes, and pursuit of future learning about the topic?

Vansteenkiste, Simons, Lens, Soenens, Matos, and Lacante (2004) compared the effects of an intrinsic, extrinsic, or both intrinsic and extrinsic goals on (1) learner perceptions of stress during study, (2) goal achievement orientations (mastery versus performance), (3) learning outcomes, and (4) engagement in future optional activities related to the lesson topic (recycling). They found that a single intrinsic goal such as "learning about recycling in order to make a contribution to the community" led to better learning outcomes. Specifically, individuals with the intrinsic goal reported less stress during study, greater mastery goal orientation, and less performance goal orientation and achieved higher scores than those under the other goal conditions. In contrast, the extrinsic goal of "learning recycling to earn money" led to greater stress, a greater tendency to adopt a performance goal orientation, and poorer test performance.

As an indicator of motivation, participants in the recycling lessons could choose to engage in some optional follow-up activities related to recycling. Seventy three percent of those in the intrinsic goal condition engaged in one or both of the free-choice activities, compared to 62 percent in the double goal and 43 percent in the extrinsic-only goal condition. The research team suggests that "only contexts that focus on the attainment of future goals that are *intrinsic in nature* facilitate the learning process, whereas contexts that value the achievement of future extrinsic goals undermine an optimal academic functioning" (p. 763, emphasis mine).

In other words, specific goals that are challenging, focus on improvement in relevant techniques over time, and are of intrinsic worth are most likely to lead to deliberate practice regimens that build expertise. Such goals will arise from beliefs that include confidence in success, control over outcomes, personal interest in the learning goal, and a value placed on goal achievement.

THE PSYCHOLOGY OF MOTIVATION

Expertise requires persistence, which is fueled by motivation. Motivation in turn depends on a cycle of self-regulation that leads to selection of learning events, adoption of goals that prompt optimal effort, and interpretation of outcomes in terms of controllable attributions. All of these events are driven by beliefs, including self-confidence, task value, interest, and reasons for outcomes as controllable or uncontrollable. In this chapter, I have summarized the main types of goals and beliefs that are likely to motivate choice, persistence, and productive adjustments during learning.

The best mix of goals to promote learning are

☐ Specific goals that are challenging (but attainable) and focus on perfecting of techniques that will in turn lead to desired outcomes,

☐ Mastery goals that focus on self-improvement

☐ Intrinsic goals that are more likely to lead to mastery goals

COMING NEXT

Motivating Your Learners

Now that we have reviewed the psychology of motivation, the next chapter looks at evidence regarding how learning professionals can build instructional environments that promote productive motivation. Specifically, we will focus on how you can support productive beliefs and goals in your learning environment, and I will discuss techniques you can use to help learners adopt productive learning goals.

Recommended Readings

Eccles, J.S., & Wigfield, A. (2002). Motivational beliefs, values, and goals. *Annual Review of Psychology, 53*, 109–132.

Greene, J.A., & Azevedo, R. (2007). A theoretical review of Winne and Hadwin's model of self-regulated learning: New perspectives and directions. *Review of Educational Research, 77,* 334–372.

Hidi, S., & Renninger, K.A. (2006). The four-phase model of interest development, *Educational Psychologist, 41*(2), 111–127.

Pintrich, P.R. (2003). A motivational science perspective on the role of student motivation in learning and teaching contexts. *Journal of Educational Psychology, 95,* 667–686.

Schunk, D.H., & Zimmerman, B.J. (2006). Competency and control beliefs: Distinguishing the means and ends. In P.A. Alexander & P.H. Winne (Eds.), *Handbook of educational psychology.* Mahwah, NJ: Lawrence Erlbaum Associates.

Zimmerman, B.J. (2006). Development and adaptation of expertise: The role of self-regulatory processes and beliefs. In K.A. Ericsson, N. Charness, P.J. Feltovich, & R.R. Hoffman (Eds.), *The Cambridge handbook of expertise and expert performance.* New York: Cambridge University Press.

CHAPTER 16 TOPICS

Instructional Environments That Motivate

Evidence for Managing Learner Beliefs

Promote Self-Confidence by Structuring for Success

> Construct Tasks of Optimal Challenge
>
> Match Learning Architectures to Learner Background
>
> Incorporate Guidance and Explanatory Feedback with Frequent Practice
>
> Incorporate Social Models of Success
>
> Help Learners Assess Prerequisites

Encourage Mastery (Progress) Goal Orientations

> Establish a Criterion-Referenced Learning Environment
>
> Encourage Attributions to Controllable Causes
>
> Establish Technique Goals As Well As Outcome Goals

Exploit Personal and Situational Interest

Techniques to Promote Cognitive Situational Interest

> Write Understandable and Coherent Lessons
>
> Use Language and Examples That Are Concrete and Vivid
>
> Engage Readers Through Personalization
>
> Present New Content in Familiar Terms

Leverage Personal Interest

> Situational Interest Can Compensate for Lack of Personal Interest

Make Values Salient

16

Motivating Your Learners

Would you persuade, speak of interest, not of reason.

BENJAMIN FRANKLIN, 1734

IN CHAPTER 15, we saw that motivation relies on a set of beliefs that fuel the selection of productive goals. How can instructional professionals promote productive beliefs and goals? In this chapter, I will summarize specific motivational techniques you can use in order to:

- Build beliefs of self-confidence and self-control

- Encourage goals that focus on learning progress

- Build lessons high in cognitive interest

- Make lesson relevance salient

Instructional Environments That Motivate

Expertise depends on a self-regulatory performance cycle that includes (1) choosing a learning activity, (2) setting productive goals, (3) investing effort congruent with those goals, and (4) reflecting on outcomes in ways that lead to refinement of goals and effort. In Chapter 15, I reviewed evidence pointing to beliefs as drivers of self-regulation. Motivational beliefs are related to self-confidence and self-control, to interest in content, and to task value. Optimal beliefs drive a cycle of activity that includes the type of deliberate practice that builds expertise. How can you shape the self-regulation learning cycle or the beliefs that drive it? How can you create motivational environments that promote learning? In this chapter, I review research that addresses these questions.

Evidence for Managing Learner Beliefs

Your instructional environment can help learners adopt productive beliefs about themselves and their outcomes. It can capitalize on personal and situational interests, and it can exploit values that will lead to investment of effort. Most of the conclusions we have today on motivation are based on *correlational evidence*. In correlational research, we identify factors that are associated with higher or lower levels of expertise. For example, Zimmerman (2006) correlated practice behaviors of basketball players with their level of expertise. Experts were defined as players who made more than 70 percent of their free throws during games, whereas non-experts made less than 55 percent. The research team surveyed the high and low performers regarding their goals, their strategy choices, their self-confidence, and their self-reflections. They then looked for associations or correlations between these factors and higher and lower levels of expertise.

They found no differences between experts and non-experts in frequency of practice, playing experience, and knowledge of techniques. However, there were differences in their methods of self-regulation. Experts set more specific goals, focused on technique-oriented strategies, made more attributions to strategy use, and expressed higher levels of self-confidence.

This research shows a relationship between performance outcomes and productive beliefs and behaviors. However, correlations are insufficient to prove a direct causal relationship. In addition to correlations, we need *experimental evidence* based on studies that manipulate the beliefs of different groups and measure the effects of those manipulations on outcomes. For example, the research by Vansteenkiste, Simons, Lens, Soenens, Matos, and Lacante (2004), summarized in Chapter 15, experimentally imposed different types of goals (*intrinsic* versus *extrinsic*) in conjunction with a lesson on recycling and measured their effects on stress during study, goal orientation, achievement, and motivation to engage in optional follow-up activities. Experiments of this type offer much stronger evidence that the type of goal assigned caused positive motivational effects. We do not yet have many experimental studies that compare instructional strategies designed to promote productive beliefs. As more experimental studies are published, we can expand our repertoire of motivational strategies proven to work. For now, I draw on my own experience and what evidence we have to suggest techniques that (1) promote self-confidence, (2) encourage *mastery* (progress) goals, (3) exploit personal and situational interest, and (4) make the relevance of the lesson salient.

Promote Self-Confidence by Structuring for Success

Success breeds confidence and confidence breeds success! A belief in your ability to succeed (self-efficacy) has consistently correlated with selection of learning options, adoption of optimal goals, and investment of effort. The best route to self-confidence is the experience of success—either directly yourself or vicariously through others who are similar to you. You can help your learners succeed by (1) constructing tasks of optimal challenge, (2) matching the instructional architecture with learner background knowledge and skills, (3) assigning relevant practice with feedback, (4) incorporating social models of success, and (5) offering guidance regarding course prerequisites.

Construct Tasks of Optimal Challenge

I mentioned in Chapter 15 that one of the important motivational elements of games is the right level of challenge. Tasks that are too easy won't sustain interest or promote learning. Tasks that are too difficult lead to dropout. Therefore, you need to structure learning tasks that are relatively short-term and attainable by your target audience with reasonable invested effort. The best tasks offer sufficient challenge to motivate effort but not so much challenge as to discourage attempts. One of my learning failures was landing an airplane. I failed because I was practicing my first landings in a complex aircraft that imposed too much cognitive load for a beginner. In my case, the challenge was too great to inspire my confidence in ultimate success.

As you structure your training, break complex and long-term goals up into small and achievable sub-goals. At the same time, maintain sufficient challenge to inspire optimal effort. For example, write lesson objectives and supporting materials that are achievable in a brief time frame. A classroom lesson should be completed in roughly sixty minutes or less. In contrast, a self-study e-learning lesson should be scaled for completion in the range of five to eight minutes.

Match Learning Architectures to Learner Background

Is your learning audience experienced in the skills of your training, or will they primarily be novice? For new learners, select a directive learning architecture that breaks tasks down into small chunks and incorporates frequent practice, guidance, and feedback. If your learners already have a track record of experience and success, consider one of the more challenging architectures such as guided discovery. "As levels of learner task-specific expertise increase, relatively less-guided exploratory, problem-solving, or game-based environments could effectively assist in learning advanced knowledge and skills in specific domains" (Kalyuga, 2007, p. 529).

Incorporate Guidance and Explanatory Feedback with Frequent Practice

Success comes from effort, and well-designed practice exercises should direct effort toward achievement of goals. Ensure successful practice outcomes by offering various types of help during practice. For example, assign case studies to small heterogeneous teams that can offer one another social guidance; provide plenty of worked examples as performance models; take a *part-task* rather than *whole-task* approach to practice; and include working aids in the form of step-by-step guides or templates.

Of course, we can't feel successful if we don't know the outcomes of our practice attempts. That's why feedback is such a critical element of practice. The best feedback is aligned to productive task goals and is informative as well as corrective.

For example, if the learning goal focuses on techniques, feedback should inform learners how frequently or how successfully they used those techniques. A video replay of an athlete or a supervisor in a role-play exercise accompanied by a discussion of specific techniques is a powerful form of feedback for demonstrable behaviors. For goals that focus on progress (mastery-achievement goals) feedback that shows goal attainment over time will be most useful. For example, a chart showing outcomes or techniques used over twenty practice attempts will focus attention to progress.

In Chapter 10, I described research by Moreno (2004) showing that useful feedback goes beyond telling learners that their responses are right or wrong. Instead, explanatory feedback gives learners the reasons the response is correct or incorrect. Moreno (2004) compared learning from corrective and explanatory feedback in a computer botany game called Design-A-Plant. She found that explanatory feedback not only resulted in more learning but that learners rated lessons with explanatory feedback as more helpful.

Incorporate Social Models of Success

Self-confidence can come from seeing others succeed. When I decided to start my own consulting business, seeing colleagues who succeeded in their consulting initiatives was a confidence booster for me. My feeling was: *"If they can do it, why not me?"* In Chapter 8, I discussed the value of including learning agents in asynchronous e-learning. One useful role for a learning agent is to provide a social model of success. For example, in Figure 16.1 an on-screen agent the same age as the intended learners acts as a social model by describing how he passed his GED test.

Help Learners Assess Prerequisites

If your course depends on prior knowledge, help learners assess themselves to be sure they meet the prerequisites before they enroll. Make statements of prerequisite knowledge and skills specific and readily accessible to your learners. Rather than stating a prerequisite as: *You should understand spreadsheets*, a more specific statement is: *You can construct formulas and graphs in Excel to calculate gross and net profit*. Because many learners are not good at accurate self-assessment, you could even include a self-assessment diagnostic test they can use to define their qualifications for your class. For a class on advanced ISD skills, a survey asked potential attendees about their experience in a number of prerequisite skills, including conducting job and task analysis and writing learning objectives. An even more accurate survey could include test-like questions such as "Which of the following is a well-written learning objective?"

Figure 16.1. An On-Screen Agent Provides a Peer Success Model
With permission from Plato Learning

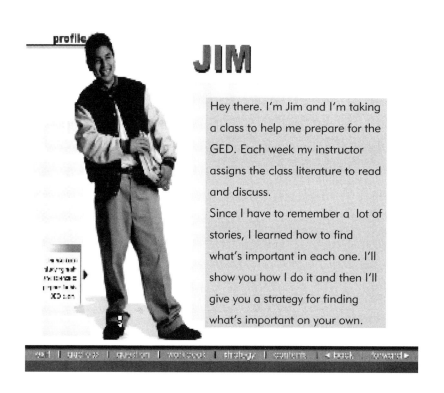

Encourage Mastery (Progress) Goal Orientations

Learners with *mastery goal orientations* direct their attention to techniques that lead to improvement over time. Mastery or progress goals lead to better learning than *performance goal orientations*. Recall that a mastery goal orientation emphasizes self-progress rather than competition with others. In contrast, a performance goal will waste limited mental resources with activities that focus on looking good relative to others. In this section, I recommend three strategies you can use to direct attention to learning progress.

Establish a Criterion-Referenced Learning Environment

In *criterion-referenced instruction,* each learner's achievements are measured against the criterion of the objective—not against other participants in the class. For example, in my basic instructional design seminar, the course objective states that learners will develop a lesson from their own content area that is (1) based on a job and task analysis, (2) includes application learning objectives and practice, (3) uses structured writing for handouts, and (4) includes a valid assessment. Each learner must produce a lesson that meets those criteria to demonstrate skill competency. An individual feedback chart lists the main components of the lesson and checks off each component as the course progresses. In this way, participants' attention is directed toward their own progress—not that of their colleagues.

Encourage Attributions to Controllable Causes

One of the benefits of a mastery goal orientation is persistence in goal achievement in the face of failure. Remember that I failed my airplane landing lessons. I could have attributed my failure to (1) lack of ability, (2) insufficient practice, (3) a poor instructor, or (4). a task that was too demanding. Because the instructor was my husband, option 3 was probably not a good choice. My explanation at the time was that I lacked spatial ability to land the airplane. In other words, I made an attribution to uncontrollable causes because there is not much I could do about lack of spatial ability. Consequently, I gave up on my goal. A more productive attribution would have been to controllable causes such as I needed more practice and I needed to simplify the task.

Although learners form their own attributions, the reaction of the instructor can shape those attributions. For example, if an instructor offers excessive assistance or expressions of sympathy, learners may interpret those behaviors as a signal that the instructor does not believe they have the ability. Instructors need to set and project high achievement expectations. Begin by presenting clear short-term learning objectives. When learners don't reach the objective, assign additional practice and make statements that attribute success to task-specific effort.

Establish Technique Goals As Well As Outcome Goals

A focus on outcomes alone can lead learners to set general goals such as *"I'll try harder"* or *"I'll concentrate more."* Technique goals that focus on a specific behavior—mental or physical—that will lead to the desired outcome are more productive. For example, I occasionally have some participants who fail a test in my instructional design class. I provide them with a supplemental practice worksheet. However, I recommend that they not plunge immediately into the worksheet right after the test. First, it is usually late in the day and they may be tired. Second, they are often feeling a bit demoralized by not meeting passing criteria. I explain that different learners need different amounts of time and practice to achieve goals. I recommend they get up a bit early the next day, read some relevant pages in their text related to the questions they missed, and then tackle the worksheet with a fresh mindset. I also recommend that they write out the reasons for their answers. In other words, I suggest some learning techniques that are likely to lead to productive outcomes.

Exploit Personal and Situational Interest

We saw in Chapter 15 that interest in lesson content correlates with greater learning. We also distinguished between personal interest and two forms of situational interest: emotional and cognitive. I recommended that you minimize techniques used to leverage emotional interest in favor of techniques that build cognitive situational interest.

Techniques to Promote Cognitive Situational Interest

What are some proven techniques you can use to enhance interest in lesson materials? In several research studies, the learning and interest ratings from different versions of instructional materials were compared to determine what text features lead to increased interest and subsequent learning (Sadoski, Goetz, & Rodriguez, 2000; Schraw & Lehman, 2001). In this section, I summarize the following features of training materials associated with increased interest and better learning:

- Understandability and coherence
- Concrete and vivid language and visuals
- Conversational tone
- Familiar content and context

Write Understandable and Coherent Lessons

Materials that are understandable and coherent use simple language. These materials avoid technical terms other than those essential to the learning goals. By adequately explaining new ideas, they minimize the need for the learner to make inferences. Such materials are often called "*considerate.*" They follow a logical sequence with ideas building on each other. They make content organization explicit with transitions, summaries, headers, and sub-headers. They use lean text and put information into tables, charts, and bulleted text when appropriate. Considerate materials illustrate ideas with graphics that are meaningful—not gratuitous. In their report on the negative effects of seductive details, Harp and Mayer (1997) conclude: "The best way to help students enjoy a passage is to help them understand it" (p. 100).

Use Language and Examples That Are Concrete and Vivid

Consider the following two phrases: *volcanic eruption* and *geological event.* Which one generates a mental image? Which one draws you in? Materials that use specific rather than abstract words and augment abstract ideas with examples are more memorable. Higher memorability is caused by a dual encoding effect that leads the reader to generate a phonetic and a visual code in memory.

In a comparison of history texts altered to make them high and low in concreteness, concrete texts were recalled more than two to one, immediately after reading as well as later (Sadoski, Goetz, & Fritz, 1993). In fact, the more concrete a lesson, the more likely it will be comprehensible and the more memorable the content. Sadoski (2001) concludes that "text material that evokes interest tends to be concrete and imaginable . . . excessive attention to abstractions without concrete, imaginable examples may be counterproductive to both learning and appreciation" (p. 269).

Your challenge is to leverage concreteness to promote interest and learning by making *important content* concrete rather than adding concrete asides that will divert the learner from the lesson objective. Strunk and White (2000) suggest: "If those who have studied the art of writing are in accord on any one point, it is this: the surest way to arouse and hold the reader's attention is by being specific, definite, and concrete" (p. 21). Compare your own reactions to the abstract and concrete versions of a social principle in Exhibit 16.1.

Engage Readers Through Personalization

Humans are inherently social—conditioned to attend to and process information from other humans. You can promote higher

EXHIBIT 16.1. EXPRESSION OF IDEAS WITH ABSTRACT
AND CONCRETE LANGUAGE

Abstract version: In proportion as the manners, customs, and amusement of a nation are cruel and barbarous, the regulations of its penal code will be severe.

Concrete version: In proportion as men delight in battles, bullfights, and combats of gladiators, will they punish by hanging, burning, and the rack.

By Herbert Spencer

Cited in Strunk and White, 2000

levels of engagement simply by using a conversational rather than a didactic tone in your training materials. Moreno and Mayer (2000b) showed that writing instructional materials with first- and second-person constructions resulted in better learning than materials that used a more impersonal tone or passive voice. Many instructional texts use a rhetorical style, perhaps to make them appear more objective. This style of writing is impersonal and does not actively engage readers. Avoid a didactic tone in favor of a relaxed conversational approach.

In Chapter 9, I recommended the use of a learning agent to promote implicit processing of content. Research summarized by Clark and Mayer (2008) shows that on-screen agents lead to better learning than comparison lessons with the same content but without the agent. For example, Herman the Bug from the Design-A-Plant game (shown in Figure 16.2) is a learning agent who teaches adaptive features of plants. Lessons that provided the same explanations without Herman resulted in less learning. Apparently the agent serves as a vicarious learning partner who can trigger learner engagement.

A third technique to promote personalization is to reveal yourself in your texts and lectures. Rather than writing or speaking in

Figure 16.2. Herman-the-Bug—A Learning Agent Improves Learning
From Moreno, Mayer, Spires, and Lester, 2001

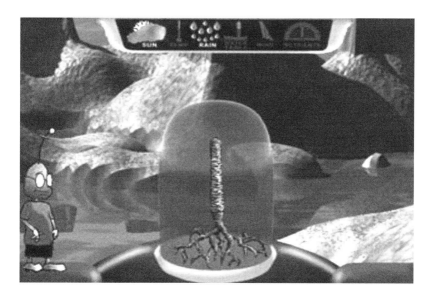

an abstract and detached manner, use first person and incorporate your own *relevant* experiences and interpretations. You might cite a personal experience that illustrates lesson content. Alternatively, you might give your own opinion about a controversial topic. Recent research summarized by Clark and Mayer (2008) demonstrates the learning benefits of what Mayer calls a *"visible author"* approach to writing.

Present New Content in Familiar Terms

Typically, lessons contain unfamiliar content. After all, learning new knowledge and skills is the point of lessons. Nevertheless, you can use devices such as analogies and metaphors to make new information more familiar. In Chapter 9, I summarized research showing that an analogy such as a ketchup squeeze packet to illustrate peristalsis improved learning (Stepich & Newby, 1988). Familiarity can also be boosted by the use of bridging statements that link related content presented at different points in a lesson or course. Some examples include phrases like: *Recall from lesson 2 that.* . . . or *Based on this research, we can modify the modality principle summarized in Chapter 5 as follows.* Familiarity and concreteness improve comprehensibility and all three—concreteness, familiarity, and comprehensibility generate interest.

Leverage Personal Interest

In addition to making your content understandable, consider ways you can use personal interest to improve learning. Leverage personal interest by contextualizing learning materials in ways that relate to learners' goals. In other words, make lessons relevant! For job-specific training, make the relationship between the lesson and the job explicit. Begin by organizing lessons around job tasks. Make the task focus of the lesson obvious by starting with a job-relevant problem or demonstration, as discussed in Chapter 13. Use personal interest to deliver the WIIFM (What's in it for me?), which can be a short activity, a problem, or a direct statement of relevance in the introductory portion of a lesson. Ask class participants to contribute a personal work situation related to the objectives of the lesson. For example, at the start of a management training lesson on handling difficult conversations, each participant summarized a difficult conversation he or she had recently faced and shared the situation with a class partner. Bringing a personal encounter to mind with this activity created a "moment of need" and made the lesson techniques much more relevant. In short, good instruction emphasizes relevance from the start.

Situational Interest Can Compensate for Lack of Personal Interest

Means, Jonassen, and Dwyer (1997) manipulated personal interest and situational interest to see their independent and combined effects on motivation and learning. Here's how their experiment worked. Two versions of a lesson on heart structure and function were developed. One took a "just the facts" didactic approach. The other promoted situational interest by adding concrete language and examples, imagery, analogies, and human interest stories. For example, the enhanced lesson used verbiage such as "*Compare this to a peach*" and "*It's accurate to say your heart is a glorified pump house*" and "*Most physical exams require a reading of your systolic and diastolic pressure.*"

To compare personal interest of the learners, students from two different classes were assigned to the high and low situational interest lesson versions. One group was drawn from a statistics class and the other from a physiology class. Learners from the statistics class were expected overall to have less personal interest and to see less relevance in the heart lesson than students in the physiology class. The research team compared the motivation and learning of four groups of learners: the physiology students—half studying the basic lesson and half studying the enhanced lesson—and the statistics students—half studying the basic lesson and half studying the enhanced lesson.

As you can see from the test scores in Figure 16.3, the enhanced version improved learning among those with lower personal interest, that is, the statistics students. However, there were no real differences between the basic and the enhanced lesson among the physiology learners who were already interested. These results illustrate the value of developing lessons high in situational interest for learners who are lacking in personal interest. However, in the presence of personal interest, situational interest is not as important. Hidi and Renninger (2006) propose that situational interest usually precedes and leads to personal interest. Therefore, invest more effort building situational interest in your materials when you anticipate the learners have not yet evolved personal interest.

Figure 16.3. Situational Interest Improves Learning of Students Low in Personal Interest

Based on data from Means, Jonassen, and Dwyer,1997

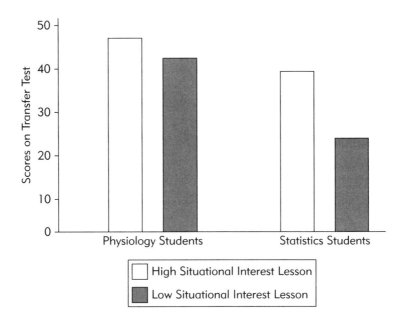

Make Values Salient

Recall that beliefs relevant to the importance of achieving the learning goal are essential to motivation. In Chapter 15, we saw that importance can stem from values that are oriented to attainment, intrinsic outcomes, or utility outcomes. The main strategy you can use to promote interest in your lesson is to make the relevance of the content explicit.

Most adults engage in a work-related learning opportunity to gain knowledge and skills that will aid them in their jobs. For example, a new supervisor needs to hire staff. Important to her are knowledge and skills that support developing and conducting hiring interviews that are legal and valid. In another situation, a new software order-entry system will replace the current system. Learning how the new software changes their current procedures is important to operators.

How can you make your lessons relevant right from the start? Build lessons around job tasks—not isolated content or theories. Medical students consistently give higher satisfaction ratings to problem-based lessons that focus on solving a medical case than they give to lessons that teach science topics out of context. Learning by working on a medical case makes the new knowledge and skills highly relevant. In the same way, learning of software programs is more satisfying when hands-on activities focus on use of software to perform realistic job tasks rather than focus on the tool bars and commands independent of a task. In other words, it's all about context! Be sure your lessons reflect the learner's values by embedding knowledge and skills in a relevant context.

COMING NEXT

Practical Applications in Building Expertise

So far in *Building Expertise,* I have presented proven instructional methods organized by their cognitive effects, including management of cognitive load and building mental models. In the next and final chapter, I summarize the key principles presented throughout the book, organized by the stages of instructional development, and summarize how I have used these principles in building lessons for three of the four architectures introduced in Chapter 2. My goal is to summarize the cognitive principles of instruction in an application context.

METHODS TO MOTIVATE LEARNERS

Motivation has a major impact on learning. In this chapter, I have reviewed the following evidence-based methods you can use to promote motivation:

☐ Make learning relevant. Engage personal interest and task values by using an introductory problem, lesson overview, learning objectives, or case studies directly related to the learners' goals. In training environments, make the instructional content explicitly job-relevant by organizing learning around job tasks.

☐ Design materials of high situational interest. As you plan and write instructional materials, use techniques to make lessons coherent, write with concrete, vivid, personal, and conversational language, and use learning agents to increase situational interest. In the class-room, become a "visible" instructor by including your own relevant experiences and opinions.

☐ Boost confidence with designs that ensure success and incorporate peer models of success. The fact that success breeds success means that you can increase confidence the most with lessons that lead to success with reasonable investment of effort. To do so, optimize les-son challenge, include practice accompanied by adequate support and explanatory feedback, and incorporate success stories of others who have achieved challenging goals.

☐ Promote mastery goal orientations by setting goals and offering feedback that directs attention to individual progress throughout the course—and minimizes performance comparisons. Help learners set goals that focus on techniques that lead to desired outcomes.

☐ Encourage reflection on learning failures to direct attention to con-trollable causes such as increased effort on relevant performance techniques.

Recommended Readings

Tollefson, N. (2000). Classroom applications of cognitive theories of motivation. *Educational Psychology Review, 12*(1) 63–81.

Zimmerman, B.J. (2006). Development and adaptation of expertise: The role of self-regulatory processes and beliefs. In K.A. Ericsson, N. Charness, P.J. Feltovich, & R.R. Hoffman (Eds.), *The Cambridge handbook of expertise and expert performance*. New York: Cambridge University Press.

Chapter 17
Practical Applications in
Building Expertise

BUILDING EXPERTISE IN ACTION

| **Chapter 13**
Problem-Centered
Instruction | **Chapter 14**
Metacognition and
Self-Regulation | **Chapter 15**
Motivation and
Expertise | **Chapter 16**
Motivating Your
Learners |

PROMOTING ADAPTIVE EXPERTISE AND MOTIVATION

Basic Learning Events Proven to Build Expertise

| **Chapter 11**
The Psychology of
Transfer | **Chapter 12**
Teaching for
Transfer |

SUPPORTING TRANSFER OF LEARNING

| **Chapter 9**
Implicit Methods | **Chapter 10**
Explicit Methods |

BUILDING NEW MENTAL MODELS

| **Chapter 7**
Managing Attention | **Chapter 8**
Leveraging
Prior Knowledge |

MANAGING EARLY EVENTS OF INSTRUCTION

| **Chapter 5**
How Working Memory
Works | **Chapter 6**
Managing Cognitive
Load |

OPTIMIZING WORKING MEMORY RESOURCES

| **Chapter 1**
Expertise in the Global
Economy | **Chapter 2**
Four Ingredients
of Instruction | **Chapter 3**
No Yellow Brick
Road | **Chapter 4**
The Psychology of
Building Expertise |

FOUNDATIONS OF BUILDING EXPERTISE

PART FOUR

Building Expertise in Action

AS AN INSTRUCTIONAL professional, it is important that you know not only what to do but the evidence and psychology behind your training decisions. Therefore, I organized this book around the main psychological events that mediate expertise. However, as you prepare and deliver training programs, your frame of reference will focus on the context of your design and development process.

In the final chapter, I summarize the main ideas of the book by illustrating how to apply the various instructional methods in the context of decisions you make as you plan and create training programs. To that end, I integrated the book's major proven guidelines into tables that focus on actions you can take during introductory lesson stages, when presenting content, and when delivering practice opportunities. In Chapter 2, I introduced four instructional architectures: receptive, directive, guided discovery, and exploratory. Now I revisit each architecture with a discussion of how I have applied instructional methods that support the key psychological events that lead to expertise.

CHAPTER 17 TOPICS

Adopting Evidence-Based Practice

Guidelines for Lesson Introductions

Guidelines for Presenting Content

Guidelines for Practice

What Is an Excellent Lesson?

Tailor for Prior Knowledge

Tailor for Outcome Goals

Sample 1: A Receptive Presentation

How It Works

Learning Tradeoffs

Sample 2: A Directive e-Lesson

How It Works

Learning Tradeoffs

Sample 3: A Guided-Discovery Classroom Workshop

How It Works

Learning Tradeoffs

Problem-Based Learning Benefits

Exploratory Architectures for Far-Transfer Learning

A Final Word

17

Practical Applications in Building Expertise

IN THIS FINAL CHAPTER, I summarize the instructional principles that appear throughout the book in the context of their application to lesson design and delivery. To illustrate practical applications, I describe some ways I have applied these guidelines to receptive, directive, and guided-discovery learning environments that I designed and taught. In the context of these examples, I review the methods needed to support the major learning processes discussed throughout the book, including:

- Motivating learners
- Gaining and sustaining attention
- Activating prior knowledge
- Managing cognitive load
- Building mental models
- Transferring new skills to the job
- Supporting metacognitive skills

As a fourth example of how these guidelines might be applied, I conclude with some thoughts of how to tackle the challenge of building adaptive forms of expertise through exploratory learning environments that promote creative and critical thinking skills.

Adopting Evidence-Based Practice

Throughout *Building Expertise* I have presented evidence for instructional modes, methods, and architectures you can use to support essential psychological learning processes. I believe we are transitioning from a craft approach to training to a professional practice based on evidence of what works. As a training professional, you must incorporate evidence as one factor in your decisions about design, development, and delivery of instruction. How many times have you been told (1) what content to train, (2) how long the training should last, (3) when the training is to be rolled out, and (4) what approach to take to the class? Because just about everyone believes he or she is an expert in learning, your challenge is to establish yourself as a professional by explaining best practices to your clients and stakeholders in terms of the psychology and evidence behind those practices.

Specifically, you need to build learning environments that trigger core psychological events of active learning that have been the focus of this book. In this summary chapter, I organize the major guidelines presented throughout the book into tables focused on techniques to consider in lesson introductions, when presenting content, and when designing and delivering practice opportunities. Then I illustrate these ideas using some lessons I have designed using receptive, directive, and guided-discovery architectures.

Guidelines for Lesson Introductions

Motivating learners, gaining attention, and activating prior knowledge are the three main psychological events that result from a successful introduction. Table 17.1 summarizes three major guidelines to get your training off to a good start.

Guidelines for Presenting Content

Whether you are using PowerPoint slides, workbooks, or e-learning screens, all lessons at some point present the content learners need to achieve lesson objectives. When presenting content you need to reduce irrelevant types of cognitive load as well as use implicit instructional methods that promote active building of new mental models. Table 17.2 summarizes the major guidelines to consider when presenting content.

Guidelines for Practice

Many learning environments incorporate opportunities for active engagement with new content with activities such as case studies,

Table 17.1. Guidelines to Apply to Lesson Introductions

Guideline	Description
Make Relevance Obvious–Chapter 16	Use a demonstration, scenario, or problem to make the application of new knowledge and skills obvious from the start
Activate Relevant Prior Knowledge–Chapter 8	Use an activity, previews, and advance organizers to help learners bring relevant knowledge into working memory
Present Learning Objectives–Chapters 7 and 14	Provide a clear statement of expected outcomes from the lesson

Table 17.2. Guidelines to Apply to Content Presentations

Guideline	Description
Optimize Mental Capacity–Chapter 7	Maintain energy levels by managing the physical environment, minimizing fatigue, and promoting accountability for learning.
Include Learning Agents– Chapter 9	Use agents to provide explanations or engage in question-answer dialogs in e-learning.
Build Situational interest–Chapter 16	Write or speak with well-organized, concrete language that engages learners.
Use Graphics– Chapter 9	Use relevant visuals to present content.
Use Audio–Chapter 6	Explain complex visuals with words presented in audio rather than text
Avoid Redundancy– Chapter 6	Avoid presenting words in text and audio that repeats the text.
Signal Attention– Chapter 7	Use cues in text, graphics, and audio to direct learner attention to important content.
Maintain Coherence– Chapters 6 and 8	Keep text succinct. Avoid words or stories that are not directly related to the instructional objective.
Keep Text and Graphics Contiguous–Chapter 6	Align text close to the visual display it describes.
Personalize Lessons– Chapter 9	Use conversational language and learning agents and include instructor point of view.

Guideline	Description
Allow Pacing Control–Chapter 6	In self-study materials, allow learners to move through the content at their own rate. For example, put a continue button on e-learning screens.
Use Pre-Training to Organize Content–Chapter 6	Teach relevant concepts prior to teaching process stages or task steps.
Include Analogies–Chapter 9	Model the features or functions of new content with illustrations from a different content domain.
Include Worked Examples–Chapter 9	Provide demonstrations to illustrate task performance.
Vary the Context–Chapter 12	Use examples that have diverse surface features but similar deep structure to promote far-transfer learning.
Include Process Content–Chapter 9	Teach how systems work to promote far-transfer learning.
Minimize Note-Taking–Chapter 10	Maximize limited instructional time and ensure accurate references by providing learners with notes or working aids that summarize the core lesson content.

group discussions, instructor questions, short-answer exercises on screens or in workbooks. Table 17.3 summarizes major guidelines to apply as you create and deliver practice opportunities.

What Is an Excellent Lesson?

As summarized in Figure 17.1, there is no yellow brick road to training excellence. The optimal choice of instructional strategies

Table 17.3. Guidelines to Apply to Practice Sessions

Guideline	Description
Support Deliberate Practice–Chapter 1	Assign tasks that are just outside the performers competence and focus on specific gaps in their knowledge and skills.
Offer Explanatory Feedback–Chapter 10	Inform learners not only of the correctness of their responses but of the reason behind a correct or incorrect response.
Manage Cognitive Load–Chapter 10	Avoid physical activities that add extraneous processing load that interferes with productive mental processing leading to learning.
Distribute Practice Throughout–Chapter 10	Space exercises throughout the course and lesson rather than all in one place.
Consider Part or Whole Task Practice–Chapters 12 and 13	Assign practice on subtasks that can be learned independently of a full task or on simplified whole tasks that must be learned in context of the entire task.
Build Automaticity–Chapter 10	Use drill and practice when fast error-free responses are needed.
Promote Elaborative Rehearsal–Chapter 10	Design practice exercises that promote deep learning; avoid regurgitation exercises.
Encourage Mastery Goal Achievement–Chapter 16	Help learners record and review their progress over time, rather than focus on the outcomes of others.
Apply Identical Elements and Mirror the Job Principles–Chapters 11 and 12	For near-transfer learning, emulate the application environment in look and response requirements of examples and exercises.

Guideline	Description
Use Operational Simulations–Chapter 12	Provide step-by-step simulations for near-transfer tasks that are unsafe or impractical to practice on the job.
Use Conceptual Simulations–Chapter 12	Provide simulations that model a real-world system or process to build knowledge and skills for far-transfer learning
Use Training Wheels–Chapter 6	Limit device functionality during early practice with operational simulations.
Apply Power Law of Practice–Chapter 10	Greatest learning gains occur during the first few practice assignments; assign the amount of practice based on task performance criticality.
Offer Memory Support and Job Aids–Chapter 6	Provide external sources of reference to facts and steps to guide practice and performance of new job tasks.
Include Self-Explanation Questions–Chapter 10	Help learners to process demonstrations and graphics by asking questions about them.
Include Collaborative Learning Opportunities–Chapter 10	Leverage social presence by offering structured exercises for small groups of learners.
Use Problem-Centered Designs–Chapter 13	Center learning opportunities around job-relevant problems for far-transfer learning of participants with some background experience.
Provide Diagnostic Tests–Chapter 14	Offer learners opportunities to assess their progress throughout the learning event.
Encourage Productive Attributions–Chapter 16	Encourage learners to attribute success and failure to controllable causes such as effort.

Figure 17.1. No Yellow Brick Road to Training Excellence

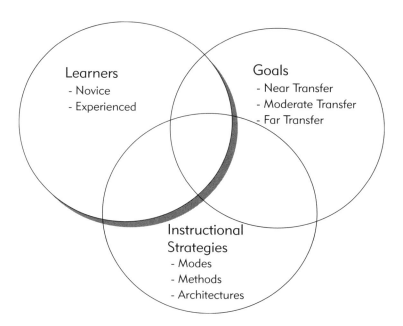

depends on differences among your learners and your instructional goals.

Tailor for Prior Knowledge

The most important learner differences are relevant background knowledge. In general, the more related prior knowledge and metacognitive skills your learners have, the less need for heavily guided instructional formats such as directive architectures. This is because these learners are able to use schemas they have in long-term memory to initiate and manage their own learning processes. Learners with high background knowledge and metacognitive skills make appropriate decisions about what they need to learn and how to learn it. In contrast, novice learners benefit from learning aids I've discussed throughout the book that compensate for their lack of schemas.

Tailor for Outcome Goals

The type of skills to be gained is a second important factor to consider when selecting instructional modes, methods, and architectures. Near-transfer skills are best learned through high-fidelity operational simulations in a directive learning architecture. In these lessons, demonstrations and practice exercises reflect performance environments similar to those of the job. Working aids introduced during the training will encourage transfer of new skills to similar tasks on the job.

In contrast, moderate transfer goals demand a range of faded worked examples using realistic work scenarios that systematically vary their surface features and remain consistent in their underlying principles. Opportunities to contrast and compare multiple cases or examples will increase the chances of deeper understanding, leading to routine expertise. Moderate transfer goals related to systems benefit from healthy doses of process or "how it works" content so that learners know not only what to do but how their actions affect the system. This deeper layer of understanding will help learners adjust their actions when circumstances require adaptation for optimal system functioning.

Finally, far transfer—the type that leads to adaptive expertise—requires a firm knowledge base but also a long-term commitment to training and organizational support that helps experts engage in creative and critical thinking within and across domains. Adaptive expertise will grow as much from experience as from formal learning opportunities.

In this final chapter, I first describe three specific lessons I designed that reflect receptive, directive, and guided-discovery architectures. I present these examples as a context to integrate some of the predominant themes and methods summarized throughout *Building Expertise*. I end with some guidelines for design of exploratory learning environments to build creative and critical thinking skills.

Sample 1: A Receptive Presentation

I'm sure that receptive forms of instruction make up the largest proportion of learning environments—certainly in educational settings as well as in workforce learning. That's because many instructors base their training on models of lecture-based courses they experienced in college settings. In addition, a briefing is about the fastest way to pull together a training event, and it allows a great deal of content to be "covered" in a relatively short time. Unfortunately, content "covered" is not necessarily content learned!

Quite often I present short receptive briefings—mostly in the form of keynote speeches. For example, I have given several forty-five or sixty-minute speeches on my book on cognitive load, *Efficiency in Learning,* to groups of thirty to three hundred. I'll illustrate my receptive design techniques based on this presentation.

How It Works

A good presentation or briefing starts with the planning phase. To trigger motivation, the presentation needs to consider the personal interests of the attendees and present ideas and examples in a relevant context. While my presentation on *Efficiency in Learning* is really about cognitive load theory, I need to contextualize it in terms that my audience considers important—namely how to develop efficient learning environments that save time and money.

I like to engage participants even before my presentation begins. Therefore I include a true-false pre-test in the handout and a place a note on my title slide urging participants to try the pre-test before the presentation starts. The five to eight pre-questions ask about training guidelines that will be discussed in the presentation. Typically, keynotes tend to be very one-sided with an active presenter and a passive audience. I insert opportunities for engagement to make a receptive architecture as interactive as practical.

After a brief introduction, I typically will ask for a show of hands on answers to the pre-test questions, often summarizing how the votes fall out—but not giving any answers! Next I show a short multimedia lesson that is included on the book's CD. The example is polished—it looks good. However, it violates just about every cognitive load principle. After showing the sample, I ask participants to grade it and list their reasons. Then I ask them to discuss their grades and reasons with others sitting close by.

Next I lay some groundwork for the content through some audience-participation demonstrations. For example, I engage participants in a couple of the experiments I described in Chapter 5. I use these demonstrations to illustrate the limitations of our working memory and how working and long-term memory work together. Then I get to the meat of the presentation, which focuses on a series of cognitive load principles. Rather than present principles in a didactic mode, I show two very brief versions of a lesson (one in violation and one congruent with the principles) and ask participants to select the one they think leads to most efficient learning. Following their vote, I show the experimental data that supports the principle as well as some examples.

At the end of the presentation, I return to the sample shown in the beginning and ask them to vote again. Then I play a multimedia commentary on the sample from Dr. John Sweller (the originator of modern cognitive load theory), which reinforces the main guidelines of my presentation. In the concluding minutes, I review the pre-test, which serves as a good summary event.

Learning Tradeoffs

There are no perfect learning architectures, and receptive environments are particularly challenging to learning because they rely on the learner to actively process the content. We've all zoned out during lectures or even well-crafted documentaries. Here is how my keynote speech stacks up.

Motivation. In a receptive learning environment, it's important to show relevance right away. I've seen conference attendees walk out on keynote speeches after five minutes, having heard nothing that engages their interest. I use the pre-test and the "grade this sample" introductory exercises to engage participants and to provide a specific context. I also make some explicit comments on the power of cognitive load theory to directly communicate the benefits participants can anticipate from my presentation. For example, I explain that cognitive load theory is the single more powerful and universal proven set of modern learning principles. We also know that motivation can be driven by interest. That's why it's important to articulate your message in the context of your audience—to call on their perspectives from the start. Explain or illustrate how your presentation solves their problems or gives them an edge.

Attention and Prior Knowledge. Receptive learning environments are famous as attention losers. It is the very talented speaker who can command attention through a receptive presentation of an hour or more! Depending on the purpose, some speakers use humor, some use stories, and some use props to hold attention. Coming from a training background, I usually rely on interactions between the audience and my content as well as among members in the audience. As I plan the topics of my presentation, I simultaneously consider the types of questions and activities I can manage with a large group that will promote attention and forward my message. To avoid split attention, I discourage note-taking during receptive presentations. Most participants cannot follow the content and at the same time take meaningful notes. Therefore, rather than including copies of the slides in my handout I provide textual summarizes of the main content points.

Regarding prior knowledge, my introductory exercises—the pre-test and the "grade this sample" exercise, along with audience discussions, will activate relevant prior knowledge because the questions and the sample are directly related to the topics to be presented and reflect a familiar context.

Cognitive Load. Receptive environments can easily overload the audience. The combination of technical information presented in a passive instructor-controlled pace can often impose more work than memory can handle. I have learned in my presentations that it's often better to say less but to say it well. While my early presentations incorporated just about everything I knew about cognitive load theory in an hour or less, I quickly realized that content covered does not translate into content learned. Participants would leave these bloated sessions feeling overwhelmed and demotivated rather than energized. I needed to do some drastic trimming and leave participants with additional follow-up resources to pursue at a later time.

Encoding and Transfer. Lacking overt engagement, receptive environments must rely on implicit encoding methods. One of the most powerful and underutilized techniques is graphics. We've all sat through lengthy presentations looking at slides of text and more text. Instead, slides should contain relevant—not gratuitous—visuals. For example, Figure 17.2 shows a visual from the cognitive load presentation. The slide visualizes a chemistry analogy to communicate the relationships among three important components of all learning environments. In addition to graphics, a conversational tone and questions—even rhetorical questions—can promote encoding during the presentation. Finally, I incorporate as many examples as possible to concretize and illustrate main points.

Even with implicit methods like these, I don't expect a great deal of learning from my keynote speeches. For the most part, keynote speeches are not really designed to build knowledge

Figure 17.2. A Slide from a Receptive Presentation Uses a Visual Analogy
Clark and Kwinn, 2007

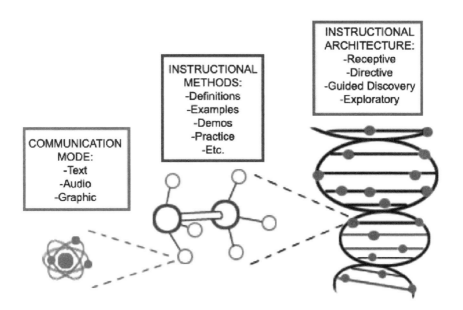

or skills. My goal is to build some awareness – perhaps spark enough interest so that some will pursue the topic at a later time. The bottom line is don't expect much learning from a briefing and don't rely too much on receptive environments when your goal is building expertise that relies on new knowledge and skills.

Transfer. With little learning, it's not realistic to expect much transfer. I do provide some working aids in my handout. For example, participants can use a checklist I include as a reminder of cognitive load techniques they can apply. Many conference organizers require presenters to include a working aid as part of their handout as a transfer-enhancer.

Metacognitive Skills. Similarly, I doubt that receptive environments will do much to build skills in goal setting, selection of strategies, or monitoring. Building metacognitive skills will require a much more learner centered architecture.

In short, receptive environments have some limits when it comes to learning. They are likely overused in many training settings that would be better served by more interactive architectures. However, we know that learning is based on mental activities—not physical activities. Therefore, well-designed receptive environments that promote those psychological learning events can be effective. In fact, for learners with relevant background knowledge, brief lectures have been shown to result in as much or more learning as formats with greater physical activity (Haidet, Morgan, O'Malley, Moran, & Richards, 2004; Mayer & Suhre, 2007).

Sample 2: A Directive e-Lesson

I had the opportunity to work with John Sweller and Frank Nguyen to design a demonstration lesson on Excel that would illustrate cognitive load principles in our book *Efficiency in Learning* (Clark, Nguyen, & Sweller, 2006). The lesson is a self-study asynchronous e-lesson on how to construct formulas in Excel.

How It Works

The Excel lesson starts with a pre-test to guide learners to lesson topics that are unfamiliar to them. One of the big advantages of self-study e-learning is the opportunity to increase instructional efficiency of heterogeneous audiences by guiding individuals to topics and lessons based on their prior knowledge. Following the pre-test, the lesson presents learning objectives and introduces Barb's Bargain Basement Boutique—a small business that will serve as a context for the various spreadsheet examples and exercises in the lesson.

The first part of the lesson applies content segmenting and pre-training principles by teaching key concepts prior to the

Figure 17.3. Directive Design for Excel Lesson

From Clark, Nguyen, and Sweller, 2006

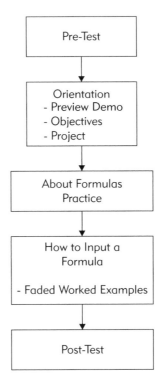

main procedure of inputting a formula into a spreadsheet. For example, the concepts of Excel operators and formula formats are taught first. We used faded worked examples to illustrate construction of formulas to accomplish various calculations for Barb's small business. We made the examples more interactive by adding self-explanation questions to some of the worked steps. Figure 17.3 summarizes the main components of this directive design.

Learning Tradeoffs

Directive lessons draw their strength from excellent management of cognitive load. By keeping lessons and topics brief and including frequent interactions with feedback, you can efficiently train novices to learn procedural skills along with supporting knowledge.

Motivation. It's easy to show relevance in directive lessons by including a "what's-in-it-for me" job-relevant demonstration right in the beginning. This need not be lengthy and, in fact, should not be too detailed. Provide just enough to illustrate the outcomes and benefits of the lesson skills. I think we could have done a better job of this in our sample lesson. Although we do start off with Barb's spreadsheet, we could have used our learning agent to briefly show the advantage Barb gained by quickly updating her calculations through the use of formulas.

Attention and Prior Knowledge. There are many opportunities to sustain attention in a directive lesson through frequent relevant learner responses to questions and exercises. In addition, when teaching procedures that involve complex interfaces such as screens or equipment, use cueing to direct the eye to the relevant portion of the graphic. Cues such as circles or arrows are especially helpful when presenting animated demonstrations of software or equipment.

By tailoring the content to individual prior knowledge through pre-tests, asynchronous e-learning can effectively adapt training to participant background knowledge. In addition, a preview of the job tasks as described under "Motivation" could serve as an advance organizer of the lesson to follow.

Cognitive Load. Mental load management is a major strength of the directive architecture. We segmented our lesson into short topics that preceded the main skill of inputting a formula into a spreadsheet. We explained relevant visuals with audio or with text placed near the graphic. For each topic we included faded worked examples that ended in full practice exercises. We added memory support to initial exercises in the form of reminders of the formula formatting guidelines.

This high level of guidance will replace the schemas that novice learners lack, enabling them to complete lesson tasks. However, for more experienced learners, too much guidance can defeat learning by making the task so easy that they fail to engage. Therefore, you should use high levels of support in beginning lessons, but remove it gradually as your course progresses.

Encoding and Transfer. These two critical processes are also well supported by directive architectures. Encoding is promoted by a combination of implicit methods, such as visuals, learning agents, and examples as well as by explicit methods—notably the frequent practice interactions and self-explanation questions used with worked examples.

You can realistically aim for near or moderate transfer with directive architectures. In our Excel lesson, our goal was moderate transfer. We wanted learners to be able to adapt formulas to various scenarios they might encounter on the job. Barb's Boutique required calculations regarding expenses, income, and inventory—a full range that allowed us to illustrate various operators and formula formats. A project that requires learners to set up a spreadsheet to accomplish their own work-related task would improve transfer even more. Such an assignment would require instructor intervention to review the work. Since our lesson was designed to be self-contained, we did not include a project.

Metacognitive Skills. Directive architectures are better at compensating for lack of metacognitive skills than for building them. Our course used pre-tests to direct learners to knowledge and skills they lacked. There was minimal learner control, as the sequence, examples and exercises were served up as the learner pressed the continue button. Of course, these elements can always be bypassed, but for most learners, who tend follow the default layout of the course, there are few choices.

The directive architecture reflects an instructional design that has been associated with behavioral models of learning since the mid-20th Century. It is not ideal for all goals. However, to teach novices procedural skills most efficiently, it is still your best bet! However, if your goal is deeper learning associated with problem solving and innovative types of expertise, you will need to move beyond directive architectures. Let's look at one alternative— guided discovery!

Sample 3: A Guided-Discovery Classroom Workshop

After reading so much about problem-based learning, I was eager to try it out for myself. Because I teach relatively brief courses (several days rather than semesters), I needed to adapt the problem-based learning approach. I wanted an interactive and effective way to teach the principles from my book *e-Learning and the Science of Instruction* written with Richard Mayer. A combination of problem-based and jig-saw collaborative learning seemed a good way to accomplish my goals. I diagram the class flow in Figure 17.4.

Figure 17.4. A Guided Discovery Collaborative Design

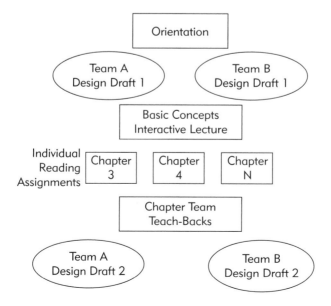

How It Works

Class starts with a brief orientation. I have found that problem-based learning and structured collaboration are unfamiliar to many participants. Therefore, I spend a little up-front time explaining the basic structure and benefits. I then present the learning objective and break the class into teams to prepare a first-draft solution to my case study problem. I allow 45 to 60 minutes for the initial case assignment.

The case consists of some poorly constructed e-learning story-boards. Designing the case required some thought and revision. First, it had to be the right level of challenge and complexity. My pilot versions were too complex for the amount of time available and I arrived at the final version after several revisions and simplifications. Second, the case study storyboards had to communicate the core content of the lesson so that teams could gain a quick understanding of the content they had to teach. The goal of my class is not to learn about the lesson content, but rather it's to focus on how to treat the content effectively. Therefore, I needed a method to communicate the core content efficiently. The storyboards along with a sample test to illustrate desired outcomes serve that purpose. Third, the topic of the case study needed to lend itself to application of the main principles of my lessons, which include visualization of content and inclusion of examples and practice.

After teams complete first drafts of the case lesson, I give an interactive PowerPoint presentation that covers basic concepts presented in the first two chapters of the book. Next I assign a chapter in *e-Learning and the Science of Instruction* to each partic-ipant. I give them about an hour to read the chapter individually and to construct a teaching aid. After my pilot sessions, I found that I obtained better results if I gave specific directions about what should be on the teaching aid as well as posted an example of an effective aid.

Following the individual chapter readings, I assemble participants into chapter teams. Thus, everyone who read Chapter 3, for example, meets as a team. The chapter teams have twenty minutes to compare their individual teaching aids and construct a common aid for a class presentation. Next, each chapter team makes a ten-minute presentation on the principles of their chapter. In total, all the presentations take around forty-five to fifty minutes. I augment the team presentations with any important points that need more emphasis.

Finally, the design teams reconvene, review their first draft case study storyboards, and edit them by applying the principles. At this stage, I pass out a checklist as a working aid of evidence-based practices in e-learning.

Learning Tradeoffs

Guided-discovery classes are fun to design and to teach. But they can be challenging for instructors (and students) who are used to an instructor-centered approach. Instructors may feel they are not doing their job because they are not "in control" of the content of the class. Participants may feel they are cheated by not hearing a lecture. Some of these perceptions are culture-specific. I recall complaints from a guided discovery type class I taught in Scandinavia. The participants wanted to learn directly from the expert—NOT through an experience with their colleagues. However, for goals of building moderate- to far-transfer learning that emphasize problem-solving skills, well-designed guided-discovery learning environments offer better opportunities than either a straight receptive or directive architecture.

Motivation. One of the strengths of problem-based learning is motivation! Research has shown that, although medical students may score equally well on knowledge tests, those who take a problem-based curriculum like it better! No doubt starting the class with a job-relevant case study along with the collaborative discussions immediately positions learning as relevant and interactive. A good recipe for learner commitment!

Attention and Prior Knowledge. Engagement in a job-relevant problem that offers the right level of challenge will, like a good game, support attention. In addition, the collaborative work has been shown to activate relevant prior knowledge.

Cognitive Load. One of the challenges of any form of guided discovery can be mental overload. Having to learn while at the same time solving a problem can impose too much on working memory. Therefore, guided discovery is most safely used with more experienced learners—say workers at a journeyman level. Alternatively, guided-discovery lessons can be supported with various learning aids commonly called scaffolds to manage the "flounder factor." Some examples of scaffolds I include are a case problem that is not too complex, heterogeneous design teams that evenly distribute more experienced participants among the teams, worked examples of a teaching aid to help participants organize their chapter readings, as well as clear directions regarding activities, deliverables, and time frames for each activity.

Encoding and Transfer. In this workshop, participants are actively engaged in job-relevant activity about 80 percent of the time. Discussing a design problem, reading a chapter while constructing a teaching aid, doing a teach-back, and revising their first draft solutions all offer explicit encoding opportunities.

The goal of the workshop is moderate transfer. In my certification program, I promote transfer by requiring participants to complete a post-class project in which participants apply the workshop principles in the workshop to their own e-learning assignments.

Additionally, I support transfer with a checklist of techniques created by the participants during the teach back sessions.

Metacognitive Skills. Problem-based learning designs offer solid opportunities to build metacognitive skills. I believe this is a facet of my workshop that I could improve. For example, I could add some "think-aloud" models of a course designer applying the principles in various situations. I could also ask design teams to consider their project and problem-solving process as well as their output. My main excuse is lack of time. I have chosen to stress the main content of the book rather than the back story of design rationale. But I suspect that many other instructional professionals also lack time and that collectively we need to weigh the tradeoffs between content coverage and building creative and critical thinking skills.

Problem-Based Learning Benefits

In summary, I have found a structured problem-based collaborative design works well for learners with some background in the target skills. The case study and the diverse collaborative activities provide a motivational context for learning. Learning success depends on (1) designing a case problem that will support the learning objectives given your constraints of time and resources, (2) structuring the class design and delivery in ways that keep participants engaged in productive activities that will support problem solution, and (3) providing ready access to supporting resources that will guide case study solution.

Exploratory Architectures for Far-Transfer Learning

As a result of my business framework and audience, I have not had the opportunity to work with exploratory architectures.

Yet I believe they have high potential as we face the challenges of building resources that encourage creative and critical thinking. Here are some thoughts on how these might play out.

Start with a design or problem assignment. Creative thinking must occur in a context—a context that allows for application of guidelines to either solve a problem or design some job-relevant artifact. The goal is not so much the solutions or designs per se—although a secondary benefit might be some useful products. Rather, the goal is to apply domain-specific techniques that leverage creative idea alternatives, along with implementation and critical evaluation of their effectiveness. *Action learning* that involves small team work on real organizational challenges is one potential model of this type of instruction.

Assemble diverse expertise in the team. A challenge that all experts face is conceptual fixation on ideas and solutions that arise from their developed schemas. For example, cardiologists tended to recommend a cardiac solution even when the problem really was not related to cardiology (Chi, 2006). Multidisciplinary teams working together on the same assignment offer an opportunity to cross-pollinate the schemas of any one expert. We are learning more about how to best leverage expertise in work teams.

Incorporate worked examples that apply problem-solving heuristics appropriate to the domain. Traditional worked examples focus on the overt steps and decisions behind a standard solution in a given domain. However, creative and critical thinking will benefit from worked examples that stress metacognitive processes—the back story behind successful innovation. The back story will typically require some form of cognitive task analysis because experts can rarely articulate the full and accurate thinking and monitoring processes they use during problem solving.

Provide access to varied resources. Innovation will rely not so much on use of a prescribed set of concepts and guidelines but on the ability to access and adapt resources within and outside organizations. Internet and intranet skills will play an important role. Being aware of available resources, both technical and personal, being able to subject such resources to critical evaluation, and to apply them to unfamiliar problems are the new soft skills of the adaptive expert of the future.

Maintain a library of problem or design solutions that illustrate both process and product outcomes. Lessons learned from a new product design or a problem resolution are lost unless some knowledge management effort is invested to capture and store them. For example, in a problem-based learning course I designed for intelligence analysts, learners were required to apply course techniques to their own work in a project. By recording those projects and housing them in an online repository, lessons learned became available to the broader community.

A Final Word

Expertise in all its forms is the bedrock of economic competitiveness in the 21st Century. As professionals who are responsible for the growth and deployment of expertise in organizations, I hope you are able to adapt the guidelines in this book to your own instructional environments. Your observations and suggestions are welcome. Please contact me at Ruth@Clarktraining.com.

REFERENCES

Anderson, J.R., Farrell, R., & Sauers, R. (1984). How subject matter knowledge affects recall and interest. *American Educational Research Journal*, 31, 313–337.

Anderson, L.W., & Torrey, P. (1995). Instructional pacing. In L.W. Anderson (Ed.), *International encyclopedia of teaching and teacher education* (2nd ed.). New York: Elsevier.

Atkinson, R.K., & Renkl, A. (2007). Interactive example-based learning environments: Using interactive elements to encourage effective processing of worked examples. *Educational Psychology Review, 19*, 375–386.

Atkinson, R.K., Renkl, A., & Merrill, M.M. (2003). Transitioning from studying examples to solving problems: Effects of self-explanation prompts and fading worked out steps. *Journal of Educational Psychology, 95*(4), 774–783.

Ausubel, D.P. (1968). *Educational psychology: A cognitive view*. New York: Holt, Rinehart and Winston.

Ausubel, D.P., & Youssef, M. (1963). The role of discriminability in meaningful parallel learning. *Journal of Educational Psychology, 54*, 331–336.

Azevedo, R., & Cromley, J.G. (2004). Does training on self-regulated learning facilitate students' learning with hypermedia? *Journal of Educational Psychology, 96*, 523–535.

Baddeley, A.D., & Logie, R.H. (1999). Working memory: The multiple component model. In A. Miyake& P. Shah (Eds.),

Models of working memory: Mechanisms of active maintenance and executive control. New York: Cambridge University Press.

Bahrick, H.P. (1987). Retention of Spanish vocabulary for eight years. *Journal of Experimental Psychology: Learning, Memory, and Cognition, 13,* 344–349.

Benton, S.L., Kiewra, K.A., Whitefill, J.M., & Dennison, R. (1993). Encoding and external-storage effects on writing processes. *Journal of Educational Psychology. 85*(2), 267–280.

Bernard, R.M., Abrami, P.C., Lou, Y., Borokhovski, E., Wade, A., Wozney, L., Wallet, P.A., Fishet, M., & Huang, B. (2004). How does distance education compare with classroom instruction? A meta-analysis of the empirical literature. *Review of Educational Research, 74*(3), 379–439.

Bielaczyc, K., Pirolli, P., & Brown, A.L. (1995). Training in self-explanation and self-regulation strategies: Investigating the effects of knowledge acquisition activities on problem solving. *Cognition and Instruction, 13,* 221–253.

Bransford, J.D., Barron, B., Pea, R.D., Meltzoff, A., Kuhl, P., Bell, P., Stevens, R., Schwartz, D.L., Vye, N., Reeves, B., Roschelle, J., & Sabelli, N.H. (2006). Foundations and opportunities for an interdisciplinary science of learning. In R.K. Sawyer (Ed), *The Cambridge handbook of the learning sciences.* New York: Cambridge University Press.

Bransford, J.D., & Johnson, M.K. (1972). Contextual prerequisites for understanding: Some investigations of comprehension and recall. *Journal of Verbal Learning and Verbal Behavior, 11,* 717–726.

Brewer, N., Harvey, S., & Semmler, C. (2004). Improving comprehension of jury instructions with audio-visual presentation. *Applied Cognitive Psychology, 18,* 765–776.

Brophy, J., & Good, T.L. (1986). Teacher behavior and student achievement. In M.C. Wittrock (Ed.), *Handbook of research on teaching* (3rd ed.). New York: Macmillan.

Brunye, T.T., Taylor, H.A., Rapp, D.N., & Spiro, A.B. (2006). Learning procedures: The role of working memory in multimedia learning experiences. *Applied Cognitive Psychology, 20*, 917–940.

Butcher, K.R. (2006). Learning from text with diagrams: Promoting mental model development and inference generation. *Journal of Educational Psychology, 98*, 182–197.

Campbell, J.P., & Oblinger, D.G. (2007). Top-ten teaching and learning issues, 2007. *Educause Quarterly, 30*(3), 15–22.

Caroll, J.M. (1992). Minimalist documentation. In H.D. Stolovitch & E.J. Keeps (Eds.), *Handbook of human performance technology.* San Francisco, CA: Jossey-Bass.

Cattell, R.B. (1943). The measurement of adult intelligence. *Psychological Bulletin, 40*, 153–193.

Cattell, R.B. (1963). Theory of fluid and crystallized intelligence: A critical experiment. *Journal of Educational Psychology, 54*, 1–22.

Cavalier, J.C., & Klein, J.D. (1998). Effects of cooperative versus individual learning and orienting activities during computer-based instruction. *ETR&D, 46*(1), 5–17.

Cerpa, N., Chandler, P.L., & Sweller, J. (1996). Some conditions under which integrated computer-based training software can facilitate learning. *Journal of Educational Computing Research, 14*(4), 344–367.

Chao, C., & Salvendy, G. (1994). Percentage of procedural knowledge acquired as a function of the number of experts from whom knowledge is acquired for diagnosis, debugging, and interpretation tasks. *International Journal of Human-Computer Interaction*, 6(3), 221–233.

Chase, W.G., & Simon, H.A. (1973). Perception in chess. *Cognitive Psychology, 4*, 55–81.

Cherry, E.C. (1953). Some experiments on the recognition of speech with one and two ears. *Journal of the Acoustical Society of America, 25*, 975–979.

Chi, M.T.H. (2000). Self-explaining expository texts: The dual processes of generating inferences and repairing mental models. In R. Glaser (Ed.), *Advances in instructional psychology: Educational design and cognitive science.* Mahwah, NJ: Lawrence Erlbaum Associates.

Chi, M.T.H. (2006). Two approaches to the study of experts' characteristics. In K.A. Ericsson, N. Charness, P.J. Feltovich, & R.R. Hoffman (Eds.), *The Cambridge handbook of expertise and expert performance.* New York: Cambridge University Press.

Chi, M.T.H., DeLeeuw, N., Chiu, M., & LaVancher, C. (1994). Eliciting self-explanations improves understanding. *Cognitive Science, 18*, 439–477.

Chi, M.T.H., Feltovich, P.J., & Glaser, R. (1981). Categorization and representation of physics problems by experts and novices. *Cognitive Science, 5*, 121–125.

Clark, R.C. (2000). Four architectures of learning. *Performance Improvement, 39*, 31–38.

Clark, R.C. (2008). *Developing technical training* (3rd ed.). San Francisco, CA: Pfeiffer.

Clark, R.C., & Kwinn, A. (2007). *The new virtual classroom.* San Francisco, CA: Pfeiffer.

Clark R.C., & Lyons, C. (2004). *Graphics for learning.* San Francisco, CA: Pfeiffer.

Clark, R.C., & Mayer, R.E. (2008). *e-Learning and the science of instruction* (2nd ed.). San Francisco, CA: Pfeiffer.

Clark, R.C., Nguyen, F., & Sweller, J. (2006). *Efficiency in learning*. San Francisco, CA: Pfeiffer.

Clark, R.E. (1994). Media will never influence learning. *Educational Technology Research and Development, 42*(2), 21–30.

Cohen, E.G. (1994). Restructuring the classroom: Conditions for productive small groups. *Review of Educational Research, 64*(1), 1–35.

Cosmides, L., & Tooby, J. (1996). Are humans good intuitive statisticians after all? Rethinking some conclusions from the literature on judgment under uncertainty. *Cognition, 58*, 1–73.

Craig, S.D., Sullings, J., Witherspoon, A., & Gholson, B. (2006). The deep-level reasoning question effect: The role of dialogue and deep-level reasoning questions during vicarious learning. *Cognition and Instruction, 24*(4), 565–591.

Craig, F.I.M., & Watkins, M.J. (1973). The role of rehearsal in short-term memory. *Journal of Verbal Learning and Verbal Behavior, 12*, 599–607.

Crandall, B., Klein, G., & Hoffman, R.R. (2006). *Working minds*. Cambridge, MA: Massachusetts Institute of Technology.

Crossman, E.R. F.W. (1959). A theory of the acquisition of speed skill. *Ergonomics, 2*, 153–166.

David, P.A., & Foray, D. (2003). Economic fundamentals of the knowledge society. *Policy Futures in Education, 1*(1), 20–49.

de Bruin, A.B.H., Rikers, R.M.J.P., & Schmidt, H.G. (2007). The effect of self-explanation and prediction on the development of principled understanding of chess in novices. *Contemporary Educational Psychology, 32*, 188–205.

deKoning, B.B., Tabbers, H.K., Rikers, R.M.J.P., & Paas, F. (2007). Attention cueing as a means to enhance learning from an animation. *Applied Cognitive Psychology, 21*, 731–746.

Dewey, J. (1916). *Democracy and education.* New York: Macmillan.

Dickey, M.D. (2005). Engaging by design: How engagement strategies in popular computer and video games can inform instructional design. *Educational Technology Research and Development, 53*(2), 1042–1629.

Dochy, F., Segers, M., & Buehl, M.M. (1999). The relation between assessment practices and outcomes of studies: The case of research on prior knowledge. *Review of Educational Research, 69*(2), 145–186.

Dochy, F., Segers, M., Van den Bossche, P., & Gijbels, D. (2003). Effects of problem-based learning: A meta-analysis. *Learning and Instruction, 13*, 533–568.

Dolmans, D.H.J.M., & Schmidt, H.G. (2006). What do we know about cognitive and motivational effects of small group tutorials in problem-based learning? *Advances in Health Sciences Education, 11*, 321–336.

Dunker, K. (1945). On problem solving. *Psychological Monographs, 58*, 270.

Eccles, J.S.,& Wigfield, A. (2002). Motivational beliefs, values, and goals. *Annual Review of Psychology, 53*, 109–132.

Ericcson, K.A. (2006). The influence of experience and deliberate practice on the development of superior expert performance. In K.A. Ericsson, N. Charness, P.J. Feltovich, & R.R. Hoffman. (Eds.), *The Cambridge handbook of expertise and expert performance.* New York: Cambridge University Press.

Ericsson, K.A., Charness, N., Feltovich, P.J., & Hoffman, R.R. (Eds.). (2006). *The Cambridge handbook of expertise and expert performance.* New York: Cambridge University Press.

Ericsson, K.A. (1990). Theoretical issues in the study of exceptional performance. In K.J. Gilhooly, M.T.G. Keane, R.H. Logie, & G. Erdos (Eds.), *Lines of thinking: Reflections on the psychology of thought* (Vol. 2). Mahwah, NJ: Lawrence Erlbaum Associates.

Eva, K.W., Cunnington, J.W., Reiter, H.I., Keane, D.R., & Norman, G.R. (2004). How can I know what I don't know? Poor self-assessment in a well-defined domain. *Advances in Health Sciences Education, 9*, 211–224.

Feldon, D.F. (2007). The implications of research on expertise for curriculum and pedagogy. *Educational Psychology Review, 19*, 91–110.

Gagne, R.M. (1985). *The conditions of learning and theory of instruction* (4th ed.). New York: Holt, Rinehart and Winston.

Gall, M.D., & Artero-Bonare, M.T. (1995). Questioning. In L.W. Anderson (Ed.), *International encyclopedia of teaching and teacher education.* New York: Elselevier.

Garner, R., Gillingham, M., & White, C. (1989). Effects of seductive details on macroprocessing and microprocessing in adults and children. *Cognition and Instruction, 6*, 41–57.

Gentner, D., Loewenstein, J., & Thompson, L. (2003). Learning and transfer: A general role for analogical encoding. *Journal of Educational Psychology, 95*(2), 393–408.

Gibbons, C. (2007, December 29). Professionals take work out of their workplaces. *The Arizona Republic*, D1.

Glenberg, A.M., Sanocki, T., Epstein, W., & Morris, C. (1987). Enhancing calibration of comprehension. *Journal of Experimental Psychology: General, 116*(2), 119–136.

Glenberg, A.M., Wilkinson, A.C., & Epstein, W. (1992). The illusion of knowing: Failure in the self-assessment of comprehension. In T.O. Nelson (Ed.), *Metacognition: Core readings.* Boston, MA: Allyn and Bacon.

Gholson, B., & Craig, S.D. (2006). Promoting constructive activities that support vicarious learning during computer-based instruction. *Educational Psychology Review, 18*, 119–139.

Gick, M.L., & Holyoak, K.J. (1980). Analogical problem solving. *Cognitive Psychology, 12*, 306–355.

Gick, M.L., & Holyoak, K.J. (1983). Schema induction and analogical transfer. *Cognitive Psychology, 15*, 1–38.

Ginns, P. (2005). Meta-analysis of the modality effect. *Learning and Instruction, 15*, 313–331.

Gott, S.P., & Lesgold, A.M. (2000). Competence in the workplace: How cognitive performance models and situated instruction can accelerate skill acquisition. In R. Glaser (Ed.), *Advances in instructional psychology: Educational design and cognitive science.* Mahwah, NJ: Lawrence Erlbaum Associates.

Greene, J.A., & Azevedo, R. (2007). A theoretical review of Winne and Hadwin's model of self-regulated learning: New perspectives and directions. *Review of Educational Research, 77*, 334–372.

Grudowski, M. (2003). The girl next door is hungry. *Men's Journal, 12*(7), 72–73.

Gurlitt, J., Renkl, A., Motes, M.A., & Hauser, S. (2006). How can we use concept maps for prior knowledge activation:Different mapping tasks lead to different cognitive processes. *In Proceedings of the 7th International Conference on Learning Sciences,* 217–221.

Hacker, D.J., Bol, L., Horgan, D.D., & Rakow, E.A. (2000). Test prediction and performance in a classroom context. *Journal of Educational Psychology, 92*(1), 160–170.

Haidet, P., Morgan, R.O., O'Malley, K., Moran, B.J., & Richards, B.F. (2004). A controlled trial of active versus passive learning strategies in a large group setting. *Advances in Health Sciences Education, 9,* 15–27.

Hale, J. (2000). *Performance-based certification.* San Francisco, CA: Pfeiffer.

Hall, W.E., & Cushing, J.R. (1947). The relative value of three methods of presenting learning material. *Journal of Psychology, 24,* 57–62.

Hamilton, P., Hockey, G.R.J., & Rejman, M. (1977). The place of the concept of activation in human information processing theory: An integrative approach. In S. Dornic (Ed.), *Attention and performance.* Mahwah, NJ: Lawrence Erlbaum Associates.

Hannafin, M.J., Hannafin, K.M., Land, S.M., & Oliver, K. (1997). Grounded practice and the design of constructivist learning environments. *Educational Technology Research and Development, 45,* 101–117.

Harp, S.F., & Mayer, R.E. (1997). The role of interest in learning from scientific text and illustrations: On the distinction between emotional interest and cognitive interest. *Journal of Educational Psychology, 89*(1), 92–102.

Harp, S.F., & Mayer, R.E. (1998). How seductive details do their damage: A theory of cognitive interest in science learning. *Journal of Educational Psychology, 90*(3), 414–434.

Harskamp, E.G., Mayer, R.E., & Suhre, C. (2007). Does the modality principle for multimedia learning apply to science classrooms? *Learning & Instruction, 17,* 465–477.

Haskell, R.E. (2001). *Transfer of learning: Cognition, instruction, and reasoning.* New York: Academic Press.

Hidi, S.E. (1995). A re-examination of the role of attention in learning from text. *Educational Psychology Review, 7*(4), 323–350.

Hidi, S., & Renninger, K.A. (2006). The four-phase model of interest development. *Educational Psychologist, 41*(2), 111–127.

Hmelo-Silver, C.E. (2004). Problem-based learning: What and how do students learn? *Educational Psychology Review, 16*(3), 235–266.

Hmelo-Silver, C.E., Duncan, R.G., & Chinn, C.A. (2007). Scaffolding and achievement in problem-based and inquiry learning: A response to Kirschner, Sweller, and Clark (2006). *Educational Psychologist, 42*(2), 99–107.

Hummel, H.G.K., Paas, F., & Koper, B. (2006). Effects of cueing and collaboration on the acquisition of complex legal skills. *British Journal of Educational Psychology, 76*, 613–631.

Independent Commission on the Los Angeles Police Department. (1991). *Report of the Independent Commission on the Los Angeles Police Department.* Los Angeles, CA: Author.

Industry Report—2007. (2007). *Training, 44*(10), 9–24.

Issenberg, S.B., McGaghle, W.C., Petrusa, E.R., Gordon, D.L., & Scalese, R.J. (2005). Features and uses of high fidelity medical simulations that lead to effective learning: a BEME systematic review. *Medical Teacher, 27*(1), 10–29.

Jeung, H., Chandler, P., & Sweller, J. (1997). The role of visual indicators in dual sensory mode instruction. *Educational Psychology, 17*(3), 329–343.

Johnson, D.W., & Johnson, R.T. (1992). *Creative controversy: Intellectual challenge in the classroom.* Edina, MN: Interaction Book Company.

Johnson, D.W., Johnson, R.T., & Smith, K. (2007). The state of cooperative learning in postsecondary and professional settings. *Educational Psychology Review, 19*, 15–20.

Jonassen, D.H. (2003). *Learning to solve problems: An instructional design guide.* San Francisco, CA: Pfeiffer.

Kalyuga, S. (2007). Expertise reversal effect and its implications for learner-tailored instruction. *Educational Psychology Review, 19*, 509–539.

Kalyuga, S., Ayres, P., Chandler, P., & Sweller, J. (2003). The expertise reversal effect. *Educational Psychologist, 38*(1), 23–31.

Kamin, C.S., O'Sullivan, P.S., Deterding, R., & Younger, M. (2003). A comparison of critical thinking in groups of third-year medical student sin text, video, and virtual PBL case modalities. *Academic Medicine, 78*(2), 204–211.

Keehner, M., Lippa, Y., Montello, D.R., Tendick, F., & Hegary, M. (2006). Learning a spatial skill for surgery: How the contribution of abilities change with practice. *Applied Cognitive Psychology, 20*, 487–503.

Kenz, I., & Hugge, S. (2002). Irrelevant speech and indoor lighting: Effects of cognitive performance and self-reported affect. *Applied Cognitive Psychology, 15*, 709–718.

Kieras, D.E., & Bovair, S. (1984). The role of a mental model in learning to operate a device. *Cognitive Science, 8*, 255–273.

Kiewra, K.A. (1989). A review of note-taking: The encoding storage paradigm and beyond. *Educational Psychology Review, 1*, 147–172.

Kirschner, P.A., Sweller, J., & Clark, R.E. (2006). Why minimal guidance during instruction does not work: An analysis of the failure of constructivist, discovery, problem-based, experiential, and inquiry-based teaching. *Educational Psychologist, 41*(2), 75–86.

Kloster, A.M., & Winne, P.H. (1989). The effects of different types of organizers on students' learning from text. *Journal of Educational Psychology, 81*(1), 9–15.

Kobayashi, K. (2005). What limits the encoding effect of note-taking? A meta-analytic examination. *Contemporary Educational Psychology, 30*, 242–262.

Kumta, S.M., Psang, P.L., Hung. L.K., & Chenge, J.C.Y. (2003). Fostering critical thinking skills through a web-based tutorial programme for first year medical students—A randomized controlled study. *Journal of Educational Multimedia and Hypermedia, 12*(3), 267–273.

Lee, H., Plass, J.L., & Homer, B.D. (2006). Optimizing cognitive load for learning from computer-based science simulations. *Journal of Educational Psychology, 98,* 902–913.

LeFevre, J.A., & Dixon, P. (1986). Do written instructions need examples? *Cognition and Instruction, 3,* 1–30.

Ley, K., & Young, D.B. (2001). Instructional principles for self-regulation. *Educational Technology Research and Development, 49*(2), 93.

Lin, A., Hmelo, C., Kinzer, C.K., & Secules, T.J. (1999). Designing technology to support reflection. *Educational Technology Research and Development, 47,* 43–62.

Locke, E.A., & Latham, G.P. (2002). Building a practically useful theory of goal setting and task motivation: A 35-year odyssey. *American Psychologist, 57*(9), 705–717.

Lou, Y., Abrami, P.C., & d'Apollonia, S. (2001). Small group and individual learning with technology: A meta-analysis. *Review of Educational Research, 71*(3), 449–521.

Malone, T.W., & Lepper, M.R. (1987). Making learning fun: A taxonomy of intrinsic motivations for learning. In R.E. Snow & M.J. Farr (Eds.), *Aptitude, learning and instruction.* Mahwah, NJ: Lawrence Erlbaum Associates.

Mamede, S., Schmidt, H.G., & Norman, G.R. (2006). Innovations in problem-based learning: What can we learn from recent studies? *Advances in Health Sciences Education, 11,* 403–422.

Marcus, N., Cooper, M., & Sweller, J. (1996). Understanding instructions. *Journal of Educational Psychology, 88*(1), 49–63.

Mautone, P.D., & Mayer, R.E. (2001). Signaling as a cognitive guide in multimedia learning. *Journal of Educational Psychology, 93*(2), 377–389.

Mayer, R.E. (1983). Can you repeat that? Qualitative and quantitative effects of repetition and advance organizers on learning from science prose. *Journal of Educational Psychology, 75*, 40–49.

Mayer, R.E. (1999). *Instructional technology.* In F.T. Durson (Ed.), *Handbook of applied cognition* (pp. 551–569). Hoboken, NJ: John Wiley & Sons.

Mayer, R.E. (2001). *Multimedia learning.* Cambridge, UK: Cambridge University Press.

Mayer, R.E. (2002). *The promise of educational psychology volume II: Teaching for meaningful learning* (pp. 127–137). Upper Saddle River, NJ: Merrill/Prentice Hall.

Mayer, R.E. (2004). Should there be a three-strikes rule against pure discovery learning: The case for guided methods of instruction. *American Psychologist, 59*(1), 14–19.

Mayer, R.E. (Ed.) (2005). *The Cambridge handbook of multimedia learning.* New York: Cambridge University Press.

Mayer, R.E. (2008). *Learning and instruction* (2nd ed.). Upper Saddle River, NJ: Pearson Merrill Prentice Hall.

Mayer, R.E., Bove, W., Bryman, A., Mars, R., & Tapangco, L. (1996). When less is more: Meaningful learning from visual and verbal summaries of science textbook lessons. *Journal of Educational Psychology, 88*(1), 64–73.

Mayer, R.E., & Chandler, P. (2001). When learning is just a click away: Does simple user interaction foster deeper understanding of multimedia messages? *Journal of Educational Psychology, 93*(2), 390–397.

Mayer, R.E., & Gallini, J.K. (1990). When is an illustration worth ten thousand words? *Journal of Educational Psychology, 88*, 64–73.

Mayer, R.E., Hegarty, M., Mayer, S., & Campbell, J. (2005). When static media promote active learning: Annotated illustrations versus narrated animations in multimedia instruction. *Journal of Experimental Psychology: Applied, 11,* 256–265.

Mayer, R.E., & Jackson, J. (2005). The case for coherence in scientific explanations: quantitative details can hurt qualitative understanding. *Journal of Experimental Psychology: Applied, 11,* 13–18.

Mayer, R.E., Mathias, A., & Wetzell, K. (2002). Fostering understanding of multimedia messages through pre-training: Evidence for a two-stage theory of mental model construction. *Journal of Experimental Psychology: Applied, 8*(3), 147–154.

Mayer, R.E., & Moreno, R. (1998). A split-attention effect in multimedia learning: Evidence for dual processing systems in working memory. *Journal of Educational Psychology, 90,* 312–320.

Mayer, R.E., Sims, V., & Tajika, H. (1995). A comparison of how textbooks teach mathematical problem solving in Japan and the United States. *American Educational Research Journal, 32,* 443–460.

Mayer, R.E., & Wittrock, M.C. (2006). Problem-solving transfer. In D.C. Berliner& R.C. Calfee (Eds.), *Handbook of educational psychology.* New York: Simon & Schuster/Macmillan.

McCrudden, M.T., & Schraw, G. (2007). Relevance and goal-focusing in text processing. *Educational Psychology Review, 19,* 113–139.

McCrudden, M.T., Schraw, G., & Kambe, G. (2005). The effect of relevance instructions on reading time and learning. *Journal of Educational Psychology, 97*(1), 88–102.

McKinsey & Co. (2005). The emerging global market. Cited in R. Uhalde & J. Strohl, *America in the global economy.* Washington, DC: National Center on Education and the Economy.

McNamara, D.W., Kintsch, E., Songer N.B., & Kintsch, W. (1996). Are good texts always better? Interactions of text coherence, background knowledge, and levels of understanding in learning from text. *Cognition and Instruction, 14*(1), 1–43

Means, T.B., Jonassen, D.H., & Dwyer, F.M. (1997). Enhancing relevance: Embedded ARCS strategies vs. purpose. *Educational Technology Research and Development, 45*(1), 5–17.

Miller, G.A. (1956). The magical number seven, plus or minus two: Some limits on our capacity for processing information. *Psychological Review, 63,* 81–97.

Moreno, R. (2004). Decreasing cognitive load for novice students: Effects of explanatory versus corrective feedback in discovery-based multimedia. *Instructional Science, 32,* 99–113.

Moreno, R., & Mayer, R.E. (1999). Cognitive principles of multimedia learning: The role of modality and contiguity. *Journal of Educational Psychology, 91,* 358–368.

Moreno, R., & Mayer R.E. (2000a). A coherence effect in multimedia learning: The case for minimizing irrelevant sounds in the design of multimedia instructional messages. *Journal of Educational Psychology, 92*(1), 117–125.

Moreno, R., & Mayer, R.E. (2000b). Engaging students in active learning: The case for personalized multimedia messages. *Journal of Educational Psychology, 92*(4), 724–733.

Moreno, R., & Mayer, R.E. (2002). Verbal redundancy in multimedia learning: When reading helps listening. *Journal of Educational Psychology, 94,* 156–163.

Moreno, R., & Mayer, R.E. (2004). Personalized messages that promote science learning in virtual environments. *Journal of Educational Psychology, 96,* 165–173.

Moreno, R., & Mayer, R.E. (2005). Role of guidance, reflection, and interactivity in an Agent-based multimedia game. *Journal of Educational Psychology, 97*(1), 117–128.

Moreno, R., Mayer, R.E., Spires, H., & Lester, J.C. (2001). The case for social agency in computer-based teaching: Do students learn more deeply when they interact with animated pedagogical agents? *Cognition and Instruction, 19*, 177–214.

Morrison, R.G. (2005). Thinking in working memory. In K.J. Holyoak & R.G. Morrison (Eds.), *The Cambridge handbook of thinking and reasoning.* New York: Cambridge University Press.

Mousavi, S., Low, R., & Sweller, J. (1995). Reducing cognitive load by mixing auditory and visual presentation modes. *Journal of Educational Psychology, 87,* 319–334

Nadolski, R.J., Krischner, P.A., van Merrienboer, J.J.G., & Hummel, H.G.K. (2001). A model for optimizing step size of learning tasks in competency-based multimedia practicals. *Educational Technology Research and Development, 49*(3), 87–103.

Natter, H.M., & Berry, D.C. (2005). Effects of active information processing on the understanding of risk information. *Applied Cognitive Psychology, 19,* 123–135.

National Research Council. (1991). D. Druckman & R.A. Bjork (Eds.), *In the mind's eye: Enhancing human performance.* Washington, DC: National Academy Press.

Newby, T.J., Ertmer, P.A., & Stepich, D.A. (1995). Instructional analogies and the learning of concepts. *ETR&D, 43*(1), 5–18.

Nietfeld, J.L., Finney, S.J., Schraw, G., & McCrudden, M.T. (2007). A test of theoretical models that account for information processing demands. *Contemporary Educational Psychology, 32,* 499–515.

Norman, G.R. (2004). Editorial: Beyond PBL. *Advances in Health Sciences Education, 9,* 257–260.

Paas, F.G., & van Merrienboer, J.G. (1996). Variability of worked examples and transfer of geometrical problem-solving skills:

A cognitive load approach. *Journal of Educational Psychology, 86*(19), 122–123.

Paivio, A. (1986). *Mental representations: A dual coding approach.* Oxford, England: Oxford University Press.

Perkins, D.N., & Salomon, G. (1989). Are cognitive skills context bound? *Educational Researcher, 18*(1), 16–25.

Peterson, L.R., & Peterson, M.J. (1959). Short-term retention of individual verbal items. *Journal of Experimental Psychology, 58,* 193–198.

Pintrich, P.R. (2003). A motivational science perspective on the role of student motivation in learning and teaching contexts. *Journal of Educational Psychology, 95,* 667–686.

Potelle, H., & Routet, J.F. (2003). Effects of content representation and readers' prior knowledge on the comprehension of hypertext. *International Journal of Human Computer Studies, 58,* 327–345.

Pressley, M., Wood, E., Woloshyn, V.E., Martin, V., King, A., & Menke, D. (1992). Encouraging mindful use of prior knowledge: Attempting to construct explanatory answers facilitates learning. *Educational Psychologist, 27*(1), 91–109.

Prins, F.J., Sluijsmans, D.M.A., & Kirschner, P.A. (2006). Feedback for general practitioners in training: Quality, styles, and preferences. *Advances in Health Sciences Education, 11,* 289–303.

Qin, A., Johnson, D.W., & Johnson, R.T. (1995). Cooperative versus competitive efforts and problem solving. *Review of Educational Research, 65*(2), 129–143.

Quilici, J.L., & Mayer, R.E. (1996). Role of examples in how students learn to categorize statistics word problems. *Journal of Educational Psychology, 88*(1), 144–161.

Ransdell, S.E., & Gilroy, L. (2001). The effects of background music on word processed writing. *Computers in Human Behavior, 17*, 141–148.

Renkl, A., Mandl, H., & Gruber, H. (1996). Inert knowledge: Analyses and remedies. *Educational Psychologist, 3*(2), 115–121.

Renkl, A., Stark, R., Gruber, H., & Mandl, H. (1998). Learning from worked-out examples: The effects of example variability and elicited self-explanations. *Contemporary Educational Psychology, 23*, 90–108.

Richart, R., & Perkins, D.N. (2005). Learning to think: The challenges of teaching thinking. In K.J. Holyoak & R.G. Morrison (Eds.), *The Cambridge handbook of thinking and reasoning.* New York: Cambridge University Press.

Rickards, J.P., Fajen, B.R., Sullivan, J.F., & Gillespie, G. (1997). Signaling, note-taking, and field independence-dependence in text comprehension and recall. *Journal of Educational Psychology, 89*(3), 508–517.

Robbins, S.B., Lauver, K., Le, H., Davis, D., Langley, R., & Carlstrom, A. (2004). Do psycho-social and study skill factors predict college outcomes? A meta-analysis. *Psychological Bulletin, 130*(2), 261–288.

Rohrer, D., & Taylor, K. (2006). The effects of over learning and distributed practice on the retention of mathematics knowledge. *Applied Cognitive Psychology, 20,* 1209–1224.

Rosenbaum, D.A., Carlson, R.A., & Gilmore, R.O. (2001). Acquisition of intellectual and perceptual-motor skills. *Annual Review of Psychology, 52,* 453–470.

Rosenshine, B., & Stevens, R. (1986). Teaching functions. In M.C. Wittrock (Ed.), *Handbook of research on teaching* (3rd ed.). New York: Macmillan.

Rothkopf, E.Z., & Billington, M.J. (1979). Goal-guided learning from text: Inferring a descriptive processing model from inspection times and eye movements. *Journal of Educational Psychology, 71,* 310–327.

Rouet, J.F., & Potelle, H. (2005). Navigational principles in multimedia learning. In R.E. Mayer (Ed.), *The Cambridge handbook of multimedia learning.* New York: Cambridge University Press.

Sadoski, M. (2001). Resolving the effects of concreteness on interest, comprehension, and learning important ideas from text. *Educational Psychology Review, 13*(3), 263–281.

Sadoski, M. Goetz, E.T., & Fritz, J.B. (1993). Impact of concreteness on comprehensibility, interest, and memory for text: Implications for dual coding theory and text design. *Journal of Educational Psychology, 85*(2), 291–304.

Sadoski, M., Goetz, E.T., & Rodriguez, M. (2000). Engaging texts: Effects of concreteness on comprehensibility, interest, and recall in four text types. *Journal of Educational Psychology, 92*(1), 85–95.

Schar, S.G., & Zimmermann, P.G (2007). Investigating means to reduce cognitive load from animations: Applying differentiated measures of knowledge representation. *Research on Technology in Education, 40,* 64–78.

Schmidt, H.G., Loyens, S.M.M., van Gog, T., & Paas, F. (2007). Problem-based learning is comparable with human cognitive architecture: Commentary on Krischner, Sweller, and Clark (2006). *Educational Psychologist, 42*(2), 91–97.

Schmidt, H.G., & Moust, J.H.C. (2000). Factors affecting small-group tutorial learning: A review of research. In D.H. Evensen & C.E. Hmelo (Eds.), *Problem-based learning.* Mahwah, NJ: Lawrence Erlbaum Associates.

Schnackenberg, H.L., & Sullivan, H.J. (2000). Learner control over full and lean computer-based instruction under differing ability levels. *Educational Technology Research and Development, 48*(2), 19–35.

Schnackenberg, H.L. Sullivan, H.J., Leader, L.R., & Jones, E.E.K. (1998). Learner preferences and achievement under differing amounts of learner practice. *Educational Technology Research and Development, 46*(2) 5–15.

Schnotz, W., & Kurschner, C. (2007). A reconsideration of cognitive load theory. *Educational Psychology Review, 19,* 469–508.

Schoenfeld, A.H. (1987). What's all the fuss about metacognition? In A. Schoenfeld (Ed.), *Cognitive science and mathematics education.* Mahwah, NJ: Lawrence Erlbaum Associates.

Schraw, G. (2006). Knowledge: Structures and processes. In P.A. Alexander & P.H. Winne (Eds.), *Handbook of educational psychology* (2nd ed.). Mahwah, NJ: Lawrence Erlbaum Associates.

Schraw, G., & Lehman, S. (2001). Situational interest: A review of the literature and directions for future research. *Educational Psychology Review, 13*(1), 2001.

Schunk, D.H., & Zimmerman, B.J. (2006). Competency and control beliefs: Distinguishing the means and ends. In P. A. Alexander & P. H. Winne (Eds.), *Handbook of educational psychology.* Mahwah, NJ: Lawrence Erlbaum Associates.

Schwartz, D.L., & Bransford, J.D. (1998). A time for telling. *Cognition and Instruction, 16*(4), 475–522.

Shapiro, A.M. (2005). The site map principle in multimedia learning. In R.E. Mayer (Ed.), *The Cambridge handbook of multimedia learning.* New York: Cambridge University Press.

Simon, H.A., & Gilmartin, K. (1973). A simulation memory for chess positions. *Cognitive Psychology, 5,* 29–46.

Slotte, V., & Lonka, K. (1999). Review and process effects of spontaneous note-taking on text comprehension. *Contemporary Educational Psychology, 24,* 1–20.

Spelke, E.S., Hirst, W.C., & Neisser, U. (1976). Skills of divided attention. *Cognition, 4,* 215–230.

Spira, J.B. (2005, September). The high cost of interruptions. *KM World.*

Springer, L., Stanne, M.E., & Donovan, S.S. (1999). Effects of small-group learning on undergraduates in science, mathematics, engineering, and technology: A meta-analysis. *Review of Educational Research, 69*(1), 21–51.

Srinivasan, M., Wilkes, M., Stevenson, F., Nguyen, T., & Slavin, S. (2007). Comparing problem-based learning with case-based learning: Effects of a major curricular shift at two institutions. *Academic Medicine, 82,* 74–82.

Stark, R., Mandl, H., Gruber, H., & Renkl, A. (2002). Conditions and effects of example elaboration. *Learning and Instruction, 12,* 39–60.

Stepich, D.A., & Newby, T.J. (1988). Analogizing as an instructional strategy. *Performance and Instruction, 27*(9), 21–23.

Stern, E., Aprea, C., & Ebner, H.G. (2003). Improving cross-content transfer in text processing by means of active graphical representation. *Learning & Instruction, 13,* 191–203.

Sternberg, R.J. (1996). Attention and consciousness. In *Cognitive psychology.* New York: Harcourt Brace.

Stone, N.J. (2000). Exploring the relationship between calibration and self-regulated learning. *Educational Psychology Review, 4,* 437–475.

Strunk, W., & White, E.B. (2000). *The elements of style* (4th ed.). Boston, MA: Allyn and Bacon.

Stull, A.T.& Mayer, R.E. (2007). Learning by doing versus learning by viewing: Three experimental comparisons of learner-generated versus author-provided graphic organizers. *Journal of Educational Psychology, 99* (4), 808–820.

Svinicki, M.D. (2007). Moving beyond "It worked": The ongoing evolution of research on problem-based learning in medical education. *Educational Psychology Review, 19,* 49–61.

Sweller, J. (2005). *Implications of cognitive load theory for multimedia learning.* In R.E. Mayer (Ed.), *The Cambridge handbook of multimedia learning.* New York: Cambridge University Press.

Sweller, J., Chandler, P., Tierney, P., & Cooper, M. (1990). Cognitive load as a factor in the structuring of technical material. *Journal of Experimental Psychology: General, 119,* 176–192.

Sweller, J., & Cooper, G.A. (1985). The use of worked examples as a substitute for problem solving in learning algebra. *Cognition and Instruction, 2,* 59–89.

Sweller, J., Kirschner, P.A., & Clark, R.E. (2007). Why minimally guided teaching techniques do not work: A reply to commentaries. *Educational Psychologist, 42*(2), 115–121.

Sweller, J., van Merrienboer, J.J.G., & Paas, F. (1998). Cognitive architectures and instructional design. *Educational Psychology Review, 10*(3), 251–296.

Tallent-Runnels, M.K., Thomas, J.A., Lan, W.Y., Cooper, S., Ahern, T.C., Shaw, S.M., & Liu, X. (2006). Teaching courses online: A review of the research. *Review of Educational Research, 76*(1), 93–135.

Taylor, R.S., & Chi, M.T.H. (2006). Simulation versus text: Acquisition of implicit and explicit information. *Journal of Educational Computing Research, 35*(3), 289–313.

Thorndike, E.L. (1932). *The fundamentals of learning.* New York: Teachers College Press.

Thorndike, E.L., & Woodworth, R.S. (1901). The influence of improvement in one mental function upon the efficiency of other functions. *Psychological Review, 8,* 247–261.

Thiagarajan, S. (2006). *Thiagi's 100 favorite games.* San Francisco, CA: Pfeiffer.

Tindall-Ford, S., Chandler, P., & Sweller, J. (1997). When two sensory modes are better than one. *Journal of Experimental Psychology: Applied, 3*(4), 257–287.

Tobin, K. (1987). The role of wait time in higher cognitive level learning. *Review of Educational Research, 57*(1), 69–95.

Tollefson, N. (2000). Classroom applications of cognitive theories of motivation. *Educational Psychology Review, 12*(1), 63–81.

Uhalde, R., & Strohl, J. (2006). *America in the global economy: A background paper for the new commission on the skills of the American workforce.* Washington, DC: National Center on Education and the Economy.

Valaitis, R.G., Sword, W.A., Jones, B., & Hodges, A. (2005). Problem-based learning online: Perceptions of heath science students. *Advances in Health Sciences Education, 10,* 231–252.

Van den Broek, P., Risden, K., Tzeng, Y., Trabasso, T., & Brasche, P. (2001). Inferential questioning: Effects of comprehension of narrative texts as a function of grade and timing. *Journal of Educational Psychology, 93*(3), 521–529.

Van Gog, T., Paas, F., & van Merrienboer, J.J.G. (2004). Process-oriented worked examples: Improving transfer performance through enhanced understanding. *Instructional Science, 32,* 83–98.

van Merroenboer, J.J.G. (1997). *Training complex cognitive skills.* Englewood Cliffs, NJ: Educational Technology Publications.

van Merrienboer, J.J.G., & Croock, M.B.M. (2002). Performance-based ISD: 10 steps to complex learning. *Performance Improvement, 41*(7), 33–38.

van Merrienboer, J.J.G., & Kester, L. (2005). The four-component instructional design model: Multimedia principles in environments for complex learning. In R.E. Mayer (Ed.), *The Cambridge handbook of multimedia learning.* New York: Cambridge University Press.

van Merrienboer, J.J.G., Kester, L., & Pass, F. (2006). Teaching complex rather than simple tasks: Balancing intrinsic and germane load to enhance transfer of learning. *Applied Cognitive Psychology, 20,* 343–352.

van Merrienboer, J.J.G., & Sweller, J. (2005). Cognitive load theory and complex learning: Recent developments and future directions. *Educational Psychology Review, 17,* 147–177.

Vansteenkiste, M., Simons, J., Lens, W., Soenens, B., Matos, L., & Lacante, M. (2004). Less is sometimes more: Goal content matters. *Journal of Educational Psychology, 96*(4), 755–764.

Vernon, D.T., & Blake, R.L. (1993). Does problem-based learning work? A meta-analysis of evaluative research. *Academic Medicine, 68,* 550–563.

Violato, C., & Lockyer, J. (2006). Self and peer assessment of pediatricians, psychiatrists, and medicine specialists: Implications for self-directed learning. *Advances in Health Sciences Education, 11,* 235–244.

Wacker, M.B., & Silverman, L.L. (2003). *Stories trainers tell.* San Francisco, CA: Pfeiffer.

Wang, M.C., Haertel, G.D., & Walberg, H.J. (1993). Toward a knowledge base for school learning. *Review of Educational Research, 63(3),* 249–294.

Weiner, B. (2000). Intrapersonal and interpersonal theory of motivation from an attribution perspective. *Educational Psychology Review, 12*(1), 1–14.

Weisberg, R.W. (2006). Modes of expertise in creative thinking: Evidence from case studies. In K.A. Ericsson, N. Charness, P.J. Feltovich, & Hoffman, R.R. (Eds.), *The Cambridge handbook of expertise and expert performance.* New York: Cambridge University Press.

Wiley, J., & Voss, J.F. (1999). Constructing arguments form multiple sources: Tasks that promote understanding and not just memory for text. *Journal of Educational Psychology, 91*(2), 301–311.

Woodward, A. (1993). Do illustrations serve an instructional purpose in U.S. textbooks? In B.K. Britton, A. Woodward, & M. Binkley (Eds.), *Learning from textbooks: Theory and practice* (pp. 115–134). Mahwah, NJ: Lawrence Erlbaum Associates.

Zimmerman, B.J. (2006). Development and adaptation of expertise: The role of self-regulatory processes and beliefs. In K.A. Ericsson, N. Charness, P.J. Feltovich, & R.R. Hoffman (Eds.), *The Cambridge handbook of expertise and expert performance.* New York: Cambridge University Press.

Absorption view of learning	A belief that learning occurs when students are exposed to content rather than actively processing it. A metaphor is student as a sponge and instruction as a pitcher of water. Related to a transmission view of teaching. Some receptive architectures reflect an absorption view of learning
Action learning	A form of project-based learning in which workplace teams take on real-world organizational problems or design challenges and use the process as a vehicle for learning.
Activation of prior knowledge	A learning process in which relevant schemas stored in long-term memory are brought into working memory prior to learning to facilitate integration of new content with existing knowledge.
Active processing	A belief that learning occurs when students engage in appropriate mental processing during learning, such as attending to relevant materials, responding to practice exercises, reflecting on examples.
Adaptive expertise	Flexible expertise that can be used to solve novel unfamiliar problems. Expertise that

supports creative problem solving by invoking new approaches to solving unfamiliar problems. Compare to routine expertise.

Advance organizer   A learning aid placed in the introductory phases of a learning event designed to activate or supply prior knowledge relevant to the lesson content. The goal is to bring relevant schema in long-term memory into consciousness in working memory. See also comparative and expository organizers.

Agents   Onscreen characters who help guide the learning process during an e-learning episode. Also called pedagogical agents.

Analogy   A learning aid that invokes a comparison between two objects or sets of objects (a familiar object and a to-be-learned object) that share structural, functional, or causal similarities.

Animation   A graphic that depicts movement such as a video of a procedure or a moving sequence of line drawings

Architecture   A course or lesson design that varies regarding the amount and type of structure, guidance, and response opportunities included in the lesson. Examples are receptive, directive, guided discovery, and exploratory.

Argumentation   An activity whereby one or more participants formulate reasons and evidence for a given position. Often argumentation can be focused around pro and con rationale for a controversy or policy.

Arousal theory	The idea that adding entertaining and interesting material to lessons stimulates emotional engagement that promotes learning. Arousal theory is the rationale for adding emotional situational interest to lessons.
Asynchronous collaborations	Opportunities for learners and/or instructors to interact with each other via computer at different times, such as in a discussion board or email.
Asynchronous e-learning	Digitized instructional resources intended for self-study. Learners can access on-line training resources any time and any place.
Attainment value	A belief that achieving an instructional goal will promote individual career or personal goals. Refers to the personal importance a learner assigns to achieving an instructional goal.
Attention	A psychological process that supports allocation of mental resources to a limited amount of information from the vast amount available to us in the environment and in our memories. One of the fundamental events of learning.
Attention support principle	Help learners optimize attentional resources during learning by maximizing capacity, focusing attention to important elements of the instruction and minimizing dividing attention among related content elements displayed in physically separate locations.
Attribution	A reason given by a performer for the outcome of their learning efforts. For example, when failing a test a learner may give themselves the reason that they were unlucky or that they did

not study hard enough. Attributions to controllable causes are generally more productive than
attributions to uncontrollable causes. See attribution theory.

Attribution theory   A motivational set of principles that predicts
persistence in learning as a result of learner's
interpretations of outcomes of learning results
to causes that are internal or external or
controllable or uncontrollable.

Auditory channel   Part of the human memory system that
processes information that enters through the
ears and is mentally represented in the form of
sounds.

Automaticity   A stage of learning in which knowledge or skills
can be applied directly from long-term memory
without using working memory capacity. Some
tasks that are commonly automatic include
driving a car, typing, and reading. Knowledge
becomes automatic only after many repetitions.

**Behavioral view
of learning**   A belief that learning is mediated by the
accrual of many small associations between
instructional questions and learner responses
strengthened by reinforcements or rewards.
Programmed learning was one of the early
instructional models that reflected a behavioral
learning view. Directive architectures reflect
a behavioral view of learning. Also known as a
response-strengthening view of learning.

Beliefs   Opinions or ideas that learners hold about
themselves, the value of achieving a task, or
their interest in a topic that are the basis of
motivation to learn.

Building mental models principle

Helping learners psychologically engage with content supports learning through constructing new mental models in long-term memory.

Calibration

The accuracy of self-estimates of knowing. If a learner estimates low knowledge and scores low on a test he or she has good calibration; similarly, if he or she estimates high knowledge and scores high on a test it indicates good calibration.

Case-based learning

An instructional strategy in which learning is initiated with review and discussion of a domain-specific authentic situation or problem. In contrast to problem-based learning, case-based learning is more structured, often requires pre-work assignments, and encourages a more directive role of the group facilitator.

Cause and effect mental model

A memory structure that is the basis for understanding how a system works.

Chunk

Groups of content or data that can be held as one element in working memory. Optimal chunk size depends on schema in long-term memory. More experienced learners with developed schemas can form large chunks.

Cognitive apprenticeship

An instructional model in which learning occurs through engagement with real-world problems under the direction and supervision of a more skilled practitioner. Cognitive apprenticeships may be set up in face-to-face classrooms or digital self-study learning environments.

Cognitive learning theory

An explanation of how people learn based on the idea of dual channels (information is processed in visual and auditory channels), limited

	capacity (only a small amount of information can be processed in each channel at one time), and active learning (meaningful learning occurs when learners pay attention to relevant information, organize it into a coherent structure, and integrate it with what they already know).
Cognitive load	The amount of mental work imposed on working memory during learning. Some forms of cognitive load are irrelevant and should be avoided, while others that are productive benefit learning.
Cognitive situational interest	A source of motivation stemming from learners' ability to make sense of the instructional materials. As a result of understanding the lesson, the learner experiences enjoyment. Contrast with emotional situational interest.
Cognitive support	Any instructional method that aids in a critical psychological learning process, such as cues that direct attention or practice exercises that promote rehearsal, encoding, and retrieval. Also called a learning aid.
Cognitive task analysis	Techniques used to define the thinking processes used by experts during real-world problem solution. One technique is asking experts to talk aloud while solving a problem.
Coherence effect	Refers to the benefits of training that minimizes content to the essential elements needed for learning. Less is more. Lessons that violate coherence impose irrelevant cognitive load during learning.
Coherence principle	People learn more deeply from multimedia lessons when distracting stories, graphics,

sounds, and extraneous words are eliminated. See coherence effect.

Collaborative learning principle	A structured instructional interaction among two or more learners to achieve a learning goal or complete an assignment can benefit learning. An example is structured controversy.
Comparative advance organizer	Familiar content in the form of text or graphics presented prior to a lesson that helps learners relate new unfamiliar ideas to it. May serve as an analogy. Ausbel's comparison of Buddhism to Christianity is a classic example.
Computer-supported collaborative learning (CSCL)	Any instructional program in which two or more individuals work together on an instructional activity or assignment using digital technology to communicate.
Concept	Lesson content that represents object or idea categories with common core features and variable irrelevant features. Some examples are computer, lesson, integrity.
Conceptual simulations	A model of a scientific or technological system that operates on the basis of principles or cause-and-effect relationships. For example, a genetics simulation shows changes in organisms when the user alters the genes or an ecological simulation shows the effects of various environmental changes on living populations. Contrast with operational simulations.
Considerate materials	Instructional materials that are high in cognitive interest as a result of clear expression of ideas and various techniques used to minimize irrelevant cognitive load.

Constructive view of learning
The belief that learning occurs through the active building of new mental models as the result of integrating new lesson content with existing knowledge in long-term memory. Widely accepted as the valid mechanism of learning. See also cognitive learning theory.

Contiguity principle
People learn more deeply when corresponding printed words and graphics are placed close to one another on the screen or when spoken words and graphics are presented at the same time. Applying the contiguity principle reduces irrelevant cognitive load.

Control
A comparison lesson that does not include the variable being studied in the treatment lesson in a research experiment. For example, a text-only lesson is a control compared to a lesson that adds graphics to the text.

Controlled studies
Research comparing the learning outcomes and/or processes of two or more groups of learners made up of individuals randomly assigned to different lesson versions; the groups are the same except for the variable(s) being studied. Also called experimental studies.

Conversational style
A writing style that uses first- and second-person constructions, active voice, and speech-like phrases. Conversational style has been shown to be an implicit learning aid that leads to productive cognitive load.

Corrective feedback
Instructional responses to learner answers to a practice exercise that tell the learners whether they answered correctly or incorrectly. Contrast with explanatory feedback.

Correlational evidence	Evidence based on observed associations between two or more variables. For example, a survey of experts finds that those with higher levels of expertise devote more daily time to practice. Correlations suggest relationships, but do not prove causality. Contrast with experimental evidence.
Course map	A type of menu or concept map that graphically represents the structure of an online course or lesson. Course maps have been shown to influence how learners organize learning content.
Creative thinking	Production of multiple ideas or solutions to novel, ill-defined problems of relatively high complexity.
Criterion–referenced learning	Instructional environments and measures in which each learner's progress is evaluated against a common criteria rather than the outcomes of other learners. Leads to mastery learning goals.
Critical thinking	The evaluation of ideas, sources, or solutions that are proposed as potential resources or solutions to unusual problems or to product design.
Crystallized intelligence	Intelligence that stems from learned knowledge and skills such as reading and mathematics and forms the basis for routine expertise.
Cueing	A physical visual or auditory technique used to draw attention to content relevant to the instructional goal. For example, a circle drawn around an important element in a complex graphic will draw the learner's attention to that element. Cueing techniques support selective attention.

Declarative knowledge   Schemas in long-term memory that represent facts and concepts. For example, concepts such as transportation, animals, and software are based on declarative memories. Declarative knowledge is easy to articulate and explain to others.

Decorative graphics   Visuals used for aesthetic purposes or to add humor such as clip art of two people talking in a lesson on communication.

Deep structures   The principle or concept that underlies an example, problem, or task. For example, a convergence principle underlies the solution to a tumor problem. Contrast with surface features. See also varied context.

Deliberate practice   A planned regiment of exercises that fall just outside the learner's level of competence focusing on specific skill gaps. Typically assigned by a teacher or coach and tailored to the individual performer. The type of practice that leads to high levels of expertise.

Dependent variable   The outcome measures in an experimental study. In many learning experiments, a test score is the dependent variable.

Design   The stage in course production in which a blueprint specifies the content sequence and main instructional methods. May be communicated with outlines, flow charts, learning objectives, and storyboards

Development   The stage in course production in which the learning materials such as workbooks, online screens, and case studies are created.

Diagnostic assessment	Tests that help learners and instructors identify specific knowledge and skill deficiencies during learning episodes.
Digit span	The number of numbers an individual can recall without memory aid. Most digit spans fall in a range of seven plus or minus two.
Directive architecture	An instructional design in which small content segments are followed by some type of practice exercise with feedback. Also called show-and-do method or rule-example-practice method. Based on a behavioral theory of learning.
Discovery learning	Experiential exploratory instructional interfaces that offer little structure or guidance.
Disruption	A process that interferes with the organization of new content in memory as a result of irrelevant content interfering with formation of new mental models.
Distraction	A process that interferes with the selection process by taking learner focus away from important instructional content or methods.
Distributed cognition	The idea that expertise can reside in multiple sources such as in a database, a working aid, a colleague, or a training course.
Distributed practice	Exercises that are placed throughout a lesson or course, rather than all in one location. Long-term learning is better under conditions of distributed practice. Also called spaced practice. Compare to massed practice.
Divided attention	The phenomena of trying to split attention across modes or media in a learning

environment. For example, when text explains a visual on the back of the page one is reading, attention is split by trying to mentally integrate the text and visual. Divided attention should be minimized during learning.

Domain   A specific arena of expertise such as medicine, basketball, or mathematics.

Drag and drop   A facility that allows the user to move objects from one part of the screen to another. Often used in e-learning practice exercises.

Drill and practice   A type of instructional activity that involves repetition of facts or skills many times until they become automated in memory. For example, repeated practice exercises in typing result in fast and accurate "touch" typing.

Dual channels   A psychological principle stating that humans have two separate channels for processing visual/pictorial material and auditory/verbal material.

Dual encoding   The idea that viewing a graphic representation and reading text about that representation results in two memory codes rather than only one and thus leads to deeper levels of learning.

Dual task experiment   A research technique in which the subject is asked to perform two simultaneous tasks. For example, the subject may be asked to read a lesson and respond periodically to a tone by pressing a computer key. Often used to assess the cognitive load of the primary task by measuring the response time to the secondary task.

Effect size   A statistic indicating the proportion of standard deviations difference between the mean score of the experimental group and the mean score of the control group. A useful metric to determine the practical significance of research results. Effect sizes of less than .2 are considered small, .5 moderate, and .8 or greater large.

Elaborative exercise   A practice activity that leads to elaborative rehearsal.

Elaborative rehearsal   A type of mental activity in which new knowledge and skills are actively processed with existing schema to result in application level learning. For example, learners solve case studies or engage in role plays. Contrast with maintenance rehearsal.

e-Learning   A combination of content and instructional methods delivered by media elements such as words and graphics on a computer intended to build job-transferable knowledge and skills linked to individual learning goals or organizational performance. May be designed for self-study or instructor-led training. See asynchronous and synchronous e-learning.

Emotional situational interest   A source of motivation stemming from lesson treatments that induce arousal in learners, such as dramatic visuals or stories. See also seductive details. Contrast with cognitive situational interest.

Encoding   Integration of new lesson information entering working memory into long-term memory for permanent storage in mental models.

Encoding specificity   A principle of memory stating that people are better able to retrieve information if the conditions at the time of original learning are similar to the conditions at the time of retrieval. For example, to enable learning of a new computer system, learners should practice in training with the same system they will use on the job so that they encode memories that are identical to the performance environment. See also identical elements transfer model.

Examples
Instances of lesson concepts, procedures, processes, or principles. See also worked example.

Expectancy-value theory
A set of motivational principles that predict selection and persistence of a learning goal based on the perceived value or worth of achieving the goal as well as on confidence that with effort, the learner will be successful.

Experimental evidence
Research conclusions based on randomly assigning a group of learners to two or more different learning environments, each of which has a different independent variable. For example, one group studies a lesson with text only while a second group studies the same lesson with text plus graphics. Experimental evidence suggests a causal relationship between the variable and the outcome. Contrast with correlational evidence.

Expertise
A person with extensive knowledge or ability in a particular area of study. Someone widely recognized as a reliable source of technique or skill.

Expertise reversal effect
Instructional methods that are helpful to novice learners may have no effect or even depress learning of high-knowledge learners.

Explanatory feedback   Instructional responses to student answers to practice exercises that tell the learners whether they are correct or incorrect and also provide the rationale or a hint guiding the learners to a correct answer. For example, "Not quite. You forgot to square the value of the radius before multiplying."

Explanatory visual   A graphic that helps learners build relationships among content elements. Includes the organizational, relational, transformational, and interpretive types of visuals.

Explicit methods   Instructional techniques that enable psychological learning processes through overt learner activity. A practice exercise or questions directed to learners are two common explicit instructional methods.

Exploratory architectures   An instructional design that allows high learner control and relies on the learners to select instructional resources they need.

Expository advance organizer (preview)   An instructional technique that provides learners with a high-level introduction to the content of a lesson to come. Site maps and outlines may serve as expository advance organizers.

Extraneous processing load   Irrelevant mental work during learning that results from ineffective instructional design of the lesson. Also called irrelevant cognitive load.

Extrinsic goal   A focus on achieving a specific learning outcome to gain an external reward such as a grade, self-image, or monetary gain. Contrast with intrinsic goal.

Fact	Lesson content that includes unique and specific information or data. For example, the codes to log into a system or a specific application screen.
Fading	An instructional technique in which learners move from fully worked examples to full practice exercises through a series of worked examples in which the learners gradually complete more of the steps.
Far-transfer tasks	Tasks that require learners to apply what they have learned in a situation that differs from the learning context, such as adjusting a general principle to resolve a new problem, for example, how to troubleshoot an unusual system failure or how to write a sales proposal. See also strategic knowledge. Also called a non-routine or strategic task.
Feedback	Information concerning the correctness of one's performance on a learning task or question. May also include explanations to guide learners to a correct response.
Fluid intelligence	A type of raw intelligence that *is not* the result of learned knowledge and skills. Fluid intelligence is an important element of adaptive expertise and creative thinking. Fluid intelligence underlies revision of existing problem-solving strategies, search for analogies, and other innovative approaches to problems or design work.
Formal discipline transfer model	The idea that training in a specific skill set will pay off in transfer to an unrelated set of skills. For example, study of Latin will boost general

mental muscle for studying languages or learning to solve insight puzzle problems will build job-specific analytic skills. Evidence does not support the formal disciple transfer model.

Four-component instructional design

An instructional design model proposed by Van Merrienboer that emphasizes a task-centered approach to designing lessons for training of complex cognitive skills.

Game

An environment that involves a competitive activity with a challenge to achieve a goal, a set of rules and constraints, and a specific context. Game features vary dramatically, including games of chance, games based on motor skills (also called twitch games), and games of strategy.

Generative processing

Relevant mental work during learning directed at deeper understanding of the content that stems from the motivation of the learner to make sense of the material or from productive sources of cognitive load.

Goal orientation

A focus of the learner's attention and effort on self-progress over time or on outperforming others. See mastery and performance goal orientations.

Graphic

Any iconic representation, including illustrations, drawings, charts, maps, photos, organizational visuals, animation, and video. Also called visual representation.

Grounded design

The practice of considering valid evidence when making instructional decisions.

Guided discovery architecture

An instructional design in which the learner is assigned an authentic job task or case study, along with guidance from the instructional environment about how to process the incoming information. Problem-based and case-based learning are two examples of guided discovery.

Heterogeneous groups   Learners who differ regarding prior knowledge, job background, culture, or other significant features. Contrast with homogeneous.

Homogeneous groups   Learners who are similar regarding prior knowledge, job background, culture, or other significant features. Contrast with heterogeneous.

Identical elements transfer model   The idea that the cues of retrieval must be embedded at the time of learning and therefore only learning environments that closely match the performance environment will build transferable skills. For example, when learning a new software system, practice environments should emulate the features of the software and its use on the job. There is good evidence for the validity of this model of transfer. See also encoding specificity. Contrast with formal discipline transfer model.

Ill-defined tasks or problems   Scenarios or cases for which there is no one correct answer or approach, for example, designing a website or developing a patient treatment plan. Ill-structured problems are considered best for problem-based learning.

Implicit methods   Instructional methods that promote learning in the absence of overt learner activity. An example is a relevant visual that helps learners build a deeper mental model through a dual encoding mental process. Contrast with explicit methods.

Independent variable   The feature that is studied in an experiment. For example, in a lesson that uses visuals and text that is compared to the same lesson that uses text alone, visuals are the independent variable.

Inductive instructional methods   Training techniques in which learners are pro vided with examples or experiential activities from which they are asked to derive content. For example, learners are provided with a group of well-designed and poorly designed websites and asked to use these samples to derive the features of an effective website. Guided discovery architectures rely more on inductive learning than directive architectures do. Contrast with instructive instructional models.

Inductive methods principle   Use inductive methods whereby learners derive new content from examples and experience when the goal is far-transfer learning and there is sufficient instructional time to support the learning activity.

Inert knowledge   Knowledge and skills that are held in long-term memory schema but which fail to activate in situations for which they could be useful. Many skills learned independently of an application context result in inert knowledge because they fail to be retrieved in an application setting.

Information acquisition   A metaphor of learning that assumes that learners absorb information that is provided to them by the instructor. This metaphor is the basis for receptive architectures of learning.

Information delivery   An explanation of how people learn based on the idea that learners directly absorb new information presented in the instructional environment. Also called the transmission view or the information acquisition view. See also information acquisition.

Instructional component One of three basic elements that make up a training environment, including modes such as text or visuals, methods such as examples and practice, and design architectures.

Instructional feedback Responses given by a trainer or program that may correct and/or offer explanations to learner responses to practice assignments. See also explanatory feedback.

Instructional method A learning aid in a lesson intended to facilitate any of the main psychological processing events that underlie learning, for example, a demonstration, a practice exercise, feedback to practice responses.

Instructional media See media

Instructional mode See mode

Instructive methods Training techniques in which learners are explicitly told rules, definitions, or steps, provided examples, and then asked to practice the new content. Instructive methods are used in directive architectures. Contrast with inductive instructional methods.

Interaction See practice.

Interdependence A condition in collaborative group work in which the rewards of each individual member depend to some degree on the outcomes of each group member. For example, your score on a test is an average of all scores in the group. Has

	been shown to be an important condition for successful collaborative learning.
Integration process	A cognitive process in which visual information and auditory information are connected with each other and with relevant memories from long-term memory.
Interpretive graphics	Visuals used to depict invisible or intangible relationships such as an animation of a bicycle pump that uses small dots to represent the flow of air.
Intrinsic feedback	The natural responses of a system to a learner's action. For example, if the customer receives a rude greeting, her body language and words show disapproval. Most simulations incorporate intrinsic feedback. Contrast with instructional feedback.
Intrinsic goal	A focus on achieving a specific learning outcome based on a core psychological or physical health need, such as competence, affiliation with others, health, or autonomy—goals that are inherently satisfying to the learner. Contrast with extrinsic goal.
Intrinsic value	A belief that achieving an instructional goal is inherently satisfying as a result of personal interest in a topic or enjoyment in the process. Many hobbies are pursued as a result of intrinsic value experienced in the activity.
Irrelevant cognitive load	Mental work imposed on working memory that wastes limited capacity that is more productively devoted to learning. Much irrelevant cognitive load can be minimized by instructional

	design decisions regarding best use of modes and methods such as worked examples.
Jigsaw collaboration	A team learning design in which pairs or small groups each study or research one aspect of a larger problem and then share individual pieces with the entire group in order to solve a problem or complete a learning task.
Job aid	A form of memory support that can be displayed in print or digital media that provides key information needed to perform a job task. Elaborate digital job aids are also known as electronic performance support systems (EPSS).
Job analysis	See task analysis
Journeyman	An individual who can perform routine work unsupervised.
Knowledge construction	A widely accepted view of learning among instructional psychologists that learners are active participants in the building of new knowledge by integrating new lesson content into existing knowledge structures. Cognitive approaches to learning are based on this metaphor.
Law of effect	An instructional principle stating that a reward will strengthen a response to a stimulus. This law serves as the basis for behavioral theories of learning. Proposed by Thorndike in 1932.
Learner control	A condition in which the learner can select or manage elements of the lesson, such as the pacing, topics, sequencing, and instructional methods. Asynchronous e-learning can provide various types of learner control. Contrast with program or instructional control.

Learning agent   An on-screen character used to guide learning in an e-learning episode. See also agent.

Learning aids   Instructional methods that guide or support one or more of the essential psychological events of learning. For example, learning aids may manage cognitive load by providing various forms of guidance during learning. Also called cognitive aids. See also scaffolds.

Learning objective   A statement of a measurable outcome of a learning episode. Learning objectives are an instructional method that support attention and metacognitive monitoring during learning.

Learning styles   The idea that individuals process information in different ways based on some specific mental differences. For example, some learners may have an auditory style and learn better from narration, while others have a visual style and learn better from graphics. There has not been solid or consistent experimental evidence to support learning styles.

Limited capacity   A psychological principle stating that humans have a small capacity in working memory, allowing them to actively process only a few pieces of information in each channel at one time. See also cognitive load.

Link   An object on a screen (text or graphic) that when accessed leads to additional information on the same or on different web pages.

Long-term memory   Part of the cognitive system that stores knowledge and skills in a permanent form.

Maintenance rehearsal A type of mental activity in working memory that involves rote repetition or regurgitation of content. Practice exercises that ask for recall of content promote maintenance rehearsal. Contrast with elaborative rehearsal.

Massed practice Practice exercises that are placed all in one location in a lesson or course. Results in poorer long-term learning than spaced practice. Compare to distributed practice.

Master An expert who can teach others; a member of an elite group of experts whose judgments set regulations, standards, or ideals.

Mastery goals Personal achievement goals that focus on improving one's individual skill level over time rather than any comparison with how others are doing. Contrast with performance goals.

Media element Text, graphics, or sounds used to convey lesson content. See also modes.

Media Any carrier of instructional modes and methods. May include digital technology such as computers as well as traditional formats such as books and instructors.

Mental model A knowledge structure stored in long-term memory that is the basis for expertise. Also called schema.

Mental models transfer model The idea that moderate levels of transfer can be achieved by building a depth of understanding during learning. For example, a learner can troubleshoot an unfamiliar equipment flaw based on an understanding of how the equipment works. Contrast with identical elements and formal discipline transfer models.

Meta-analysis

A statistical technique in which the outcomes from multiple experimental comparisons are synthesized by evaluating effect sizes. Because the recommendations are based on multiple experiments, practitioners can have greater confidence in the results from an effective meta-analysis.

Metacognition

Awareness and control of one's learning or thinking processing that support setting goals, monitoring progress, and adjusting strategies as needed. Also called metacognitive skill and metaskill.

Methods

Instructional techniques that support one or more key learning processes, including attention, rehearsal, encoding, or retrieval. Some examples include examples, practice, feedback, and analogies. Also called instructional methods or learning aids.

Mirror the job principle

Design examples and practice exercises that emulate the job interface and require learners to respond as they would in the work environment. Based on the identical elements transfer principle.

Modality principle

People learn more deeply from multimedia lessons when graphics are explained by audio narration rather than onscreen text. Exceptions include situations in which learners are familiar with the content, are not native speakers of the narration language, or when only printed words appear on the screen.

Modes

The basic communication elements of instruction to include graphics (still and animated), text, and audio. All instructional materials make use of one or more modes to communicate content and provide instructional methods. Also called media elements.

Motivation
Any internal or external factor that prompts a learner to select, initiate, persist, and complete a learning event or achieve a learning goal.

Multimedia presentation
Any presentation containing words (such as narration or onscreen text) and graphics (such as illustrations, photos, animation, or video).

Multimedia principle
People learn more deeply from words and graphics than from words alone. A strongly supported effect recommending that all lessons use a combination of words and visuals for best learning.

Near-transfer tasks
Tasks that require the learner to apply a well-known procedure in the same way as it was learned, for example, how to access your email, how to complete a routine customer order. See also procedures. Also called a routine task.

Novice
Someone with minimal exposure to a given domain or field.

Operational goals
Bottom-line indicators of organizational success such as increased sales, decreased product errors, or increased customer satisfaction.

Operational simulations
A model of a real-world system that looks like and responds like the actual system, for example, a flight simulator. Operational simulations are useful for practice of procedures that are not safe or practical in actual operations.

Organizational graphics
Visuals used to show qualitative relationships among lesson topics or concepts, for example, a tree diagram.

Outcome goal	A focus on the final results of a learning or practice episode, such as a grade or the number of baskets made during shooting practice.
Pedagogical agent	See agents.
Part task practice	An instructional system in which learning is segmented into sections such that elements of a whole task are learned and practiced independently before being integrated. For example, a learner may practice serves in tennis independently of back strokes. Contrast with whole task practice.
Performance analysis	Research to determine factors that will support organizational goals and, when training is one factor, to identify high-level instructional goals.
Performance goals	Achievement goals that are based on doing better than others. For example, a learner wants to receive a higher score or grade than his or her classmates. Contrast with mastery goals.
Personal interest	Motivation to engage in an instructional environment as a result of previous internal interest in a specific topic or knowledge domain. For example, a sports enthusiast reads a poorly crafted article about a team he or she has been following. Contrast with situational interest.
Personalization principle	People learn more deeply from multimedia lessons when learners experience heightened social presence, as when a conversational script or learning agents are included.
Polite speech	Narration that includes courteous phrases.
Power law of practice	Learners become more proficient at a task the more they practice, although the improvement occurs at a logarithmic rate. Greatest

	improvements occur during initial practice exercises, with diminishing improvements over time.
Practical significance	An inference of the real-world applicability of experimental results based on effect size. Effect sizes greater than .5 indicate sufficient magnitude for practitioners to consider applying the experimental results to their training decisions. See also effect size. Contrast with statistical significance.
Practice	Structured opportunities for the learner to engage with the content by responding to a question or taking an action to solve a problem. Also called interaction.
Pre-training principle	People learn more deeply when lessons present key concepts prior to presenting the processes or procedures related to those concepts.
Principle-based lessons	Lessons based on guidelines that must be adapted to various job situations. These lessons teach strategic knowledge, for example, how to close a sale, how to design a web page. See also strategic knowledge or far transfer.
Prior knowledge	The amount of domain-specific knowledge a learner has that is relevant to a lesson. Prior knowledge is the most important individual difference for adaptation of training techniques. See expertise reversal.
Prior knowledge principle	Optimize learning by activating or supplying relevant prior knowledge in the introductory phases of a lesson. See also advance organizer.
Probability	A statistic indicating the chances of erroneously concluding that there is a real difference

between the mean scores of the experimental and control groups. Typically probabilities of .05 or less are considered evidence sufficient to infer real differences in outcomes.

Problem-based learning An instructional strategy in which learners initiate a lesson by discussing or reviewing a domain-relevant authentic case and then acquiring sufficient knowledge to resolve the case. A popular instructional methodology in medical education.

Problem-centered design An instructional plan in which domain-specific case studies are presented in the introductory phases of learning and serve as the kickoff or context for learning new knowledge and skills.

Problem-centered learning A type of learning design in which individuals or groups learn new knowledge and skills while they work to resolve a realistic case scenario or problem. Some examples include problem-based learning and cognitive apprenticeship designs.

Procedural lessons Lessons designed to teach step-by-step skills that are performed the same way each time. See also near transfer.

Procedural knowledge A type of mental model in long-term memory that stores knowledge of how to complete tasks. Procedural memory underlies skills such as driving a car, calculating the area of a rectangle, and cooking a meal.

Process Lesson content that refers to a flow of events such as in a business or scientific process, for example, how new staff are hired, how lightning is formed.

Process worksheet	A template used to guide learners through solution of a realistic problem during a problem- or case-based learning episode. Process worksheets may specify high-level stages of problem solution or pose questions learners should answer as part of their solution process.
Program control	A condition in which the topics, sequencing, instructional methods, and pacing are managed by the instructional environment and not by the learner. Instructor-led sessions generally are presented under program control. Also called instructional control. Contrast with learner control.
Promotive interaction	The design of collaborative group activities to encourage responsibility for each member of the group. For example, a grade should NOT be dependent on the group outcome alone but rather on learning evidence from each member of the group. See also Interdependence.
Receptive architecture	An instructional design that relies primarily on presentation of content without explicit practice opportunities. Also called the show-and-tell method. Briefings or video documentaries are common examples.
Redundant modes	Onscreen text that contains the same words as corresponding audio narration.
Redundancy principle	People learn more deeply from a multimedia lesson when graphics are explained by audio narration alone rather than audio narration and onscreen text. Some exceptions to the redundancy principle involve screens with no visuals

or learners who are not native speakers of the course language.

Reference-based training

An instructional environment in which most facts and procedures are documented in a reference guide (print or online) separate from training materials that include objectives, explanations, case studies, and other exercises. The training materials point learners to the reference guides as needed to complete tasks.

Regurgitative interactions

Practice questions that require learners to repeat content provided in the lesson. Will not generally lead to deep understanding. Also called maintenance rehearsal.

Rehearsal

Active processing of new content in working memory, including mentally organizing the material. Effective rehearsal results in integration of new content with existing mental models in long-term memory.

Relational graphics

Visuals used to summarize quantitative relationships such as bar charts and pie graphs.

Representational graphics

Visuals used to show what an object looks like, such as a computer screen or a piece of equipment.

Retrieval

Transferring information stored in long-term memory to working memory. Also called retrieving process.

Response strengthening

A learning metaphor that focuses on strengthening or weakening of associations based on rewards or punishments provided during the learning event. Is the historical rationale for directive instructional architectures.

Routine expertise   Expertise that effectively solves problems or completes tasks that are commonplace to a specific domain. Contrast with adaptive expertise.

Routine task   See near transfer.

Scaffold   A learning aid that provides guidance to learners. Scaffolds are often used in guided discovery learning architectures to help learners achieve instructional objectives. Some examples of scaffolds include worked examples, hints, and templates.

Schemas   Memories in long-term memory that include knowledge and skills that are the basis for expertise. Also called mental models.

Seductive details   Text or graphics added to a lesson in order to increase the learner's interest but that is not essential to the learning objective.

Segmenting principle   People learn more deeply when content is broken into small chunks and learners can control the rate at which they access the chunks. A good strategy for managing cognitive load stemming from complex content.

Selective attention   A cognitive process in which the learner attends to relevant material in the lesson.

Self-efficacy   The belief that one has the ability to achieve an instructional goal given reasonable invested effort. Similar to the concept of self-confidence.

Self-explanation questions   An instructional technique designed to promote processing of worked examples in which the learner responses to questions asking about worked-out steps.

Self-explanation support principle	Help learners optimize learning from worked examples by requiring them to identify or provide the correct principle underlying a worked-out step.
Self-regulation	A process whereby learners can set learning goals, monitor their progress, invest effort to achieve goals, and adjust tactics as needed. The degree to which learners are metacognitively, motivationally, and behaviorally active participants in their learning.
Sensory memory	Part of the cognitive system that briefly stores visual information received by the eyes and auditory information received by the ears.
Shadowing	An experimental manipulation in which the subject paraphrases back a message read into one ear while a secondary message is read into the other ear. Used to make inferences about selective attention abilities.
Signaling	An instructional technique used to draw attention to critical elements of the instruction. Common techniques include use of arrows, circles, bolding of text, or emphasis in narration.
Signaling principle	Use signals to focus learner attention to relevant content, especially when the materials are complex and/or paced outside the control of the learner.
Simulation	An interactive environment that models a real-world system. Simulations may be conceptual, such as a simulation of genetic inheritance, or operational, such as a flight simulator. See operational simulation and conceptual simulation.

Simulation pacing   The rate at which a learner engages in a
                          simulation. For example, arcade-game types
                          of simulations are fast-paced, whereas strategy
                          games generally move at a slow rate.

Site map   A graphic representation to illustrate the
                          organization of topics or sections of a website.

Situational interest Motivation to engage in an instructional
                          environment as a result of inherent appeal of
                          the interface. For example, you watch a well-
                          crafted documentary because it uses compelling
                          examples and an engaging story line rather than
                          any interest you previously had in the topic.
                          Contrast with personal interest.

Social software   Computer facilities that allow individuals to
                          correspond or collaborate with others. Some
                          examples include wikis, blogs, discussion
                          boards, online conferencing.

**Spaced practice   Delayed learning is better when practice
principle**   opportunities are spread throughout a learn-
                          ing event rather than all in one time or place.
                          Contrast with massed practice. Also called the
                          spacing effect.

**Spatial contiguity   Align related content such as text and pictures
principle**   so that they can readily be seen in one physical
                          location rather than split across pages, screens,
                          or media.

Standard deviation   The degree of dispersion of a group of scores
                          around the average. If most scores are close
                          to the average, the standard deviation is low.
                          Conversely, if the scores are widely dispersed,
                          the standard deviation is large.

Statistical significance	A measure of the probability that the differences in the outcome results in the test and control groups are real and are not a chance difference.
Storyboard	A layout that outlines the content and instructional methods of a lesson, typically used for preview purposes before programming.
Strategic knowledge	Guidelines that help in problem solving or completion of tasks that require judgment and reflection. For example, developing a sales proposal, writing an analytic report. See also far transfer.
Structure emphasizing examples	Worked examples that vary their cover stories to help learners acquire the principles or deep structure of the content. Useful for far-transfer learning. Contrast with surface emphasizing examples. See also varied context.
Structured controversy	A structured collaborative learning structure involving argumentation and synthesis of perspectives.
Summative evaluation	Evaluation of the impact of the courseware conducted at the end of the project; may include cost-benefit analysis.
Surface emphasizing examples	Worked examples that use similar cover stories to illustrate a task. Useful for near but not far-transfer learning. Contrast with structure-emphasizing examples.
Surface features	The cover story of an example or problem. A series of examples on calculation of correlations that all use data about rain and crop growth have similar surface features. See also varied context examples.

Synchronous e-learning	Electronic delivery of instructor-led training available to geographically dispersed learners at the same time. Delivered through specialized software such as WebEx, Elluminate, Adobe Acrobat Professional Connect. Synchronous sessions can be recorded and accessed for asynchronous review after the event. Also called virtual classrooms.
Task analysis	Research to define the knowledge and skills to be included in training, based on observations of performance and interviews of performers.
Technique goal	A focus on a specific methodology used during a learning or practice episode, for example, how to position elbows during basketball shooting practice or how to self-explain examples to gain maximum benefit from them.
Training wheels	A technique introduced by John Carroll in which learners work with software simulations that are initially of limited functionality and progress to higher-fidelity simulations as they master lower-level skills.
Transfer	Application of previously learned knowledge and skills to situations encountered after the learning event. Relies on retrieval of new knowledge and skills from long-term memory during performance.
Transfer appropriate interactions	Activities that require the learners to perform during training as they would on the job. For example, when learning a new computer system, learners practice with case examples and software interfaces that are identical or very similar to the job. See encoding specificity.

Transformational graphics	Visuals used to show changes in time or space such as a weather cycle diagram or an animated illustration of a computer procedure.
Transmission view of teaching	The idea that instruction consists primarily of delivering content. Often associated with a receptive instructional architecture.
Treatment	A variable or factor incorporated in an experimental lesson to determine its impact on learners.
Twitch games	Online games that rely on fast and accurate motor responses on a game device such as a joy stick for success. Various arcade games are typical examples.
Utility value	A belief that achieving an instructional goal will lead to achievement of a future goal of value to the learner such as receiving a promotion, earning more money, and so forth.
Varied context examples and practice	A series of examples or practice exercises with different surface features but that illustrate the same principles. For example, a series of examples illustrating statistical correlations use data related to: rainfall and crop growth, age and weight, and practice time and speed. See also deep structure.
Vicarious learning	Instructional environments that promote building of new mental models by observing the actions or hearing dialogs of others.
Virtual classroom	See synchronous e-learning.
Visible author	A personal style of writing in which the authors reveal information about themselves or about personal perspectives regarding the content.

Visual channel   Part of the human memory system that
                           processes information received through the eyes
                           and mentally represented in pictorial form.

Whole task practice   An instructional plan in which learners practice
                           a task in its entirety usually with some form of
                           help or scaffolding on early attempts. For exam-
                           ple, when learning tennis, all phases are prac-
                           ticed together. Contrast with part-task practice.

Wikis   A website that allows visitors to edit its con-
                           tents. Can be controlled for editing/viewing by
                           a small group or by all.

Worked example   Step-by-step demonstration of how to solve a
                           problem or accomplish a task.

Worked example effect Learning is more efficient when some practice
                           exercises are replaced with worked examples.
                           Studying a worked example offers an efficient
                           way for learners to build new schema.

Working memory   Part of the cognitive system in which the
                           learner actively (consciously) processes incom-
                           ing information from the environment and
                           retrieves information from long-term memory.
                           Working memory has two channels (visual and
                           auditory) and is limited in capacity.

NAME INDEX

A

Abrami, P. C., 18, 223
Adams, H., 313
Ahren, T. C., 17, 18
Anderson, L. W., 119, 186
Aprea, C., 219
Artero-Bonare, M. T., 217
Atkinson, R. K., 221, 222
Ausubel, D. P., 145, 146, 153
Ayers, P., 192
Azevedo, R., 316, 322, 323, 352

B

Baddeley, A. D., 80
Bahrick, H. P., 212
Barnsford, J. D., 149, 151
Barron, B., 150
Baum, L. F., 33
Bell, P., 150
Benton, S. L., 226
Bernard, R. M., 18
Berry, D. C., 219
Bielaczye, K., 330
Billington, M. J., 128
Blake, R. L., 284
Bohr, N., 5
Bol, L., 319
Borokhovski, E., 18
Bovair, S., 189, 190
Bove, W., 94
Bransford, J. D., 13, 150, 152, 153, 159, 247, 315
Bronowski, J., 49

Brophy, J., 119, 124
Brown, A. L., 330
Bryman, A., 94
Buehl, M. M., 139

C

Caen, H., 111
Campbell, J. P., 42, 99
Carlson, R. A., 210
Carlstrom, A., 343
Cattell, R. B., 13, 249
Cavalier, J. C., 128
Cerpa, N., 135
Chandler, P. L., 102, 132, 133, 135, 192
Chao, C., 78
Chenge, J.C.Y., 293
Cherry, E. C., 120
Chi, M.T.H., 8, 12, 186
Chinn, C. A., 307
Chiu, M., 186
Clark, R. C., 95, 97, 98, 134, 154, 156, 158, 181, 273, 325, 345, 368, 369, 392, 393, 397
Clark, R. E., 282, 285, 306
Cohen, E. G., 223
Cooper, G. A., 102
Cooper, M., 104, 105
Cooper, S., 17, 18
Cosmides, L., 219
Coughlin, N., 351
Craig, F.I.M., 206
Craig, S. D., 183, 185

SUBJECT INDEX

A

Absorption learning view, 21–22
Accountability, 116–117
Achievement-learning relationship,
128–129
Action learning, 402
Active engagement strategies
argumentation as, 209
collaborative learning as, 223–226
instructional methods promoting
mental models through, 229
maintenance vs. elaborative rehearsal
as, 205–207
minimizing note-taking as,
226–227
practice exercises as, 207–214,
227–228
promoting psychological engagement
with graphics as, 219–220
providing explanatory feedback as,
214–217
self-explanations as, 220–222*fig*
See also Engagement
Active learning cases
1: lecture vs. problem-based
discussions, 198–199*fig*
2: text reading vs. computer
simulation, 199–200*fig*
3: author-provided vs. learner-
generated graphic organizers,
200–202
Adaptive expertise
description of, 13

domain-specific metacognitive skills
needed for, 327–334
problem solving through, 316
Adaptive experts, 247
Advance organizers
comparative, 145–146, 147*fig*
definition of, 145
expository, 146, 153–155*fig*
features of effective, 146–148
Alzheimer's disease, 80
Analogies
chemistry, 19*fig*
definition of, 187
flashlight, 113–114
providing instructional, 187–189
Animations, 98–100
Apollo 13 problem solving (1970), 315
Architecture. *See* Instructional
architectures
Argumentation, 209
Aristotle, 197
Attainment value, 342
Attention
definition of, 113
directed to lesson elements, 60
directive e-lesson component of, 395
divided, 114, 129–135*fig*
early and late, 113
flashlight analogy of, 113–114
focusing goals to direct, 124–125
guided discovery/problem-based
learning component of, 400
guidelines for managing, 136

Content (*Continued*)
  using familiar terms to present new,
    369–370
  lesson guidelines for presenting, 381,
    382*t*–383*t*
  motivation and interest in, 343–345
  presenting concrete and vivid
    examples of, 367
  promoting explicit self-explanations
    of, 220–222
  transformation into knowledge and
    skills, 54–59
  visuals used to represent spatial,
    104–105*fig*
  working memory and short shelf life
    of new, 69–71
  See also Lessons
Content minimizing
  by avoiding redundant modes, 97–98
  by minimizing animations, 98–100
  by omitting tangential stories and
    visuals, 97, 98*fig*
  by omitting unnecessary audio,
    including music, 95–96
  by omitting unnecessary technical
    details, 94–95*fig*
  by writing concisely, 94
Context-learning relationship, 240–241,
    253–254
Control panel
  interpretive schematic diagram of,
    190*fig*
  as process content example, 189*fig*–191
Creative thinking
  definition of, 234
  failure of training for, 235–236*fig*
  See also Innovation
Criterion-referenced instruction, 364
Critical thinking
  definition of, 234
  problem-centered design focus on, 286
Crystallized intelligence, 13, 249
Culture of transfer, 238–239

D
Declaration knowledge, 52–53
Deliberate practice
  expertise reached through, 338–339
  performance proficiency linked to, 211
  practice vs., 202–203
  teaching self-regulation to promote,
    332–333
Design phase, 21
Design-A-Plant (e-learning game), 181,
    214, 274, 368, 369*fig*
Development phase, 21
Digit span, 79*fig*–80
Directive e-lesson
  attention and prior knowledge
    components of, 395
  cognitive load component of, 395–396
  encoding and transfer components
    of, 396
  how it works, 393–394*fig*
  metacognitive skills component of,
    396–397
  motivation component of, 395
Directive instructional architectures
  description of, 24*t*, 25–26*fig*
  directive e-lesson example of, 393–397
Distributed cognition, 14
Divided attention
  definition of, 129
  goal to minimize, 114
  integrating instruction in same
    medium to minimize,
    134–135*fig*, 137
  integrating visuals/text to minimize,
    131–134
  methods to minimize, 131–135*fig*, 137
  note-taking as, 226–227
  research on, 129–131
Domain-specific metacognitive skills
  using guided-discovery architectures
    to build, 331–332
  including worked examples to build,
    329–330

how it works, 388–389

motivation component of, 390

visual analogy slide used in, 392*fig*

Redundant modes, 97–98

Reference-based training, 90–91*fig*

Rehearsal

decreasing recall due to blocked, 70*fig*

elaborative, 206–209

maintenance, 205–206*fig*, 208*fig*

working memory, 56, 69–71

See also Drill and practice

Routine expertise, 13, 315–316

Routine tasks, 40–41

S

Scaffolding, 400

Seductive details

avoiding negative, 155–156

countermeasures combined with effects of, 157*fig*

psychological effects of, 156–158

Selective attention

goal to maximize, 114

incorporating cues in visuals and text for, 121*fig*–124

research on, 120

summary of techniques for, 129

Self-assessment, 318

Self-Confidence Theory of Motivation, 340*t*–341

Self-efficacy, 343

Self-Explanation Support Principle, 222

Self-explanations

chess move learning and, 220–221

of correct responses in guided discovery learning, 221

of worked-out steps in math examples, 221–222*fig*

Self-regulated learners, 58–59

Self-regulation skills

cycle of learning and, 317*fig*

definition of, 317–318

examining learner lack of, 318–321

metacognition and role of, 58–59, 316–317

role of beliefs in, 338–339*fig*

supported during learning, 321–327

taught as part of training, 322–324

See also Skills

Shadowing, 120

Sherlock multimedia tutorial, 287*t*, 298–299, 331–332

Signaling classroom techniques, 124

Signaling Principle, 122

Simple mental models, 165, 203, 204

Simulations

Boyle's Law, 274, 275

Charles' Law, 274

keeping interfaces simple, 275, 276*fig*

learning aids for guided discovery, 273–275

optimizing pacing of, 274–275

Site maps

as expository organizer, 154

three different layouts of, 155*fig*

Situational interest

compensating for lack of personal interest, 370–372

description of, 343

emotional and cognitive, 344–345

evolution of, 344*fig*

motivating learners by exploiting, 365–370

Skills

metacognitive, 58–59

transfer from general to specific, 239–240

transformation of content into, 54–59

See also Metacognitive skills; Self-regulation skills

Spaced Practice Principle, 214

Spacing Effect, 212–214

Spatial Contiguity Principle, 132

START (Strategic Assessment of Readiness for Training), 321

Statistical significance, 44

RUTH COLVIN CLARK, Ed.D., has focused her professional efforts on bridging the gap between academic research on instructional methods and application of that research by training and performance support professionals in corporate and government organizations. Dr. Clark has developed a number of seminars and has written six books, including *e-Learning and the Science of Instruction, Developing Technical Training,* and *Efficiency in Learning,* that translate important research programs into practitioner guidelines.

A science undergraduate, she completed her doctorate in instructional psychology/educational technology in 1988 at the University of Southern California. Dr. Clark is a past president of the International Society of Performance Improvement and a member of the American Educational Research Association. She was honored with the 2006 Thomas F. Gilbert Distinguished Professional Achievement Award by the International Society for Performance Improvement and is an invited *Training Legend* Speaker at the ASTD 2006 International Conference. Dr. Clark is currently a dual resident of Southwest Colorado and Phoenix, Arizona, and divides her professional time among speaking, teaching, and writing. For more information, consult her website at www.clarktraining.com.

International Society for Performance Improvement

ABOUT ISPI

The International Society for Performance Improvement (ISPI) *is dedicated to improving individual, organizational, and societal performance.* Founded in 1962, ISPI is the leading international association dedicated to improving productivity and performance in the workplace. ISPI represents more than 10,000 international and chapter members throughout the United States, Canada, and 40 other countries.

ISPI's mission is to develop and recognize the proficiency of our members and advocate the use of Human Performance Technology. This systematic approach to improving productivity and competence uses a set of methods and procedures and a strategy for solving problems for realizing opportunities related to the performance of people. It is a systematic combination of performance analysis, cause analysis, intervention design and development, implementation, and evaluation that can be applied to individuals, small groups, and large organizations.

Website: www.ispi.org

Mail: International Society for Performance Improvement
1400 Spring Street, Suite 260
Silver Spring, Maryland 20910 USA

Phone: 1.301.587.8570

Fax: 1.301.587.8573

E-mail: info@ispi.org